yearning wild

R. Glendon Brunk

yearning
wild

Exploring the
Last Frontier
and the
Landscape of
the Heart

invisible cities press
montpelier, vermont

Invisible Cities Press
50 State Street
Montpelier, VT 05602
www.invisiblecitiespress.com

Library of Congress Cataloging-in-Publication Data

Brunk, R. Glendon.
Yearning wild : exploring the last frontier and the landscape of the heart /
R. Glendon Brunk.—1st ed.
  p. cm.
ISBN 1-931229-06-6 — ISBN 1-931229-12-0 (pbk.)
1. Brunk, R. Glendon. 2. Brunk, R. Glendon—Philosophy. 3. Pioneers—Alaska—
Fairbanks Region—Biography. 4. Environmentalists—Alaska—Fairbanks Region—
Biography. 5. Frontier and pioneer life—Alaska—Fairbanks Region. 6. Fairbanks
Region (Alaska)—Description and travel. 7. Alaska—Description and travel. 8.
Trans-Alaska Pipeline (Alaska) 9. Arctic National Wildlife Refuge (Alaska)—En-
vironmental conditions. 10. Alaska—Environmental conditions. I. Title.

F914.F16 B78 2001
979.8'051'092—DC21
2001046337

Note: A few excerpts are included from the essay "Facing East," published in the
Summer 1996 issue of *Wild Earth,* and the essay "Grizzly Fears," published in the
Vol. 14, No. 3, 1997 issue of *Trumpeter,* and republished in the Spring 1999 issue
of *Wild Earth.* Lines are included from the poem "To My Brothers," first published in the Summer 2000 issue of *Wild Earth.*

MANUFACTURED IN THE UNITED STATES OF AMERICA
PRINTED ON RECYCLED PAPER

Book design by Tim Jones
for Sterling Hill Productions

FIRST EDITION

To Cara, who has taught me many things.

contents

acknowledgments

Gratitude and appreciation all these years later to John Graves of Glen Rose, Texas, a fine writer and man of the land, who first showed me how to write about a river, and who suggested over a bottle of good whiskey that I had a story to tell and I should get to telling it. And to William Kittredge, who also encouraged the telling, who mentored a middle-aged man through graduate school, and who taught him many essential things about writing. And to friends and colleagues Colin Chisholm, Helen Harris, and Susan Watrous, who have also encouraged me, and with their own savvy writing have been great sources of inspiration. To Tom Butler, editor of *Wild Earth*, who liked what he saw, and who told others about it. And to Rowan Jacobsen, editor extraordinaire, whose enthusiasm for this project got me started. To Blanche Brunk, former wife and wonderful friend, who spent the early years in Alaska with me and lived to tell about it. And last of all to Maria Sonett, who listened to every turn of this project, who read first drafts and fed them back to me in honest, wise, and capable fashion. For her loving partnership I am blessed.

prologue

Yet it is the best and worst that one remembers, seldom the
mediocrities that lie between and demand no attention.
GAVIN MAXWELL, *Ring of Bright Water*

Remembering. How at midday the winter sun hung low
and weak on the southern horizon, a tepid glow just
above the wild, white mountains to the south, a tease of a
sun casting a thin, pale yellow light over the snow. And how
on the most bitter days the air glistened with ice crystals,
cutting nostrils and lungs like knives, freezing the hairs in
your nose, breath coming hard, accumulating on your beard,
frozen white clusters of frost. How at fifty, sixty, seventy below the sled dogs curled into tight balls, their noses buried
in the bush of their tails, not moving for hours on end. En-
during. Cold.

I am remembering a dog team. Fourteen athletes running
strong over a packed trail, moving so achingly smooth, like a
woman's soft hand over fine silk. I am there on the runners

of the sled, and for an infinite moment I feel for the first time in my life the interconnectedness of all things. There are no boundaries between me and my dogs and the world I travel through. In that moment I feel the utter rightness of my life, and out loud I say to the wind, "I am exactly where I need to be. There can be no better life." In that moment I know this to be true, and I cannot imagine that it will ever end.

I'm sitting here in my study in Arizona and I'm looking at a black-and-white photograph retrieved from a red suitcase full of memories. Two young people stand in front of a soft-top Toyota Land Cruiser with a little travel trailer hitched behind. The young man has an arm around the young woman, the other behind his back. They're both smiling. He with—what would I call it?—a certain toughness. She perhaps a bit tentatively. She stands with her feet close together. Her dark hair is cut short. She's lovely, dressed simply in faded Levi's and a black turtleneck. The young man beside her is taller than she, though not much taller. His stance is wide. He's dark, with a full beard, decked out in cowboy boots, Levi's, a big belt buckle, and a light, long-sleeve, button-down shirt. And he's thin as a twig.

I must admit that in some ways I'm envious of the young man in the picture. I miss him, at least miss parts of him: that athletic body that could drink hard and smoke a pack of cigarettes a day and go without sleep, and still climb mountains with ease; the eyes free of glasses; the sure way he stands there, with no thoughts of mortality. I miss, also, the pure passion he carried into everything he undertook. I say all this, and I know that I would not want him back. No, I would not want to have that many hard things to learn again.

Looking back. Such desire and longing well up in me when I do. Such a sense of privilege, also. I may not want the hard edges of that young man back, but I would take those first years in Alaska again, in a heartbeat. We lived on the Last Frontier. It said so on our license plates. The land of the rugged American individual, the last grand saga of the European conquerors' push west. One last gasp of the American notion of Manifest Destiny, a last place to subdue and alter. Like it wasn't good enough the way it was.

Today, with fifty-six years of life behind me, I am taken by many questions. One, though, always leads: What is this compulsion of industrialized man for altering things, for taking something pure and unspoiled and simple, and turning it into something complicated and soiled? What is this need to create something else out of what is already close to perfection? How tamed does a place have to be before it's altered enough to be predictable and bland, before the soul of it is snuffed?

Although I know in many ways it was a destructive thing I participated in, I would give anything to feel again a world still so intact and alive, the seduction of virgin country. These are all selfish reasons, I know. But I cannot deny them. I felt the tail end of something that no one in North America will ever, ever feel again. I have at least that story.

yearning wild

departure

I

the highway home

It is difficult, in this mostly wildless age, to explain how powerfully binding can become a union between a man or a woman and wildness itself. Most of us sense it, I think; with our canine molars we bite down on meat with a genetic nostalgia for chaos, and for the great extinct tests of our mettle that lay in solitude, in the wild.

GRANT SIMS, *Leaving Alaska*

The world we drive through today is turning toward winter. In the far distance, wild, roughshod mountains spill away beyond the horizon. In the foreground the earth undulates in great, ranging folds adorned in the brilliant golds, browns, and rust-reds of subarctic autumn. It's the scale of things here that always moves me. Space. The miles of nothing and everything. Country that goes on and on until it meets the barrier of the sea or the teeth of advancing civilization. I have loved these northern lands, been awed by them, since I first entered them thirty-two years ago.

We're headed south today, leaving Alaska, an act that over the last number of years has become my autumn ritual. How many times have I driven this Alcan? Fifteen? Twenty? More? So much has changed in my life, in Alaska, in the world since I first came north. The woman I sit beside now is a different woman from the one I came to Alaska with all those years ago. Maria drives and I work this laptop. Few of us dreamed of such a thing as a laptop thirty-two years ago, a personal computer, the computer age, phone menus, the pace, the frenzy of modern life. I could not have imagined writing this or even having anything I wanted to say.

I stop ticking away at my laptop, and Maria says to me, "Don't you feel like we're moving through an oil painting, a Turner maybe, with all the colors?" She pauses and stares off across the expanse. "The landscape feels so rich and fat, like I can almost taste it. It just fills me up."

She gets it, gets how this north country can enter a person and take hold, won't let go, even when you want it to. Such a pleasure to be with someone who understands how I've been held captive by this place for all these years.

The highway is paved now, an easy trip for the thousands of recreational vehicles that lumber their way to Alaska every summer. The curves are straightened and interpretive signs stand at strategic points alongside the road. Nicely painted litter barrels, organic colors, grace most of the turn-outs. There's a roadhouse every hundred miles or so, too many with cappuccinos. It's a tamed pathway now. The adventure of traveling it feels gone, though so much of the country it passes through is still so achingly beautiful, so much of it still wild. Beyond Fairbanks to somewhere in central British Columbia, for fifteen hundred miles, this highway is a thin thread of settlement humbling its way through an ocean of wild land. Though every year the distance shrinks, every year in Canada the clear-cuts and farms and mines move farther north, the cities and towns and oil fields in Alaska grow larger.

This is the highway that took me away from my childhood thirty-two years ago. It's a strange tempo that I live now, back and forth, five months here, seven months there, leaving a place I call home to inhabit a desert place that's alien to me, to work at a job that I've convinced myself is important. It is always amazing to me, and sometimes a little frightening, how the paths we travel take us to unexpected places.

I cannot travel this highway and help but recall the young man who came north thirty-two years ago. He was angry and scared and determined to forge a dream. His senior year of high school he kept a calendar above the head of his bed and marked off the days until graduation. All he wanted was escape. He went to his graduation ceremony in the high school gym wearing Levi's and a T-shirt under his gown. As soon as the ceremony was over he went out in the lobby and said good-bye to his parents. They looked both relieved and sad; he'd actually made it through high school, yet he was so determined to leave. He turned in his gown, said good-bye to a couple of classmates, then sprinted to the parking lot where a friend waited in a green, '57 Ford station wagon. In that Ford he had everything he thought he would need to start a new life. With no glances back he spun out of the parking lot and headed west.

Today, on this highway south, I recall the feeling of leaving that early-June afternoon, because it's still the same feeling I get today when I'm leaving somewhere, striking out for another. There's a bit of scared and lonely in it, but more so there's a sense of excitement, like none other, of possibilities and the potential for grand adventure. There's also the terrible recognition, beneath it all, that true freedom has so much responsibility mixed in with it. Even then I could feel it. I was responsible for me, and, like it or not, other people's expectations of me.

The roads we choose. A few miles back we stopped to watch a large black bear devour rose hips in the ditch alongside the road. The bear knew we were there, only yards away, but it studiously ignored us. Lips grimaced over white teeth, long, pinkish tongue curling ravenously, it stripped the tiny red fruits with a careful delicacy. As I watched it, I couldn't help but think that somewhere south of here we would stop seeing wildlife. I'm always struck by it when I come south, how somewhere in central-to-southern British Columbia you cross a line and there you begin to leave the wild world behind. You leave an ecosystem that is still pretty much intact, at least as far as what meets the eye, and you abruptly enter one that is increasingly shattered and degraded, fragmented and altered. It's all relative, of course. People from places even more settled would still call those borderlands wild and open. But you have entered anything but wild. The equation changes. From small islands of civilization lost in a sea of wilderness, as you go south you enter a sea of development that contains only occasional islands of pseudo-wildness that we call national parks, the bits of rocks and ice that we have labeled "wilderness areas," all managed, manipulated remnants of a former world. In short, what you have done is enter what we so proudly call civilization.

And as you do, the feeling changes. Not for the better. You leave a silent deep stillness and transition into dis-ease. It's like the breath is taken out of it. The world speeds up and closes in. This energy remains muted in the hinterlands of Canada, but when you cross the border the more frenzied the feeling becomes. Enter Seattle, and the memory of the wild world is smothered beneath the concrete and the vacuous mania of the dot.com, information age. You have entered a place where you have to be more concerned about the presence and actions of humans than about the presence of bears.

David Abram, in his book *The Spell of the Sensuous,* speaks of returning to the United States after being away for a year in the Third World, studying indigenous peoples and their sensual relationships with the natural world: "I began to feel—particularly in my chest and abdomen—as though I were being cut off from vital sources of nourishment. I was indeed reacclimating to my own culture, becoming more attuned to its styles of discourse and interaction, yet my bodily senses seemed to be losing their acuteness, becoming less awake to subtle changes and patterns."

Even though Alaska is much diminished from when I first came north, it's still true, every year I experience something similar when I return to the lower 48. It's as if something essential is pulled from me. The world turns flat and too busy, and I feel myself settle for less. Life without bears, I call it. Certainly, frantic America exists in Alaska; one only need visit Anchorage to know that. But, as the saying goes, Alaska starts just outside the city limits. And the wild world still penetrates the city's barriers at every opportunity. Bears visit suburban porches and pull pet dogs off chains. Moose tramp through people's gardens. The untamed Chugach Mountains form a formidable backdrop, looming over the city like dark prophets. I know the talk of other Alaskans, even those from Anchorage, the dread of going "outside," as we call the lower 48. It's a mixed-up world we've made out there, a convoluted story.

I know when I return to my house in Arizona in a few days I will yearn for Alaska. It's always like this. Every year I come away and beneath the activities of my day resides a smoldering discontent, the old yearning, a longing for something missing. I know I will berate myself. You should be able to settle here. This is a beautiful place, a great job, a nice house. It's warm in the winter. No winter darkness, no crazy temperatures.

But in my mind always lurks the question, How long before I can return? The life of the exile. Self-imposed exile, because I feel I'm doing something necessary here. Perhaps, also, the only way to write about yearning is to be feeling it.

It's an interesting story how this highway got built. So many of the things that seriously affect our world today were dreamed up, constructed, and delivered in response to one war or another. The idea of an overland route to Alaska was considered long before World War II, but it was the impetus of that war, the fear of the dreaded Japanese entering North America through Alaska, that got the idea off the ground. The government needed to move a lot of goods and men north, fast.

The highway's construction was a monumental human feat. On February 14, 1942, the U.S. war department issued a directive, in agreement with the Canadians, for work to begin using mostly American troops and equipment. (It's a curious thing to me that this directive came on Valentine's Day—a day for lovers, and my birthday.) America immediately moved in, with all its ingenuity and money. Against daunting obstacles, through miles of trackless mountains, muskeg and forest, over 133 river and stream crossings and eight thouand smaller water-courses, through rain, snow, and plummeting temperatures, the troops built over twelve hundred miles of pioneer road, as it was called. They did it in eight months and twelve days. Men died, equipment and horses and mules were lost in the mud and on river crossings. The road cost $138 million.

On this road today I ask myself, What if it had never been built? How would Alaska be different today if the only access was still by boat or plane? I think about the nature of projects in this north country. Always high stakes. Gold, copper, oil, the sea, tourism. Most often the projects are monumental, of great scale, man against the elements, against the odds, against an uncaring and harsh nature. Man, of course, prevails, conquers.

Without this road, development would have gone a lot slower. Fewer people would have come north. I believe I would have come, though, highway or not. This road just made it easier; it delivered me home and it has taken me away.

Traveling it today, I can't help but think of other trips I've made. One January, early seventies, driving north alone in a new Ford pickup, the faded half-light of early afternoon, through the truck's steel cab I can feel the cold deepening. The heater is turned on full blast and still the cold penetrates. I can hear my young man's voice now, cursing the Ford Motor Company. "God damn, pay forty-five hundred dollars cash for a new truck and the damn thing doesn't have a heater that could keep your dick warm." The side windows are sheets of white frost. The windshield view has closed in to where I'm peering straight ahead through a glazed porthole the size of a tea saucer. Behind, exhaust billows white and thin into the bitter air, turning instantly to ice crystals. And then things get worse. The truck gets so hard to steer on the curves that I have to slow to fifteen or twenty miles an hour and haul on the steering wheel for all I'm worth. I know it's a foolish thing to continue on, but I don't want to stop, don't want to be defeated by winter.

For once, though, I do the smart thing, don't bull ahead, don't ignore the odds. I pull into the roadhouse at Liard River, leave the truck running, get out and walk to the door. I'm wearing a down parka and fur hat, have on mittens and Sorrel boots. Less than a hundred feet to the roadhouse and I can feel the cold penetrate my chest and arms, feel my thighs beneath long underwear and wool pants stiffen, feel my cheeks already going numb. The air sears my nose and lungs.

A pile of tires burn beneath the roadhouse's propane tank. A black smudge of acrid smoke hangs like a funeral shroud in the air. Propane I know quits flowing at forty below; it has to be at least that cold for someone to build a fire under his tank. As I walk to the roadhouse, I notice a horse, a big Yukoner, standing spraddle-legged and head down, rear end pushed up tight against the side door of the garage. The horse is trying to take advantage of whatever pitiful heat leaks through the door's crack. Inside I ask the proprietor, a man with a soot-darkened face, how cold it is.

"Sixty-eight below and dropping," he says.

"You got a room?" I ask.

"A good decision," the proprietor says, "a hell of a lot better than some of these GIs who have to make their assigned duty day in Fairbanks, eh? The fools, families and all, just keep going. Damned overworked guardian angels those GIs got." He shakes his head. "Somebody's gonna die out there."

I go back outside, gas up my truck so I can leave it idling for the night. Inside, the roadhouse heat is welcome. Though always in the back of your mind is the recognition that it's a thin, tentative comfort against the frightening cold.

The next morning I get up and notice the horse is still standing against the door, hasn't moved an inch, and for the next forty-eight hours that I stay there, until it finally warms up to fifty-five below and I hit the road again, it doesn't move.

So what purpose does this memory serve? Why does it stand out from a hundred possibilities? I guess because it sums up what I came north for. Adventure, something out of the ordinary. The danger, the risks, the wildness of it. A place that pushes you. That says, Stay alert. Pay attention. This is your life.

2

growing up mennonite

Please Jesus, Save Us From Your Followers.

I'm not sure if my earliest memory is truly a recollection or just the way I want to hold things, my private fiction. It occurs on the southern Michigan farm where I was born. I must have been three or four. I stand on a sloping lawn that stretches out behind an old weathered farmhouse and gaze past a leaning red barn to a lush green pasture lined on its far side by the brushy curve of a small creek. I can smell the sour tang of cow manure from the barnyard, and fainter, farther away, the sweet musk of sun beating on newly mown hay. Beyond the creek, tall deciduous trees break the horizon. Through the muggy heat-haze of a midwestern summer afternoon, my eyes hold those trees, revel in their lush coolness, feel their invitation. The sense of this memory is one of yearning, of feeling a deep desire to enter those woods, of being drawn to some mystery there. It's a pleasant feeling, for with it also is an impression of being drawn to something entirely right for me.

I suppose, like everyone else, my memory is selective, given to convenience. Mine, I know, resists recalling a childhood too often difficult. Perhaps no one, though, remembers much of his youth. I've heard it said by psychologists who study such things that our memories are selective; something essential in the human psyche holds on to those details that serve us in some way and discards or buries those that may not, that may be too painful or complicated. Memories that serve the stories we want to believe in we repeat to ourselves, stacking them on top of one another, the building blocks of our identities and our cultures. In the interest of protecting our own stories we deny and avoid, push away details that aren't comfortable to carry.

When I was six years old my parents moved the family from southern Michigan to a town of neatly aligned north–south, east–west streets in northern Indiana. The town harbored a large community of Mennonites. My parents enrolled me in the first grade in an old redbrick school, saturated with public school stink—a concoction of chalk dust and floor wax, sloppy joes and ripe little bodies—that to this day, when I whiff it, sends me into spasms of resistance. Waterford Grade School was an institutional nightmare, so overcrowded with war babies that the first-graders were made to gather in what had once been a cloakroom. Thirty children stagnated elbow to elbow, five desks wide, six rows deep, in a twelve-by-twenty-four room with one dirt-stained window. To exit the room, we first-graders had to crawl over the rows of scarred desks between us and the only door.

My family settled south of town in a house that my father built. There were no woods nearby. We lived among a checkerboard of corn and soybean fields, and postwar, cracker-box houses built on land as flat and featureless as a book cover. The closest woods were more than a mile away, along a polluted brown slog of a river. From my first days in Indiana I missed Michigan terribly. I daydreamed of the pasture below the farmhouse where I was born, the deep green of the woods.

After only a few days in school I was labeled a troublemaker by my new teacher because I had followed another boy's lead and pitched a paper airplane across the room. The teacher, Miss Mast, assigned me to the front row, the seat closest to her desk, so she could keep a strict eye on me.

Miss Mast was an emaciated, mousy old woman, with dust-colored hair pulled into a severe bun. When I think of her now she seems a complete caricature of the old maid schoolteacher, except for one thing: she sported a colossal goiter, a knob of flesh and gristle at her throat about the size and color of a small cantaloupe. I was fascinated by Miss Mast's throat. In some way, in its strangeness, I identified with it. I watched her goiter float up and down as she talked. I tried to imagine what it would feel like to have a lump that size in my own throat. I see the metaphor now in that fascination. In one way I lived most of my childhood and adolescence with a lump in my own throat, mourning for something lost, something I could not define then, but yearning to find it again.

Looking back now I know there is no simple answer for what went on in that small boy's heart and mind. The only thing I know is that if I had a saving grace at that time, it was my attraction to the natural world. I could not articulate this then, of course, and certainly I had little encouragement toward the development of any interest. But nature was the one thing that soothed me, that pulled me in. At times the grace of it came in unexpected ways.

One day in early spring, Miss Mast announced that she

had a new bird book to give away if a student was willing to take on the task of learning all the names and identifications of the common birds of Indiana. It's extra work, she said, it will require the student to give up recesses in order to study.

My hand lifted itself into the air. I seemed to have no control of it; my arm was in open rebellion, a Judas of an appendage. Against my most common instinct not to volunteer for anything, I asked to be the one allowed to learn birds. Miss Mast wanted to ignore me, I know, but there were no other hands in the air. She covered her disappointment gracefully, solemnly acknowledged me, and reminded me that this was not work to be taken lightly. I nodded seriously, and for all the following weeks of precious spring bursting full beyond the thick walls of the cloakroom, I studied birds. I memorized the characteristics and habits of mourning doves, gray catbirds, bobwhite quail, and brown thrashers. By mid-May I had all the common birds of Indiana, all their names and habits, colors and calls in my little head. I was a first-grade bird savant.

Miss Mast, in a fit of unaccustomed kindness, acknowledged my dedication and asked me to make a presentation to the class. I crawled over my desk, stood up straight in front of my colleagues, and gave them an irresolute primer on the birds they might see outside the cloakroom: robins and cardinals, redheaded woodpeckers, perhaps even a blue heron if one of them could manage to escape to the river. When I finished, Miss Mast presented the book. I took it solemnly (a book I still possess), thanked her, then crawled back over the top of my desk into my seat. I looked at the cover. Two robins perched on a blooming apple branch. 112 BIRDS IN FULL COLOR, the cover read. A GUIDE TO THE MOST FAMILIAR AMERICAN BIRDS. A GOLDEN NATURE GUIDE. For the first time in my life I felt the letdown of a goal achieved, the process gone.

This is all there is? I asked myself. This is it, this tiny little book? That afternoon I emerged again onto the asphalt playground for recess, even then plotting my escape.

My experience in first grade mushroomed into a growing resistance to the unimpassioned, grim, and spiritless tedium of public education. My aversion to it set me on a path that in time fired into open rebellion. I gouged my way through school, fought with my classmates, and resisted my teachers. Each day was a test of my mother's will that I go to school against my own that I run away and live in a place of my own imagination. I squirmed through the class hours, waiting for recess, when I could play along the fence bordering the railroad tracks behind the school. I was drawn to the tracks, not because of a love of trains, but because the tracks harbored a tangle of red sumac and elderberry and dung-colored weeds, the only uncultivated and unhoused strip of land that could be seen in any direction. Running straight as a yardstick, the tracks cut through a land of solid predictability.

Had they been paying attention my parents would have seen the restlessness emerging in my young life. Early on it was clear to me that whatever it was I desired was not to be found within the confines of my parents' religion, in the bland geography of northern Indiana, in a town of tidy, tree-lined streets that could pass for a thousand other towns in the Midwest. I've often wondered if there is something to the idea that landscapes and people in landscapes reflect one another. Are cautious people attracted to cautious landscapes? Do cautious people shape cautious landscapes? Or if a landscape is inherently bland, does it eventually take the edge out of the people who settle there?

Mennonites came to America in the late 1700s and early 1800s, from Germany, Switzerland, Holland, and some later from Russia. They brought with them a determination to live quietly—safe, they hoped, from Catholic persecution. How is it, though, that those who flee oppression so often turn to some form of it again in their own communities? I know much has changed for the Mennonite church these last years. There has been some self-examination. When I was a boy, though, to live in a Mennonite community was to live in a tight circle of control and judgment. It was rarely said, though inherently understood, that one must always be aware of what others might think of one's actions. There was an overriding dictate of simplicity expected in every act. It was not a simplicity born of thoughtful choice derived from a spiritual center, but one dictated by a rigid code of "shoulds" and "should-nots." These dicta were interpreted from the scriptures of a judgmental male God by a male, pastoral hierarchy that, it was just understood, had an inside track on God's desires. These elders expected that in all matters one should be humble. One should not associate with sinful people. One should tithe all income. One should not smoke, drink, dance, go to movies, or fornicate. One should practice stewardship in worldly affairs, but one should *not* derive satisfaction from worldly things. One should honor one's father and mother. To live in a Mennonite community was in many ways to live in a community of eyes.

I detested those eyes and I dreaded Sunday, which meant two church services, both morning and evening. Sunday morning felt so heavy. Cars—Chevrolets, Plymouths, Buicks, and Fords—all subdued colors, pulled slowly into the church parking lot. Men in dark suits, women in plain dresses, the older women wearing coverings—little white cheesecloth caps—on their heads (to signify humility and the subservient place of women before God), emerged and walked silently into the sanctuary. People took their seats and waited quietly for the service to begin. In those days there was no organ, because an organ was considered too worldly. (Later, the congregation voted, after a long and intense debate, to purchase one. But it could be used only pre-service, not during the actual service.) Besides, Catholics used organs, and everybody knew that Catholics weren't full-fledged Christians but instruments of the pope, in reality idol worshipers; they had all those statues and such. And Catholics had persecuted Mennonites unmercifully in the fifteenth and sixteenth centuries; this was not to be forgotten.

I hear my judgment of those chosen lives, the same judgment that I rebelled against. Here I am a man in his fifty-sixth year, and the same shadows still shape me. Even after all these years I feel a resistance to the place I grew up, still feel the discontent; I would not wish to return there.

Perhaps, though, it was only me, my temperament, my constitution, the way that I came into this world that made living there so entirely uncomfortable. As a youth I felt surrounded by an immense pandering docility. My spirit yearned for expansiveness, but there was no way for it to soar in a community that pushed against change, that mistrusted anything but the patently familiar. *Heaviness* is the word. Even the seasons spoke of it. Summer: stifling heat, mugginess, torpor, a time of pushing-down density, of an atmosphere saturated to dripping. Nights, when the still air settled thick as sludge, I would lie between sheets in my upstairs bedroom, soaked in my own sweat, dreaming of other worlds.

Winter was the worst, though. Northern Indiana winter is a gray beast of a season that never seriously commits itself to anything. Instead, it slogs through a dreary succession of rain and sleet and ice storms, with clouds scudding across dull skies like sacks of dirty laundry. And at that time, before any air pollution laws, if snow fell, for a miraculous short time the world was pure, but within hours the white turned black from the soot and fly ash that spewed from the stacks of a dozen factories. It was those factories that spoke to me of winter, of the heaviness of impending doom. Many of my school acquaintances expected to graduate and take up lives in a factory, no questions asked. Their perception of life, their story, was that one works for the man; you do the robotic, mind-numbing, mundane repetitions of industrial production. Friday night, take the paycheck home to the wife and kids, pull up the recliner and tune into the TV. Zone out.

If I had a favorite season it would be spring. With spring I felt a ray of hope. For a few short weeks nature did its best to reclaim the land. The roadside ditches bloomed with flowers, songbirds called from the hedgerows, and for a short time the pungent smells of new life outdid the smells of industry. But I remember no celebration of spring, other than the obligatory Easter services. In short, those with Germanic roots are not people who trust a lot in a season of rejuvenation, or people much given to whooping it up.

Heaviness, living on a flatness that isn't space, but is instead a hemmed in-ness, a geography of prediction, of neat, ordered rows, blocks, and sections. It is oppressive trying to survive in a culture that insists upon sameness, a people who consider provincial caution a saintly virtue, who speak in hushed tones. A place of close horizons.

I must have been eleven or twelve years old when I made up my mind to go to Alaska. My mother, at the time, was doing her best to instill in me some level of sophistication by dragging me, protesting loudly, to a lecture series at the Mennonite college. "You're old enough to be introduced to culture," was the way she put it. "Culture" in Mennonite Indiana was the drone of a lecture given by a noted theologian on the challenges to Christianity occurring in the evil empire of the Soviet Union; several second-rate symphony orchestras that played what I called at the time "too serious music"; and a black gospel singer with an immense bosom (a definite high point for me) who sang hand-clapping spirituals deemed right on the racy edge for a Mennonite audience. My mother made me wear a gray wool suit to every event, which for a free-spirited youth was nothing less than a medieval hair shirt, an instrument of pure and simple torture. The short of it is, I dreaded the lecture series and I vowed that if I ever had children of my own I would certainly let them grow up entirely ignorant if that's what they wanted.

But one night proved different. We drove to yet another lecture through feathery flakes of snow falling softly in the headlights of the family Oldsmobile. The event that night was to be a slide show delivered by a couple who lived in Alaska. The lights dimmed and I sat immediately entranced, riveted, by the world of Bud and Connie Helmericks as they traveled the length of the Yukon River in a canoe. Images of moose and bear, herds of caribou, snow-capped mountains all filled my imagination. For a child raised without TV, one who had spent most of his days living in the settled, checkerboard predictability of the Midwest, that night was pure magic. I was fascinated, enthralled, captured by this place called Alaska, by the actual knowledge that a place so wild existed.

On the way home, from the backseat I told my parents that as soon as I was old enough I would be heading north. I was going to build a log cabin on a river, get a dog team, hunt and fish and live off the land. My father peered hard through the windshield into snow still falling. "Yes," he said, "once I thought I'd do something like that, too. But things change, you know. You'll probably change your mind."

"I'm going," I said firmly.

"We'll see," my father said, the same as his father before him, words to muzzle imagination, a way of discounting a young boy's dreams, words that either defeated you or added greatly to your determination to escape.

3

a war story

A true war story is never moral. It does not instruct, nor encourage virtue, nor suggest models of proper human behavior, nor restrain men from doing things men have always done. If a story seems moral, do not believe it. If at the end of a war story you feel uplifted, or if you feel that some bit of rectitude has been salvaged from the larger waste, then you have been made the victim of a very old and terrible lie. There is no rectitude whatsoever. There is no virtue. As a first rule of thumb, therefore, you can tell a true war story by its absolute and uncompromising allegiance to obscenity and evil.

TIM O'BRIEN, *The Things They Carried*

I resist writing about my father. A part of me feels that in exposing his human frailty I somehow betray him, belittle his memory. What once seemed so unforgivable has been forgiven, so why bring it up again? Also, I am reluctant to acknowledge that he passed on the imperfections of his father and grandfather and great-grandfather before him, that for all the ways I resisted him, damn it, I too took them on. I know these are not reasonable, objective emotions, particularly given that I now have some perspective on my life. They are, though, what I have. And they are, I know, the very place I must begin if I want to speak of men's ways in the world; I must start with the men who taught me.

My father was a good Mennonite, an obedient man, a servant of authority. He voted Republican, not because he had a logical affinity for the party, but because he detested Franklin Roosevelt. "He was a sinful man, the one who let Communism into America," he said on several occasions. That perception of Roosevelt and the Democrats pandering to the godless Communists was reason enough to vote Republican. My father would not dance, drink, smoke, swear, or fornicate. As were all good Mennonite men, he was a pacifist. He refused to go to war, would not take human life, would not raise his hand against another man in any way. He would, though, strike his own children. He did so often, impulsively, a hard knot of anger twisting his handsome face. I know now that he struck his children not because he thought it was the right thing to do, but because he knew no way not to. Easiest said, unexamined anger owned my father, turned him against himself and those he loved. Of the childhood memories I have, too many of them are of my father striking out in impulsive and unpredictable ways.

There's one memory in particular that came to hold a lot of meaning for me. Once we had a dog that had come to us as a stray, a simple-minded cocker spaniel that cowered and peed at the slightest hint of conflict. One summer day it crawled up on an old couch in our basement. I watched, horrified, as my father swung a claw hammer full arc against the dog's head, driving it to the floor.

"Why'd you do that?" I yelled.

My father bristled. "Don't raise your voice to me." He turned away from me. "You know that dog should not be on that couch. Get it out of here."

I carried the dog up the stairs and out into the backyard, to my favorite spot under a spreading Siberian elm, and sat with it in my arms. With my shirtsleeve I blotted blood oozing from an ear, convinced the dog was dead. Eventually, I felt it stir, watched it dazedly shake its head and come to life. As it did, my own rage grew, turned inward and festered against all authority, against a God who would make men in the form of my father, a God who was the center of a religion that held him so.

My father was a product of his own father: a rageful, Bible-toting, hellfire and brimstone preacher, who thought it his God-given duty to level harsh judgment on his family and anyone else who he deemed deserved it. In his old age his bitter ire had grown so large that he could no longer find a Mennonite church to minister to. Rejecting the Mennonites as too meek and biblically cautious, he joined a more fundamentalist faith. From that pulpit he railed against any who were vain enough to doubt his God of judgment and vengeance.

My father cowered in his father's shadow, and suffered serious self-doubt from his endless criticisms. All others in the family were expected to cower also, but my steadfast mother resisted. For this she paid a heavy toll. My grandfather was open in his disregard of her. "She should obey you," I once heard him say to my father. "She took the vows to do so, and she should obey you." My father said nothing to my grandfather in return.

Contrary to what one might expect, my father seemed not relieved by my grandfather's death, but lost. He struck more and criticized harder, as if afraid in some way that he was not living up to his father's expectations. He labored under a visible conflict between his anger and another part of him that

I know longed to prevail. As I say this, I hear the sound of my own judgment, what could be taken as a condemnation of him. In no way is this my intention. In all fairness I must say that anger was not all there was to him. Because as often as his eyes could cloud with frustration and rage, oddly close to these emotions was an infectiously charming humor.

Perhaps for people filled with rage, to maintain some semblance of sanity (whatever "sanity" might mean), humor has to be the counterbalance, the balm that keeps the fire of rage from consuming all. My father could come up with the unexpected and laugh like no one I've ever known. Certainly, though, his humor could take some odd turns.

Once, before we moved to Indiana, I traveled with him from Michigan, just the two of us in a dark blue Oldsmobile. We were going to investigate our prospective new home in Indiana. Pre-interstate, we followed a two-lane road that ran straight south through miles of empty winter fields, and the little look-alike main streets of the central Midwest. In a small town close to the Indiana border my father slowed and pulled left into the parking lot of a Dairy Queen, the new choice in midwestern dining, the first of the fast-food, fast-life franchises that would before long forever alter the character of American communities.

I was interested in what my father might be up to, but not willing to believe that I might truly be getting a treat without asking. He looked over at me. "What'll you have?"

"You mean an ice-cream cone?"

"Anything you want."

"Anything?"

"Anything," he said. "A cone, a malted. How about a fudge sundae?"

I was astounded. This was not my father. The best strategy for living with him was to not hope for anything too good. Thus, anything above disappointment was a bonus. But this was too good to pass up. I gave it some thought. "I'll have a large cone," I said, "dipped in chocolate."

My father got out and returned shortly with two large, chocolate-dipped cones. He handed mine through the window on my side, then stepped around the rear of the car and slid in behind the steering wheel. We ate in silence. Ice cream and chocolate dripped down my chin, over my hands and arms.

I finished, secretly pleased with my good fortune. My father looked over at me, eyes twinkling. "Want another one?" he asked.

This was beyond understanding. "Another?" I replied weakly. "Another," he nodded.

I was convinced there had to be a major hitch somewhere, but I also didn't want to blow it if there wasn't. "Okay," I said.

He got out again, this time returned with just one cone. He slid in on his side and handed it across to me. I began again. My father just watched.

This is turning out okay, I thought to myself. If it was possible, I relished the second cone even more than the first, taking it slower, getting into the gestalt of licking and dripping. By the time I finished I was my mother's worst nightmare; I had Dairy Queen armpits, and my T-shirt was no longer Christian white. I could tell my father was trying not to laugh. And I was trying to decide if that was good or bad. Am I the dunce or have I done something right?

"You want another?" he asked.

I was too far gone to be astounded. I really didn't want one. I felt terminally full and on the edge of nausea, but with instincts honed by five years of scarcity, I agreed.

"Large with chocolate?" he asked.

"No, maybe a medium," I said.

"Okay." He got out, and shortly returned with the third cone.

I began slowly this time, took a couple of licks, then rested. I was clearly not going to be fast enough; gravity was going to be the winner on this one. The cone and its contents slid down my arms, spread an abstract expressionist splay of vanilla and Hershey across the front of my white T-shirt and into my lap. My father began to laugh, full and out of control. He slumped forward and banged his head on the steering wheel. He struggled for breath. Tears came to his eyes. I had been a big hit, and I didn't have a clue why. Between gasps he turned to me. "You've had enough?"

"I have," I said.

"You sure?"

"I'm sure."

It was weeks before I could bear the thought of vanilla ice cream again. Months before the word *chocolate* ceased to set off Pavlovian eruptions in my stomach. On the surface my father possessed a charming rascality, but beneath it, I think now, was a certain maliciousness. I say this, and yet I know at a most essential level maliciousness would not have been what he wanted for himself.

My father did not go to World War II. He was given a deferment because he was a farmer. Thus his own pacifism was not tested. I suspect he suffered more self-doubt because of this, because a part of him thought that his faith, his pacifism, *should* be tested. But a bigger part, the part that ruled him, must have been terrified that it might be. Of course, as I write these words I'm aware of how little I actually know of my father's inner life, how little he revealed of himself. I'm aware, also, that my experience is the same as most other men I know. Men in our culture, perhaps in most modern cultures, suffer much from a misguided set of perceptions that rule our lives. Even in our play we are so often destructive. Fathers and sons are too often not connected in positive ways. There is little open, honest emotion shared.

Years after I'd left home and was living in Alaska, my father, recently retired, came north with my mother to visit me and my family in Fairbanks. We were fishing together, just he and I, the only activity we ever really shared. We were talking about what it was like to live in Alaska. My father acknowledged how much he liked the place, how he wished he'd been able to come up when he was young. I said something to him about how determined I was not to give in to a predictable life, saying something, I'm sure, that was unintentionally critical of him. My father was quiet for a moment. His big hands gripped the bail of his spinning rod and turned it down for the next cast. Then it rushed out of him. "I hated farming, hated the confinement of it. Hated milking a dozen cows morning and evening, hated fifteen years working nights in the Oldsmobile plant in Lansing, just to make ends meet." He held his cast, stared straight ahead out over the water. "But there I was with a wife and kids. What choice did I have?"

I don't recall exactly what I said to him then, though I know it was most likely not as understanding as I now wish it could have been.

"You don't know what it was like to live through the Depression," he went on. "You can't imagine what it felt like to be without a job for months at a time. After the Depression ended I vowed I'd never be without a job again. That's why I took up farming. I figured I'd always have work. It's why I took up working nights at the Oldsmobile plant." He put his rod down on the edge of the boat. "One night, though, I was working the assembly line, putting front bumpers on, one after the next. I'd never liked working there. But that night it just hit me, my whole life I might do nothing else but put bumpers on cars." He stared into the water a moment, then turned and looked directly at me. "That was one of the worst feelings I ever remember having. I came home and told your mother I couldn't do it any longer. We had to find another way."

The solution to my father's Michigan despair was to pick up and take his family to Indiana, where he again took on a long line of jobs that brought him little satisfaction. My father's story is a familiar one. Men and women trapped by their circumstances, or at least by what they perceive as their circumstances, clear out and create the same circumstances elsewhere. My father tried; he did his best to open to a new life. But the weight of the same fearful perceptions kept him trapped. I know his father's criticisms hung over his head like a guillotine. Out of deep-seated self-doubt he held on to ways of being and living that were wrong for him, ways that denied his true spirit. Whatever his circumstances, whatever his fears, they kept him from doing what he most wanted with his life. This I know, because he told me.

It hurts to admit this, but for a long time I felt ashamed of my father. I resented his caution, the fear of life I saw in him. Why, I reasoned, couldn't I have a father who accomplished something significant? Why not a father who lived an adventure? By extension, the shame I felt for him, I felt for myself. Thus, I had to act and act big, because he never did. I was determined that I would not become like him. In this unintended way he gave me a gift, painful but still a gift, one I'm thankful for.

I know my father was no different from millions of other men and women, who, as Thoreau said, live lives of quiet desperation. I'm not so sure about the word *quiet*, though. Perhaps quiet in one way, that of not rocking the collective boat. But in another way the anger, and the emotional numbness, that accompanies desperation is anything but quiet. It's more like a silent roar that in time spills into loud acts of violence and confusion that affect families and children. Quiet desperation, too, can underlie lives that appear entirely on track. The most fundamental tragedy of it all is that whatever the circumstances, desperation gets handed on generation to generation, father to son, mother to daughter. It does unless someone along the line decides enough's enough and determines to break the chain. What I know, also, is that breaking the chain is never an easy task.

During the early sixties and my adolescent years, lurking like a thief in the shadows of my awareness was always the reality of war. Those were the first vainglory days of the so-called conflict in Vietnam. Feelings ran high in favor of kicking some Communist butt in some obscure little country in Southeast Asia. Get over there and get it over with, was the way the talk went. The grasping hand of American imperialism was yet to be questioned by the masses, and it was every young man's duty to march off in lockstep to war, no questions asked.

Ironically enough, given my resistance to my father's direction, at age eighteen I chose pacifism. It was not an easy decision. I agonized long and hard over the idea. I knew I would not make a good soldier; I doubted if I was capable of following someone else's orders. But, given my determination and a sense of my own anger, I imagined that I might make a fairly tenacious warrior. In the end, mine was not a religious decision, though certainly my religious background influenced me, at least introduced me to the possibility of an alternative. My decision to resist military service was not based on my father's obedient pacifism. It was more about resistance to the authority of a central government, and an unwillingness to give my life to some ideology that even then made no sense. I decided there was no way I was going to Vietnam.

I was still in high school when I stood for the first time in front of my draft board and declared my pacifist intentions. The board was made up of World War II veterans. The board chairman was a dark man with a permanent scowl etched on his face, the shop teacher in my high school. He had spent most of World War II as a German prisoner, and he publicly made no bones about the fact that he had little use for conscientious objectors.

I was scared. I waited in a poorly lit antechamber with several other young men. A clerk called my name. I entered a large, dim, windowless room that smelled of cigar smoke and cheap aftershave. Four board members sat unsmiling behind a long wooden table. One of the members motioned for me to move to the middle of the room. I stepped forward and waited. Finally the chairman looked up from some papers he'd been studying and addressed me. "So it says here you're afraid to go to war. Is that right?"

I had carefully rehearsed responses to anticipated questions. I took a deep breath and did my best to reply as articulately as I could. "No," I said, "I'm not afraid to go to war. I object for other reasons."

"What makes you think you know enough to refuse to serve your country?"

He had a point. Although I had thought a lot about the issue, and had memorized the literature provided by various pacifist organizations, truthfully, what does any eighteen-year-old know of the philosophical and ethical implications of war? On the other hand, who better to send off to the battlefields than the young, who don't know enough to resist?

I delivered the lines that I'd practiced. "I was brought up in a Mennonite home," I said. "This background has led me to consider the moral and ethical implications of war."

"And what might those moral and ethical implications be?" the chairman asked.

"I have moral objections to taking human life under any circumstances. I also consider modern war a tool of the military-industrial complex, a tool that serves the wealthy and victimizes the poor. I believe it is not a rational or moral alternative in this nuclear age, nor do we have the right to impose our political agendas on other people." I took a deep breath. "I will not go to war."

There was a long silence. The chairman's scowl deepened. Finally, one of the other members, a gray-haired man with a cigar clamped between stubby fingers, asked me what I'd do if a Communist came into my house and tried to rape my mother. "Would you let him do that?" he asked. "You wouldn't resist?"

"I don't know what I'd do," I said. And I didn't. The question seemed to have so little relevance to what I saw as the issue. I repeated the answer that the pacifist literature had suggested. "It's a hypothetical question that I find impossible to answer."

They never asked me if I actually still considered myself a Mennonite; I suppose they just assumed that I was. If they had asked, I would have been caught in a quandary, a choice to lie and take the easy way out or be honest and answer that I no longer considered myself a Mennonite, really never had, that truth be told I had developed a quickening aversion to religion.

The board members conferred among themselves, then the chairman spoke. "I hope you know what you're getting into here, young man. Prison is not a nice way to spend your youth. Do you hear what I'm saying to you?"

"I do," I said, and was dismissed.

A month after my hearing I got a notice to report for my Army physical. This was routine procedure. All males of draft age, pacifist or not, had to take a preliminary examination to see if there was any physical reason they were unfit to serve. In the half-light of dawn, a Saturday morning in April, several dozen of the county's brightest and best gathered beneath newly budding maple trees on the courthouse square. The draft board clerk called our names, handed each of us a folder of papers, then told us to board a bus. I took a seat in the rear. Even though I had yet to be given conscientious objector status, stamped on the outside of my folder, in black, were the letters C-O. *Chicken, coward, traitor,* the letters seemed to say. I knew it was going to be a long day at the Army induction center in Chicago.

That day there were probably a dozen Mennonite and Amish boys on the bus with C-O stamped on their folders. The soldiers at the Chicago center had a field day with us. Clad only in our underwear, we shuffled from station to station. The soldiers at the stations belittled us, called us girls and chickenshits. When we would make it to the head of a line, the soldiers would send us to the back, over and over, until all the non–C-Os had made it through. It was late in the evening before the C-Os were done. The other inductees stared coldly at us as we boarded the bus. I remember thinking at the time that some of them were already well on their way to becoming good and obedient soldiers.

If ever I had any notion of letting go of my pacifist stance, the bullying and taunts at the induction center that day sealed my determination not to go into the Army. Once again I came up against the smug self-righteousness of assumed authority. Fundamentalist Christianity or military, they both simply seemed opposite ends of the same spectrum. Both relied on a sheeplike willingness of people to follow, to not ask questions.

For some reason, an accident of birth I guess, it was my nature to ask questions. From an early age I *had* to think about things, to consider questions that most of my peers seemed uninterested in. For me, growing up Mennonite intensified this tendency. I understand now that beneath the surface dogma of the religion there was a vital connection to a history of serious contemplation; the essential reasoning of the Mennonite faith was underlain by some highly ethical principles. We were encouraged to live a life of social service, of simplicity, of peace and quietness. In what might seem a contradiction, we were told how to believe, yet those beliefs dictated that we live and think outside the norm. Of course, living outside the norm, for one inclined to ask questions, can take one to unintended places. As far as my pacifism went, the contradiction of my father's professed pacifism and his private violence pushed me into going beyond the rhetoric of pacifism to examine what it actually meant. I know this: my choice to resist the military was my choice, not my father's.

Saying this I also reveal the ultimate paradox of my resistance. I resisted the military, an institution entirely dependent upon the manufacture and manipulation of men's fear and rage. Yet it was my own rage—rage passed from my father, my grandfather, and generations of fathers before them—that ultimately pushed me up against the institution of the military. My rehearsed performance in front of the draft board was a patina over the hard shell of my own anger. In some ways those hardened surfaces meant survival. In other ways they would haunt me, distract me for a long time from truly living from my inner voice, armor me against so much of what I actually desired to experience. If I were asked to define the most essential contradiction in my life, it would be my professed pacifism and all the ways that I have subsequently made war.

The next three years I bummed around the country—drove a dozer in a sawmill in Oregon, worked ranches in California and Arizona, followed the wheat harvest from Texas to Montana. When I was about to be drafted I would head back to Indiana and enroll in the Mennonite college. I made it through three separate, half-hearted and rebellious semesters before the dean of students called me into his office one winter afternoon and suggested in the most gentle, Mennonite fashion that a Mennonite college might not be exactly what I needed. Perhaps I was better suited for some other institution. In short, I was being kicked out.

A month later, in January 1966, I appeared once again before my draft board, in the windowless room on the first floor of the county courthouse. The scowling chairman told me to step to the center of the room and face the table. "I remember you in high school," he said. "You were a troublemaker then, and in my mind you still are. You're a goddamned troublemaker." He swiveled in his chair, looked at the other members and then back to me. "We've considered your case; we've decided you're just ornery enough to go through with this C-O thing. We've also decided that you ending up in jail's not going to do anybody any good. It galls me to say so, but you've got thirty days to find a job that's considered in the public interest. Find that job and report back to us. You serve two years, and you serve with damn good behavior. If there's anything but good behavior, anytime, son, you go immediately to prison." He held the papers out to me. I stepped forward and took them. "Get out of here," he said.

A few days later I headed west in a red Volkswagen bug that I'd bought from my father. Given my resistance to authority, I don't recall how I rationalized taking orders from my draft board. It's curious to me now that I didn't go to Canada. In retrospect it seems odd, but I don't recall that doing so ever crossed my mind. How different might my life be if I had turned north the day of my departure from Indiana, instead of heading west? The truth is, all noble intents and philosophical stances aside, it was Alaska that took me west. Even though Canada was immensely wild and held much of what I desired, Canada was not Alaska. My simple reasoning: I had two years of forced labor to get out of the way before I could head to the place of my dreams.

Big D, we called it. Denver. The brightly lit city on the western plains where so many Mennonite boys from farms and

small towns in the Midwest and East went to do their "alternative service." Alternative to the sweltering, terror-ridden jungles
of Vietnam. Alternative to the places we came from. Denver had
lots of hospitals. As the city sent its own young men off to war,
it developed a growing need for honest workers to take on the
menial jobs. Denver, a place where so many guileless Mennonite boys were turned loose for the first time in their lives. The
city smiled and pulled us in, welcomed us, and taught us a lot.
Some of us worked as orderlies in hospitals, others of us went
to work in mental institutions, a few got jobs as guinea pigs in
military experiments.

Big D changed all of us in ways the elders back home
would not have approved of. It opened most of us to new
possibilities in the world. The work we did was only a small
part of it. Denver had a reputation, sin city, a place that
turned good Mennonite boys into men of the world. But that
wasn't the idea. The idea was go there, and sure, if you had
to, maybe sow some wild oats. But get the wild oats out of
the way, do your twenty-four months, then head back home
and settle into the life of the church. A lot of us never made
it back home, though.

Within two days of arriving in Denver I got a job as a technician at Colorado Psychiatric Hospital, or CPH. Why did I
pick a mental hospital out of a dozen other possibilities? Part
of it, I know, was that I wanted to do something besides
empty bedpans. I was intrigued by the idea of working with
the so-called insane. I was curious to know more about the
mind. I know, also, that in some way I was unconsciously
drawn to the possibility of working with those who fell outside the cultural norms.

With no training or orientation, a couple of weeks shy of my
twenty-first birthday, tragically naive and scared out of my
wits, I stepped into Ward 2 South, the adolescent treatment facility I'd been assigned to. I checked in at the nurse's station.

The head nurse was busy charting. "Go out and introduce yourself to the patients," she said. "I'll show you around later."

I went out and found the dayroom, an institutional-green, high-ceilinged chamber with rusted steel grates over all the windows. There must have been twenty adolescents there, both boys and girls, some sitting quietly just staring into space, others playing pool, a couple engaged in a game of cards. I noted that I wasn't much older than the oldest of them. They all pointedly ignored me. I sat down by a particularly quiet boy off in a corner by himself. His hair looked as if it had been hacked off with a hoe. "Hi," I said, but he gave me no notice, just sat there and stared straight ahead with empty eyes. I felt utterly out of place. It crossed my mind that this might be a long two years.

We didn't wear uniforms. None of the staff did. The reasoning was that we shouldn't set up a barrier between patients and staff. Uniforms or not, at Colorado Psychiatric I was rapidly introduced to the world of the broken, the lost, the diagnosed crazy. I learned quickly how to be a psychiatric technician. I learned the adrenaline rush of Code-3: that urgent call over the public address system for technicians to drop whatever they were doing and run to subdue a wild patient. In time, I felt some pride in being the one they called if special attention was needed for a particularly difficult patient, if a situation was considered dangerous. I came to be known as tough, determined, fearless.

My first months there I participated in electroshock therapy, held protesting patients tightly as a psychiatrist attached electrodes to their temples and zapped them with a quick and massive electrical jolt. The patients would erupt in violent seizures, flop on the table like fish pulled from the water. When they came to, their minds would be fried and rearranged and increasingly confused. But they were also more compliant after a treatment, more manageable. I don't know what kind of mind came up with electroshock therapy. Whoever he was, though, it seems a safe bet that his sense of self bordered on the divine.

Early in my second year at CPH, with the burgeoning development of chemical drugs, electroshock therapy slid quickly into disfavor with the medical people. By the time I left, psychiatrists who had once used it routinely began to speak derisively about it. The new drugs opened a whole new world of possibility for creating passivity. Patients shuffled along the halls, zombielike, their mouths cotton-dry and chalky from the side effects of the drugs. Certainly they were more manageable, more compliant. But I wonder if some day we'll look back, just as we do now with electroshock therapy, and ask ourselves how we could have been so barbaric as to chemically alter people so, to be so deaf to the actual messages the insane are shouting to us.

My second year at CPH, acid and other hallucinogens hit the streets in a big way. With the introduction of acid and other drugs, some people in the culture were opened to something mystical and large, a world that ran counter to accepted reality. For others, in an attempt to escape a difficult world, the drug kicked them hard, set into motion a collective, free-floating confusion and anger. At CPH I watched adolescents, and adult men and women on other wards, all rage against their parents, against the world, or, in times of complete breakdown, rage against dinner or a TV show or the way another patient happened to cut her hair.

I can't honestly say to this day that I understand all that went on then. The craziness we dealt with the first year intensified the second. How could it change so quickly? Suddenly we were forced to deal with the fallout of a culture turned against itself. Patients seemed ever more determined to self-destruct. Once I cut a thirteen-year-old sprite of a boy named Dougie down from a closet rod, a knotted tie around his neck, seconds away from death. Another time I held the gushing razor-cut veins of a macho, eighteen-year-old rodeo cowboy until the emergency medics could take over and save his life. Another time, through a thick, wire-reinforced Plexiglas window, I watched a ninety-pound girl, stark naked, rip the leg from a metal hospital bed and punch it through the solid wood door of a seclusion room. "I want out of here!" she kept screaming. "I'm not crazy! You fuckers are the crazy ones! You're all goddamned crazy!"

But she was "out of control." Two other technicians joined me. I nodded and they flung open the door. Armed with a mattress, I charged the girl with it and fell on her, pinning her to the floor. The two technicians followed. It took the three of us to hold the girl while a nurse jammed a hypodermic full of tranquilizer into her hip. Pacifists we might have been, but we technicians participated in a war.

For the first time in my life I was forced to step outside my own story enough to begin to understand the stories of others. Beneath all the various diagnoses of mental illness there seemed to be one pervasive commonality, that of a modern culture confused and turned against itself. Mental illness seemed rampant and ill-defined. I began to notice that the lines between patients and staff, between patients and people I met on the street, seemed thin and at times arbitrarily drawn. It was as if some souls escaped a free-floating cultural anxiety while others bearing a more acute sensitivity to it had no choice but to cave in. One common denominator, though, for those adolescents incarcerated, was that most came from broken homes. The stories I heard—the physical abuse, the sexual perversions, the absence of love in any form—made my own upbringing seem like a picnic. Still, by observing others I was forced for the first time in my life to begin to look honestly at myself. I can't say that I gained much insight into the depth of my own anger. But feeling the pain and wounds of others, I began to develop some notion of my own. It was only the very beginning of a process, though, the creaking open of a door to let in a thin shaft of light.

It was all fascinating, but I wanted to escape it. The job took so much, and the city smothered me. My base salary was $265 a month. After taxes it barely covered rent and food, left nothing for recreation. My mother kindly lent me some money, and I bought an old Army jeep. On long weekends I would head up into the Rockies to camp and fish. In the autumn, with yellow aspen leaves spiraling to the ground, I hunted and killed my first deer. But the Rockies were just a temporary respite. They weren't enough. I lay awake nights thinking of Alaska, vowed that as soon as I was discharged I was heading north.

For all the ways I wanted to escape it, I see now that my two years in Big D were a great gift. It was there that I first began to think about the contrasts between the natural world, the cool peace of it that pulled at me so, and what I began to call the manufactured world. There was some quality in the natural world, a neutral receptiveness, a spiritual energy, that was the antithesis of the frantic, dominating energy that I felt around me in the city, the creeping anxiety that I daily witnessed in the mental hospital.

I began to see that hospital as a place that took in only a few of the most acute victims of a modern war being waged on many fronts. It was a war that resided in attitudes and perceptions that were distorted and inaccurate, that were built on a single insane idea: that by making war we can somehow have peace. Ultimately, I was just beginning to see that battlefields the world over, large and small, begin and end in the human heart.

4

the fires of youth

Fire, like the wolf, performs the role of predator, a sort of
megapredator that balances the hand of life with death.
RICHARD MANNING, "The Failure of Literature"

My second year at Colorado Psychiatric I first saw B. She
sat in front of me at a staff meeting, tall and slender,
dark hair to her shoulders. In a meeting room, crowded with
doctors, psychologists, nurses, and technicians, she stood out,
an unfamiliar face, yet at the same time somehow familiar.
The head psychiatrist introduced her, said she was a student
nurse who'd been assigned to 2-South. She stood gracefully,
and in a wonderfully soft voice told us a little about herself.
She seemed confident, at ease, had an immediate sense of humor. I was struck by her beauty, her high cheekbones and
green eyes.

The next day after the staff meeting I was in the dayroom
playing pool with a schizophrenic boy named Scott when B
walked in and sat down. Scott's technique was to take a shot,

and if he missed to just pick up the ball and put it in the pocket. I was trying to get him to play by the rules, patiently explaining after each shot that he couldn't just pick up the balls like that. Scott was having none of my suggestions. "It's the way I play pool," he said. "Scott's rules."

Yeah?" I said, appealing with logic. "What if I do the same thing?"

"You can't, you're not Scott. I'm only Scott."

I gave in and let him play by his rules, which brought the game to a quick finish. I put my pool cue back in the wall rack, summoned my courage, and introduced myself to her. She smiled. "Oh, you're the one who's supposed to orient me."

I was delighted, though I tried not to let on. I showed her around the ward, explained what I knew about working there. "You were good with that boy," she said. "I hope I can do as well."

I don't recall how I asked her out the first time, but at some point I did. She accepted. Within a couple of weeks we were in love, or at least what we thought was love.

Her parents, who lived in Denver, objected immediately to the idea of her going out with a conscientious objector. Her father, a retired Navy officer and veteran of World War Two, thought my pacifism was an abomination. A couple of months after B and I met we decided to get married. Her father told B that he wanted nothing to do with either of us if she married me. Her mother basically agreed with him.

I suspect that if they hadn't been so set against me, B and I would most likely not have gone ahead with the wedding. As it was, though, I represented an alternative for her, a statement of independence, a chance to flee two very domineering people. She said as much years later when our marriage was on the way down.

And I was such an innocent with women. True, I'd had a couple of girlfriends in high school, and I'd dated a woman

40

at the Mennonite college, but none of them had been a high-scale romance. I was riddled with hormonal pulses, but routinely abstained from sex. My abstinence was an almost pathological fear of being tied down, of getting someone pregnant and losing my freedom. While I yearned for connection, at the same time I was deathly afraid of being connected too much. But this woman offered something different. She was taken by my enthusiasm for heading to Alaska. She saw me as an adventurer, both my desire for a different life and my pacifism, different from the boys she had dated in high school and college. And I saw a good, kind woman who was attracted to my dream. And it struck me hard, the idea of a companion; it had never occurred to me before that I might do anything but head north on my own. The agreement that underpinned our June 1967 marriage: once I was free of my draft obligation, we would head for Alaska together.

We were married in the mountains outside Denver, on a beautiful, sun-strewn day, the air tinted with the smell of pines. The chapel, a glass-fronted edifice that looked up onto the alpine slopes of Long's Peak, was full of friends from the hospital and her college. Neither set of parents was there. We hadn't asked them. In fact I hadn't even told my parents we were getting married until a day or two before the wedding.

We stood at the altar. The minister began the ceremony. B looked radiant, wearing a very sixties above-the-knee white dress and a short lace veil. I did my best to appear casual and involved, but I was scared, petrified really. *I should not be doing this* kept tripping over and over in my mind. When the minister asked if I would take this woman in sickness or in health, my mind said *No*, but "I do" came out of my mouth.

Such a convoluted mix of pure stubbornness and some misplaced sense of duty carried me through that ceremony. I still don't understand all of it, though I know there was a big dose of Mennonite "should" in it. I *should* be ready to be married. I *should* be ready to settle down. After all, I reasoned, I'm of that age. People get married when they fall in love. And there was the old resistance to authority in it. To hell with what her parents thought of it, we're going ahead anyway. Ironically, even though we married in spite of her parents objections, and didn't even consider my own parents, in another way we married to accommodate all of them, to make ourselves right in their eyes. Both sets of parents would have certainly been horrified to think of us living together in sin.

B, I know, had her doubts also. But she kept them to herself. We saw no other option; we were caught on the cusp between people getting married for traditional reasons and a newly budding time when people were just beginning to experiment with relationship as something else.

I was discharged from alternative service early in February 1968. We went back to Indiana, where we both took short jobs, B as a temporary nurse in the local hospital, me as a carpenter's helper. My parents liked B immediately. We stayed with them and saved everything we made the next two months. Toward the end of April we bought a tiny travel trailer, a hedge against the rumor we'd heard that housing was hard to find in Alaska. We loaded it with canned goods, our winter clothes, fishing gear, my guns, and a supply of shells. I hitched it to our Toyota Land Cruiser. We figured we were ready.

Late April 1968 we left, two youngsters on our way to start a new life. My parents stood together on their back lawn and waved good-bye as we pulled away. I recall no sadness in that moment, no regret. The feeling was more one of taking a deep breath after holding it far too long.

We passed west and north, through the checkerboard fields of the Midwest, left the bland predictability of the place that had always made me feel closed in and dull, left it behind and crossed the Canadian border. Up into Saskatchewan we went, west through Manitoba, north through Alberta, turning northwest at the shining new city of Edmonton. Somewhere beyond Edmonton the country began to feel better. More forest than field now, a sense of bigness, feeling even bigger than the Great Plains, if that could be possible. There was a deep calm to it, unfathomable yet right, a balm that began to soothe the restlessness in me. At Dawson Creek, British Columbia, six hundred miles north of the U.S. border a large white concrete obelisk sat in the middle of the main street. MILE 'O' ALASKA HIGHWAY, it read, FAIRBANKS, 1,523 MILES.

The highway was mostly gravel then, a spring-busting hellhole, choking dust, windshields and headlights spidering with cracks from the flying rocks. We drove north, escaped the predictable, and came to a place that finally fit, as if it had been held in keeping for me.

I was just turned twenty-three, B still twenty-two, on our way to start a new life together. She sat beside me, trusting my lead, though I know there must have been a part of her that was scared and unsure. There were so many unknowns ahead of us. For me, only once on the trip did the unknowns rise above my excitement. We were camped just north of Dawson Creek. I sat at the table in our little trailer, watching B work at the stove. She turned and smiled at me. I saw her illuminated then, caught in my dream. Suddenly I felt the full weight of that responsibility, all the ways that I had sold her on an idea, and how in that moment I wasn't so sure of it. "I don't know if we're doing the right thing," I said.

B turned away from the stove, concern in her expression. "What's wrong?" she asked. "What is it?

"I don't know," I said.

"Tell me."

I tried. "We're doing what I've always wanted to do, and I'm . . ." I couldn't finish it, couldn't tell her what I really felt because I didn't know enough to know about feelings. Instead I repeated it. "I don't know if we're doing the right thing."

She shook her head. "Please don't say that. It *has* to be the right thing. It's what we're doing."

"Yes," I said. But I couldn't come up with the feeling of right inside me at that moment. Instead, I felt the responsibility of both my life and hers, when I wanted only to be responsible for mine. I was held by the comfort and companionship she offered, and at the same time was torn between the romanticized story of how men go off to the frontier, alone or in the company of other men, and the other story I had taken on at the altar in Denver.

B came over and sat with me at our tiny table, reached across and took my hands in hers. "We'll be all right," she said.

"We will be," I said, though right then I could not feel it in my heart.

I look back at those moments in that tiny travel trailer, our home on wheels, and I know at some level I was scared, petrified really, that my youthful bluster wouldn't protect us in some new place. I felt the real fear of a young man truly faced with the opening of his life, the reality of stepping up to dreams and seeing that dreams are only choices, and that choices can lead you in so many complicated directions.

North we went, through places with names that read like a Robert Service poem: Fort St. John, Fort Nelson, Watson Lake, Muncho Lake, Whitehorse, Destruction Bay, Beaver Creek. North to the future. We left a place where gas sold for twenty-six cents a gallon to come to a place where roadhouses along the highway sold it for an unbelievable ninety cents. We watched our money dwindle. But it's a Canadian gallon, we would remind each other, a quart bigger.

We traveled on and marveled at a sun that barely set. The first week of May we'd made it far enough north that at midnight you could read a newspaper outside.

We saw moose standing in ponds alongside the road, big gangly-looking brutes, plunging their ugly, roman-nosed heads beneath the surface and coming up with mouthfuls of dark green sedge, water streaming from their ears and antlers. In one camp in northern British Columbia I awoke to a thud against the side of the trailer. I sat up and faced a black bear peering through the window inches away. I was thrilled. The next morning muddy bear prints on the side of the trailer affirmed that we had indeed left Indiana. In the southern Yukon we sighted a mature bald eagle sitting in a cottonwood snag, its fierce yellow eyes and feet and curved beak bright as egg yolks in the sunlight. I was terribly excited at the sight of an eagle, such a rarity in the sixties because of the toll DDT had wrought. "That's a sign we're getting north," I told B. Once, just shy of the Alaska border, a lynx loped high-assed across the road in front of us, stopped once to look back, then melted like a tawny ghost into the stunted shadows of a black spruce forest.

It took us twelve days to make the Alaska border from Indiana. We passed through customs and continued on. A few miles past the border we stopped and walked a ways off the road. The two of us stood there looking south at the big Wrangell–St. Elias Mountains off in the distance and I felt myself come home. Is this real? I asked myself. How could a place that I had only dreamed of, schemed about, read of, in the instant of entering feel so right? Back at the rig I watched B standing there at the edge of the highway, looking so soft and vulnerable and pretty, and wondered if it was the same for her. Wondered, but couldn't ask. Because so many young men don't know how to ask things that matter.

We had a hundred and fifty dollars left. At Tok Junction, the first town across the border, the Alaska Highway continued on to Fairbanks, and another highway, the Tok Cut-off, headed south toward Anchorage. I pulled off the road at the junction. "Where do we go?" I asked B.

She sat there dusty and tired. "Remember those people from Fairbanks we met on the highway?" she said. "Remember they offered us a shower? I *really* want a shower."

So of all the places we could have ended up in Alaska, Fairbanks won on the promise of a shower. We headed northwest along the valley of the Tanana River, through the delicate greens of newly leafed birch and aspen. South of the highway, the white peaks of the Alaska Range towered like sentinels over the broad reach of the valley. Here and there unnamed lakes glistened at a distance. On that single day between Tok and Fairbanks, I wanted to turn into those mountains to the south. I wanted to walk for days, until I could breathe fully, until the yearning was satiated.

But we traveled on; we had only that pitiful ration of money left.

We pulled into Fairbanks early afternoon, the sixth day of May, to an exceptionally early spring. The soft green blanket of aspens on the hillsides north of town stood in sharp contrast to the city itself. Fairbanks had a raw, temporary feel to it. Buildings looked like they'd been thrown together in a high wind. Most of the outlying roads were still gravel. Downtown, among the bars and churches and small businesses, tiny log cabins sat askew, settling into the silt like tired elders, relics of the early gold rush.

But it was all new for us; a feeling of possibility permeated everything. The place was big, lots of room, plenty of room for sixties idealists. In the whole state there were 250,000 residents—fewer people than lived in, say, Omaha, Nebraska, then.

We joined the old-timers, the boomers of the thirties, forties, and fifties already there, the Chamber of Commerce suits who were even then trying their best to turn it into

California, and the GIs protecting everyone from the Red
Menace. We got down to the business of making a life for
ourselves.

The people who offered us a shower were generous, the
way most everyone was generous in Fairbanks then. We
parked our trailer on a piece of land they owned out on the
edge of town. On the second day I inquired at the Federal
Bureau of Land Management, the BLM, and was told by a
clerk that they had an opening for a dozer operator, fighting
forest fires. I made an appointment to see the man hiring. I
was full of hope, excited, particularly given that the U.S. Customs officials at the border had discouraged us about finding any work in Alaska.

I showed up on time. The man hiring sat behind a wide
wooden desk. He motioned for me to sit down in a chair opposite. He was a bulldog of a man, fat, old, weathered. As he
studied what I assumed was my one-page application he
rhythmically tapped a cigarette in a copper ashtray set in a
circle of deer hooves. Smoke curled up and around his face.
He looked up. "Says here you know something about operating a dozer. That so?"

I told him my experience with dozers, that I'd run a John
Deere on the farm I'd worked on one summer, had operated
a D-6 another summer backfilling gas line through Indiana,
told him my experience operating a dozer in a sawmill in
Oregon when I was out on the road bumming around. It was
all true, but I glossed it up a bit, took some risks with the actual facts, like I'd only run the D-7 in the sawmill ten days or
so before the outfit had gone on strike and I'd been laid off.

"You don't look like a goddamned Cat operator to me," the
man said. "You look too damned young."

I rose to the bait. "I'm a good operator," I said.

"You say."

"I do."

"You sure you ain't making things up here, just 'cause you need a job bad?"

I rankled. "I do need a job," I said, "but not bad enough to lie to you. You can either hire me or not. I'm a damn good operator. Put me on a dozer, I'll prove it. I can't prove anything standing here."

"I guess that's true," the man said. And that was it, the interview was over almost before it began. I left feeling like I'd blown any chance of a job with BLM, ever. I berated myself on the ride out of town. *Why the hell couldn't I just get it right, just let some things go once in a while?*

No way did I want to face B, so I drove around awhile, discouraged and mad. When I finally got back to the trailer she was gone, out walking, I supposed. There was a note taped to the door, from our friends with the shower. "Call the man at BLM," it said, "ASAP."

I called. The man answered. "We'll give you a try on that dozer," he said. "Report out to the fire base tomorrow morning at eight."

I felt exhilarated, but I pulled it in. "Thanks a lot," I said. "I apologize for getting short with you."

"No problem," the man said. "I like your spunk. You'll probably make it up here."

I reported to the fire base at eight the next morning. The boys in the shop were expecting me. The equipment boss took me out to the dozer. When I saw it, an ancient, cable-blade, D-8 Caterpillar, a monster relic from World War II, my hopes plummeted. I didn't have a clue how to start it. This is it, I thought, fired before I even begin. The equipment boss waited.

"I don't believe I know how to start this model," I said.

He smiled. "Yeah, this model can be tough."

He showed me how to crank the gas-powered pony engine, how to work two levers that engaged a clutch that engaged a flywheel that turned the big diesel engine. The diesel sputtered and roared into life. I crawled up into the seat.

I've always had a feel for equipment. It's like I can sense the mechanical heart, the rhythm of the machine, can just slip down into a zone that reveals what it needs to operate smoothly. I must admit, too, that there is a seduction to the feel of power, the roar and clatter, the poetry of levers and pedals all in sync, a daunting, destructive efficiency. Operating big machines can be an addictive thing. I know there's so much irony in this, because I've come so to detest what big machines are doing to the planet. I wish them all gone now.

The foreman stood down on the ground and watched me. I worked the hand clutches and brakes a couple of times, then opened the throttle and popped it into gear, pulled back, and engaged the main clutch. The big machine lurched forward. I let it run a few feet before I stopped it, backed up, and spun it once. I pulled forward again and dropped the blade, skimmed it along the ground, raised it, backed up again, and rocked to a stop alongside the foreman. He looked up at me, smiled, said, "You'll do."

I had a job. A week later B got a nursing job at St. Joseph's Hospital. She was delighted, though the wages were not what she had hoped for, less than she would have made back in Colorado.

That summer I fought fires all over the road system of Alaska, making the unbelievable wage of $4.25 an hour, the highest wage paid to any of the emergency firefighters. The dozer was hopeless in soft ground, slow as glacial ice.

But I felt like I'd been given a gift, to finally be in Alaska and working out in wild country, and to actually be paid for it. I loved fire fighting, loved the acidy smell of tundra and spruce burning, the adrenaline rush, the combatlike excitement, though once I nearly lost my life on a fire up the Elliot Highway north of Fairbanks.

I was running tandem with another Cat, pushing hard to cut a line around a couple-thousand-acre blaze. The other Cat broke down. I suppose it would have been all right to stop then, that from a safety standpoint it would have been permissible. But I continued on alone, pushing and backing, pushing and backing, leveling acres of spruce and birch, opening a wound across the country that would take a century or more to heal.

It never occurred to me that I was devastating the boreal forest in a way that a fire never would or could, that a lightning fire might be part of an ecological plan. None of the ecological ramifications of fire occurred to anybody in the land management business then, and if they had, nobody would have listened. We were men who had a job to do. This was combat, war. We were holding fast against the brutal, destructive forces of nature, and we were heroes for it.

I'd just made it to the back side of the fire, about to cut it off, when the wind shifted ninety degrees and began to blow hard in my direction. In no time I could see the fire racing toward me, orange flames torching the tops of the spruce, hissing and crackling, white smoke billowing up above the flames into an immense anvil cloud. I spun the Cat and popped it into high gear, pushed it as hard as I could, attempting to retrace the fire line back to the road.

The Cat's tracks slapped loose, clanked like demons. Just as I thought I might make it, within a minute of escape, the fire jumped the line ahead, shooting enormous wild flames a hundred feet into the air. I could feel the angry heat of the fire, the full danger, but I was determined not to leave the Cat. My only recourse then was to turn and run at an angle from the fire, over the lip of a slope that pitched miserably steep into a rough tangle of rocks and brush below.

I headed down, chancing it, but in less than a hundred yards came to a steep drop-off that was guaranteed suicide to take with any kind of a machine.

I locked the brakes, the dozer pitched so steeply forward that sitting in the seat I was almost standing upright. I turned and watched the fire crown the hill above me. "I'm screwed," I said out loud, feeling the bottomless fear of complete helplessness, of total vulnerability.

But then just as quickly the fire lost power as it dropped below the drive of the wind. It was still coming at me, only a lot slower.

Off to the east, two redardant planes came in low, their engines booming against the snap of the flames. The planes passed close overhead, circled once, then dove low, dropping great red misting clouds of redardant across the leading edge of the fire. I wondered if they could see me, considered trying to get their attention, though I had no notion how I might do that. It didn't matter anyway, because as soon as their cargo was discharged they pulled up steep and disappeared into the clouds, back toward the fire base in Fairbanks.

I studied my situation, figured all I could do was wait to see if the wind might shift again, or the fire might just burn itself out on the slope. I knew if it got too close I would have to abandon the Cat. I would have to scramble like hell, do my best to find some way down the cliff.

But again, things turned lucky. The wind switched once more, quartered across the slope, and above me the fire died. It's now or never, I thought to myself. Get the hell uphill and out of here the same way I came in.

I tried backing the Cat, but the tracks just spun helplessly in the loose soil.

I had two choices. The first, shut the Cat off and leave it there, hoping the other dozer could come later and cable me back up the hillside, hope that I could make my way on foot back to the road. But that idea of leaving it didn't appeal at all. I wanted to get out my own way, didn't want to admit I'd been beaten.

The other choice, because I thought the Cat could pull itself if it was pointed frontward uphill, was to spin it around. I knew that spinning was going to be a risky proposition, because the hill was clearly steeper than what a Cat could take sideways. I didn't let myself think about what would happen if I didn't pull it off: the Cat rolling with me on it, twelve tons of steel, bouncing and careening off the cliff all the way to the bottom of the ravine. The key, I knew, was to spin it faster than it could tip.

I didn't think about anything beyond that, didn't want to think about anything. I was a kid trying to be a man, and I just acted. I pushed down on the brakes with both feet, reached down, and unlocked them. I pulled the throttle back full. The stack belched black smoke. I pumped the hand clutch on the left side, then grabbed the main clutch with my right. I took a deep breath, then in one simultaneous motion engaged the main clutch, disengaged the left hand clutch, and pulled my foot off the right brake. The Cat began to spin, the right track gripping and driving, pivoting hard off the left. We hit the full slope sideways, the big machine rocked sickeningly downhill, the uphill track came up off the ground way too far. "Come on baby!" I hollered. The Cat hung there a split second—what seemed an hour or more—then still pivoting it rocked the other way and slammed down hard into a full uphill position. It was almost as if there had been a hand there that pushed it back down.

There was no celebrating, no stopping. I kept the machine going full throttle, tracks spinning and gripping, bouncing, rocking against the slope, slowly gaining the ridge. We punched through the smoking remains of the fire at the rim of the slope, up and over, where we turned and headed for the road, pressing through the black heat of trees and tundra smoldering.

The whole pivoting process could not have taken more than a couple of seconds. The uphill run, twenty. My heart raced. My mouth was cotton dry. Nausea boiled in me from adrenaline pumping through my veins. Only when I'd made it back to the road, had shut the Cat down and crawled off it, did I let myself think how close it had all been. It was the closest I'd ever come to dying.

I never told anyone what really went on that day, just told the fire boss that I'd been cut off and couldn't go forward, so I had to come back to the road. When I got back to Fairbanks a few days later I didn't tell B either, didn't want to worry her. That's the way it was for me back then. My idea of what it meant to be a man, you didn't talk about things like almost dying; even when it stared you in the face it was still held as an abstract notion. You only talked about ways you wanted to live.

The fires and the work that summer, making more money than I ever had before, all were an opening for me. I gained confidence, began to imagine that I could do just about anything if I put my mind to it. And I was getting to know more about Native Alaskans. Eskimos and Indians were the grunts, the ground troops of the fire wars. Every village, no matter how remote, had a crew of men ready to leave on a moment's notice. For many it was their only cash income of the year. I felt drawn to the Native men, liked their stories and their ways. I learned the difference between Athabascan Indians and Eskimos, learned that there are two Eskimo language groups:

Yupik and Inupiat. I learned that Indians and Eskimos have been traditional enemies for centuries, observed how they still glanced suspiciously at one another on the fire lines.

Once, on a fire down on the Kenai Peninsula, I was taking a break close to an Indian crew camped in the lee of a birch grove. An Eskimo crew passed by, coming off the fire, pulaskis and chain saws and piss bags over their shoulders. A young Indian tending a pail of coffee over a campfire called out, "Heh, look at them little Eskimos. They sure are funny-looking little guys, aren't they?" The Indians laughed, and the Eskimos kept walking. The next day I heard that the two crews got into a fight, and one of the Indians was cut badly.

I liked my work, but there was one problem. One of the foremen in the equipment shop, a hard rock of a man, ex-Navy, ex–smoke jumper, rabid nigger hater, gook hater, a hater of most anyone or anything that wasn't white Irish Catholic like himself, found out that I'd resisted Vietnam. It was an odd thing, because I knew that in private the foreman liked me. But the absolutes the man carried wouldn't allow him to admit anything like that in public. He seemed to take it as his God-given duty to berate me, of course always with bystanders present. Eyes squinted, teeth clenched: "You were one of those too chickenshit to fight in the war."

"That's not it," I'd say.

"Bullshit, too fucking scared to stand up for your country."

"That's not it, it was an unjust war."

"The hell, there's no such thing as an unjust war when it's your country telling you to fight. You go, period. It's your duty."

The foreman's blind allegiance to country was anathema to me. Even then I could not understand what it was in the human spirit that leads so many to mindless obedience. The irony of the foreman's ranting was that, although he had been in the Navy, he had never gone to Vietnam either. At some level I knew that the punishment he inflicted on me was more about his own self-doubts. But knowing that was not enough. I felt my own hard anger. I wanted to fight him, but I held my temper. It would do no good, I reasoned. Besides, there were my own doubts about my own choices pulling me back.

Times were changing. That year a young woman from Fairbanks demanded to be put on a fire crew. This was unheard of. The foreman was livid. He threatened to quit if women were allowed on fires. But she insisted and before long other women joined her in her demands. They wanted the work, the money, said they had the same rights as men, that they could do it. There was a lot of muttering among the veteran firefighters. But the women prevailed; the district manager relented and formed an all-woman crew—headed, of course, by a man. "How'd it go?" guys asked him when he came back from their first fire. Everyone had fantasies of him on the fire participating in wild sex orgies. "They were good workers," he said. "A few of you could learn something from them."

By the middle of August the fires slowed. I'd had enough. A friend at BLM, a man still a close friend today, agreed with me that there had to be more to life than working sixteen-hour days, seven days a week. A year earlier Tom had hitch-hiked north from Michigan. In Fairbanks he teamed up with an old fur trapper known as Herman the German and spent the winter with the German on his trapline up on Beaver Creek, a fine, wild stream that bends west and north around the base of the White Mountains north of Fairbanks. Tom had some wonderful stories of his winter in the bush, stories I wanted for myself.

I told B that I was quitting BLM, that Tom and I were heading off for two or three weeks. She was concerned. "Won't we need the money this winter?"

"The hell with the money," I said. "I didn't come up here to spend my life sitting on the seat of a dozer. We'll figure some way to make it."

"Go ahead," she shrugged, "if it's what you want."

That was B's way then, to yield to my dreams. And my dreams often took me away from her. She was the home fire, one I could return to but seldom tended. We're friends now. Last week in Fairbanks, Maria and I had dinner with her. I told her I was going to write this book. She was pleased. "Don't make me look too good," she said.

I looked across the table at her, the woman who had borne our child. Here she was now, over thirty years later, distinguished-looking and so very capable. In her eyes, along with the sensual and straightforward kindness and compassion that had always been there, life's trials had settled in. But in a good way, one that projected a learned unwillingness to tolerate much in the way of bullshit. She might have followed me for a while, but she was really never a follower. When we ended, she went on to make a life for herself. She's still in Alaska.

5

infatuation

One thing I noticed quickly was that Alaska was almost an
obsession to many of the people living there. It was not simply a place in which they happened to reside: it was a loved
one, a family member, by which their emotions were mo-
nopolized; about which they fretted and dreamed.

JOE MCGINNISS, *Going to Extremes*

Tom and I drove the Land Cruiser back along the Alaska
Highway. Close to the Canadian border, above the Indian village of Northway, we put a canoe in on the upper
Tanana River. It felt good to be on the river, to be away from
town and the fire wars. On that float I saw my first wolf, a
beautiful black creature sunning itself on a sandbar, laid out
like a dog in front of a fireplace. One of us scraped a paddle
against the side of the canoe and the wolf stood quickly. To
our surprise it didn't run, but just peered watchfully at us
from the tops of sloe eyes. We floated closer and the wolf
turned and trotted a few paces. I called softly to it, "Wolf." It

wheeled to face us, lowered its head, and stared again. We came within seventy-five feet of it, maybe less, before it turned quickly and disappeared like a phantom into the willows. Tom and I were elated.

When I recall my first wolf, I can't help but think of Aldo Leopold writing in *A Sand County Almanac* the essay "Thinking Like a Mountain." As a young man he and his traveling companions spotted a pack of wolves and blazed away at them. "In those days," Leopold says, "we had never passed up a chance to kill a wolf." They shot two, and, he recounts, "We reached the old wolf in time to watch a fierce green fire dying in its eyes. I realized then, and have known ever since, that there was something new to me in those eyes—something known only to her and to the mountain. I was young then, and full of trigger itch. I thought that because fewer wolves mean more deer, that no wolves would mean hunters' paradise. But after seeing the green fire die, I sensed that neither the wolf nor the mountain agreed with such a view."

I've seen many wolves since that first one. On several occasions I've observed them kill with great delight and efficiency. Once, on one of the coldest nights of winter, I was awakened by my sled dogs *whoofing* scared. I hurried to the front window. Beneath the liquid light of a cold, yellow moon, a pair of wolves circled my kennel. Thinking they were hungry and after my dogs, I grabbed my rifle and pushed open the front door. The pair melted quickly into the moon's shadows. On several occasions I've had wolves in the Arctic walk right into camp to stand and stare intently at me, no more than fifteen feet away. It has always been those eyes that have fascinated me, some beckoning mystery, a unity of spirit that calls on the observer to pay attention.

Yet wolves have been so misunderstood and maligned. We contemporary humans seem to detest those animals that be-

have most like us—wanton killers, efficient and ruthless predators; we see ourselves in the mirror. Or as Richard Nelson
says in *The Island Within,* "In the end . . . it seems that an animal is regarded as 'killer' when people empathize with its
prey or believe it competes for something they prey on themselves." We hold on to old visions.

Despite their predatory ways, in the eyes of wolves resides
an intelligence that lives beyond the capacity of our rational
minds. Even though I was a hook and bullet devotee when I
saw my first wolf, I didn't reach for my rifle. I had read *A
Sand County Almanac* a couple of years earlier; perhaps
Leopold eased the way. Even though I would have willingly
shot at them if I thought they were trying to kill my dogs,
there was just some common sense in me that had no desire
to kill a wolf just for the sake of killing it.

I know it would be easy to go off here on some mystical
binge, to fall into the trap of romanticizing the wolf with the
same fervor with which it's been villainized throughout the
centuries. Still, I have to say that there's a quality represented
in the wolf, and the grizzly as well, that symbolizes the essential spirit of the North American wilderness that I was
drawn to. When both the wolf and the grizzly are gone from
a place, then it becomes very difficult to make a case for calling that place wilderness. The land in their absence becomes
something else, a place that may still harbor some wild qualities, but a place seriously diminished.

Perhaps a day will come when we moderns can find it in
ourselves to embrace different intelligences. Then, I imagine,
we will have come to a place of healing connectedness, of ex-
panded consciousness.

Tom and I finished the canoe trip, hitchhiked back to the
Land Cruiser, drove back and picked up the canoe, then

headed south to the Kenai Peninsula. On the way we passed through Anchorage. At the end of the sixties, Anchorage was a gray, hardscrabble city, caught economically on the cusp between the World War II construction boom and the oil boom soon to come. A square grid of streets that harbored trailer parks, ramshackle churches transplanted from the Bible belt, and cheap housing tracts right out of New Jersey. The downtown was given to pawnshops and strip joints and a multitude of hard-duty bars. Indians and Eskimos, caught by the white man's alcohol, slept in alleys and staggered through the downtown streets. In my growing allegiance to a place, Anchorage wasn't Alaska but an alien presence that felt plunked down and at odds with its surroundings. It left an impression that still lingers with me today: the pernicious works of industrial humans posed against a backdrop of wild beauty.

We left Anchorage and carried on south to the Kenai: the temperate rain forest, gray skies, mild and maritime climate of south-central, coastal Alaska. We launched the canoe on a huge, glacier-fed lake, paddled through turquoise water to a deep clear-water stream that flowed from lush mountains to the east. We fished for silver salmon. At night, Tom and I sat around a fire and talked about how much we cared for this place called Alaska. We had both found something that seemed to fit us well. But Tom was facing the draft. He wasn't sure what he would do about it. "Maybe," he said, "I could just stay out on the trapline with the German. They'd never find me there."

I liked the feel of south-central Alaska. The glaciated mountains and gray seascapes were dramatically beautiful. But south-central didn't grab me the way the Interior did. There was just something about the Interior that felt right: space and more space; a round-the-clock sun circling boundless skies; in the afternoon those skies building with great, tumbling ranks of black and gray cumulus. The Interior fit me. Of course, I had yet to experience a winter there.

We headed north again, to the village of Talkeetna. We parked the rig alongside the village airstrip, shouldered packs, and walked tie to tie, north along the Alaska Railroad. After several miles we came to a rough jeep trail that cut east into a small river reputed to be great fishing. Twice on the trail we saw black bears lope off into the woods ahead of us.

Late August. The sun disappeared late in the evening. Through a moonless and cloudy night we walked. Like blind men we felt our way along the trail. Finally, below us we heard the sound of rushing water. "We'd better stop," Tom said. It was so dark that we had to get down on our hands and knees and feel around for a spot level and clear enough to camp.

We settled into our bags, but sleep was difficult; all night large creatures crashed through the woods around us. Finally, early morning, the light grew enough that I could just make out the gray shapes of trees close. Tom was sleeping, breathing softly. I heard a stick break. I sat up in my bag. There, less than fifteen feet away, stood a black bear up on its hind legs, staring curiously. "Hello bear," I said. The bear snorted, turned and scrambled into the trees. I scooted out of my bag for a look around. We were camped just a few feet from the edge of a steep bluff that ran down to the creek. Our two bags lay to each side of a rutted and muddy game trail, which was solidly covered with bear tracks.

Later in the morning we climbed down to the creek. The water boiled crimson, filled bank to bank with migrating salmon. We caught fish until our arms ached, salmon and rainbow trout both. The sandbars and mud along the edge of the creek were a jumble of bear tracks, both black and grizzly (one of the only places I've seen both species intermingle).

By the end of that trip, even though we had never ventured far from the road system—I had not yet entered deep wilderness—I was even more infatuated with Alaska. I only wanted more of it. Secretly, I made a vow: till death do us part.

But infatuation disallows the sight of any blemishes. It holds you numb, dumb, and unwilling to see the truth. Infatuation, also, is only partly about the object of one's affections. It's also about how one is reflected in the mirror of that object. I was legitimately drawn to a place that fit me in many ways, but one of those ways was how it allowed my new fantasy to thrive—my willingness to play the thunderstruck lover in a drama called frontier. I had yet to see that defining any place as frontier is an invitation to its end, an ironclad guarantee that it will fall to the same economic forces that every other frontier has fallen to during five hundred years of European colonization. It's a hard irony: the very qualities that draw us to frontier in our conquering of it are the first qualities to be lost. Define something as the *last* frontier, and it's assured that anyone who did not get his chance elsewhere will show up now, for one last big go at it.

Back in Fairbanks, by the middle of September, the tundra on the hills had turned to reds and rusts, the aspen and birch brittle yellows. Sandhill cranes warbled insanely as they kettled upward through the thin fall air to gain altitude for their escape south. Off the big river flats—the Yukon and Tanana—white-fronted geese and Canadas, pintail ducks and mallards and wigeons and shovelers and green-winged teal, set their wings and dropped into the farm fields at the university. Once a flock of tundra swans filed overhead, bleating their anxious cries. All of it made me even happier to be alive in this place.

I tried hunting moose on weekends, but I had no knowledge of how or where, so came up empty-handed. But I determined I would learn what I needed to be able to live off wild game.

We sold our trailer and I used the money to pay nonresident tuition at the university. I wanted to study wildlife management, badly enough that I was willing to risk the boredom of school again.

The seasons moved much faster than I was accustomed to. One day it was summer, the next fall, and then before you knew it the snow came and the Chena River, passing tannin-stained through town, began flowing ice: long, jagged crystals tinkling and coalescing into bigger and bigger chunks, until the whole waterway was one solid band of white running out to the big Tanana River at the edge of town, down the Tanana to the Yukon, hundreds of miles down the Yukon all the way out to the great, mysterious Bering Sea.

That winter, 1968/69, the first Hercules cargo planes began roaring overhead, hauling load after load of construction materials up to the North Slope, as the locals called it. Development had begun of what was rumored to be a massive new oil discovery, one of the biggest ever found in North America. *The Daily News-Miner,* the Fairbanks paper, touted the new find as the boom that would finally put Alaska on the map, the best thing since the gold rush. The metaphors used by the developers and schemers were all about control, domination. Men battling nature. War. Humans, against great odds, subduing the Arctic for its oil, gas, and mineral potential. A battle against the elements. An army of workers. The earth reluctantly surrendering its wealth.

The activities that winter were just the simplest warnings of big changes soon to come. But I had no clear sense of any warnings, no idea this place that I had made a vow to could be altered all that much. Those big planes roaring overhead were only a small distraction from my infatuation with a place so big and wild, a life that felt so right. How could anything much be altered?

The only immediate sign of change that affected B and me was an influx of people into town, boomers, a hard lot of construction migrants looking for work up on the North Slope. With them came a fools' ship full of con men and pimps and prostitutes, all dedicated to taking the workers' wages. With all the new folks in town, rentals were harder to find, rents started to climb. Still, we managed to find a dilapidated, one-room frame cabin close to downtown—faded military green on the outside, a depressing pus-yellow inside, one crooked door and four minuscule windows. We bought some used walnut-veneer furniture from the surplus yard on the Army base, and settled in with our meager possessions. We felt lucky to have a place to live, although eighty-five dollars a month seemed like a lot for what it was.

It was a complete dump, in a part of town where there was no city water or sewer. The neighborhood was a mishmash of frame houses and log cabins and mobile homes, all packed together on tiny city lots. Each lot had its own well and septic tank. Our first clue that we might not be living in the best of circumstances came when we noticed that if the water sat in the toilet for more than a few minutes it turned brown, with a vile blue-green scum floating on top. A month or so after we moved in, the water started coming out of the kitchen tap, frothing soap suds and smelling like sewage. When I investigated I discovered that the shallow well we were getting our water from was about twenty-five feet away from the neighbor's septic tank.

Our landlady was from Fort Smith, Arkansas. Every conversation with her, she let you know that she wished she was still there. She carried a tangerine-colored, geriatric toy poodle around with her wherever she went, and she had the biggest beehive hairdo I had ever seen on a woman. On the coldest days of the winter she still wore her gold lamé go-go boots inside or out. "Hell's bells, don't worry about it," she said when

I brought up the water situation. "It won't hurt you. I've been using it for years. Look at me, healthy as a runnin' horse."

The winter of 1968/69 was also one of the coldest ever in Fairbanks. The middle of December, one night we went to bed with snow falling softly outside, the temperature just below freezing. The next morning the snow had stopped and the sky was clear. The cabin was freezing. I turned the heater up before going outside in my shirtsleeves to burn the trash. As soon as I stepped out the door I sensed something new was afoot; the air burnt my skin, prickled the hair in my nose. When I bumped the plastic wastebasket against the side of the burn barrel the basket shattered in my hands. I hurried back to our hovel and checked the thermometer hanging outside the door. It read sixty below. Overnight the temperature had plunged ninety degrees, and the vise of an Interior Alaska winter was closed fully upon us.

The tiny windows of the cabin frosted over on the inside, solid translucent crystal. Frost crept up the inside walls, halfway to the ceiling in the corners. Water spilled on the floor would freeze solid in a matter of minutes.

We passed the winter solstice, December 21, a day that all Alaskans note fondly, when the free fall into darkness ends and the light slowly begins to return. B and I were intrigued by the radio and newspaper reports each day, detailing the hours of light and how many minutes of gain or loss there were from the day before. For thirty-four straight days the mercury never rose above minus forty. The air stood still as death, glittering with tiny ice crystals. Exposed skin would freeze in a matter of seconds. The sun, only a short midday tease, hung low on the south horizon. It set less than two hours after it rose. At night, ice-fog, a frozen soup of car exhaust and chimney smoke, got so thick that it was impossible to see the stars or the moon or even the lights of the next-door neighbor. Much of that time we lived in a dark, surrealistic haze.

We cranked up the old oil burner in our cabin. The flame flickered along. But every now and then something got into the burner, and it would start to rock back and forth, making loud *whooshing* noises, like the whole operation was about to launch itself into space.

For two and a half months I couldn't start the Land Cruiser. Even if I had been able to, it would have been miserably cold if not impossible to drive under the flapping canvas top. B had to take a cab to work, which ate up a good deal of our budget. I invested in some Army surplus cold-weather gear, and hitchhiked the five miles to the university. Some mornings the ice-fog was so thick that a car couldn't have seen me hitchhiking if I had been wearing flashing neon lights. I walked and walked, and learned how to take care of myself in the cold. I learned how to move slowly, how to breathe shallow and keep all but a small portion of my face and beard covered with my parka hood. Truthfully, I minded almost none of it. It was all a big adventure, survival, a time to prove my toughness.

Only one small part of it began to irritate me. The stove oil (which we paid close to a dollar a gallon for) was stored outside in fifty-five-gallon drums. An exposed copper line connected the drums, then ran through a hole in the back wall inside to the stove. The system worked fine until the temperature hit sixty-three below. Then the paraffin in the oil turned to sludge, which would block the lines. The fire, that pitifully small, flickering element that was the focal point of our survival, would flutter out. Within minutes our shack would be freezing.

Of course, the temperature only dropped to sixty-three or colder in the middle of the night. B would shake me awake. "The stove's out again," she'd say in her soft voice. I would creep out from under our monstrous pile of Army surplus blankets, dance from foot to foot as I put on my winter gear and pulled on my boots. I would grab a propane torch that I kept inside by the stove to keep it from freezing and clump to the door, which would always be frosted shut. I would kick it open, then stagger outside, the air stabbing at my nostrils, my breath charging out in huge vaporous clouds reflected in the dim yard light. Around behind the cabin, swearing liberally at the night, the cold, the landlady, I labored down on my hands and knees, rolled over on my back, then scooted under the oil barrels far enough to reach the lines. The cold clawed at my backside and seeped beneath my parka. The feeble blue flame of the torch pulsed against the darkness. Sometimes I would have to pull my mittens off and hold the torch in my bare hands just to keep it from freezing up before the job was done. Within seconds my hands would feel like wooden clubs. Several nights I went out three or four times. Once, just at the end of the worst of it, I went out five times. That night, at 6 A.M., I shined the flashlight on the thermometer hanging outside the front door. Through the dense clouds of my breath I read it: minus seventy, the thermometer's bottom limit. That day it was past noon before the sun finally shone enough to warm things up to sixty-two below, and the oil began to flow on its own.

We scraped along our first winter. The cab fare and oil costs kept us on the edge financially. One week, just before B's paycheck, we were down to peanut butter and white bread and a single can of tuna. Most people in Fairbanks were amazingly friendly and generous, always figuring how to help a "cheechako," as they called a greenhorn, someone trying to get through his first winter. Once a kind neighbor must have sensed our plight. We came home one evening to find the front quarter of a moose propped up against the wall inside our door, still perfectly frozen. To this day I don't know who it was that gave us the meat.

Some nights I would get restless, filled with cabin fever. I would pull on my winter gear and walk through the cold, my parka hood drawn tight about my face. Beyond the edge of town I would stop. Away from the noise and the lights, I watched the Aurora Borealis dance and flicker back and forth across the sky, a great heavenly fire, faint blues and greens and yellows, alive and flowing, as if driven by some mysterious cosmic wind. The experts say you cannot hear them, but I swear I could, a faint swishing sound or a whirring, in an odd way more a knowing of sound than an actual noise. Those nights were complete for me. Magic, a reckoning with some mystery of the universe that pulled at me. I knew then, even though my immediate circumstances were short of what I wanted for myself and my wife, that none of it really mattered. I was enthralled by a bigger thing.

But that bigger thing was becoming complicated. The first blemish on the face of Alaska was my growing recognition of the power of cold. For modern humans in winter, fire was the sole difference between life and death. Without it, one slip and life could be gone in minutes. I became aware that I was both afraid of and attracted to the cold. There was an edge of terrible loneliness with that feeling, a sense that I faced a force that was immense and impartial, a universe that ultimately laughed at the puny notions of men. In the exaggeration of the Interior Alaska winter, I could not help but begin to feel for the first time the sadness of my own inevitable mortality. To be so alive, to be so in love with life, and to think it all would be lost some day.

Those nights I would come back from walking, undress quietly in the cold, then slip into bed with my young wife. I would pull her to me. I wanted her to feel what I felt, to reassure me. But she could not know what was in me, because I could not articulate it. I was lost in the muteness of my own childish manhood.

When the cold spell finally broke at the end of January, the temperature shot up to minus twenty, a regular heat wave. Neighbors walked around outside in their shirt-sleeves. Children romped in the sooty snow. We were both relieved, yet proud that we had made it through, that we had proved we could handle the worst of it and survive.

How both of us could maintain such optimism in the face of the reality we lived that winter was a testimony to how we were both connected by a common dream. But my part of that connection was tentative, conditional. Because in my in-fatuation with a place, with all the possibilities of it and the freedom that it promised, little room was left for anything or anyone else.

6

the lure of antlers

Hunting in my experience—and by hunting I simply mean
being out on the land—is a state of mind . . . To hunt means
to have the land around you like clothing. To engage in a
wordless dialogue with it, one so absorbing that you cease to
talk with your human companions. It means to release yourself from rational images of what something "means" and to
be concerned only that it "is." And then to realize that things
exist only insofar as they can be related to other things.

BARRY LOPEZ, *Arctic Dreams*

I'm looking at two faded photos. One is of a young man
kneeling over a bull caribou sprawled on the ground.
Patches of snow dot a tundra plain and a mountainside behind. The pale blue sky is streaked with thin cirrus clouds.
The young man smiles crookedly, his eyes alive and happy.
He's dressed in Levi's and a gray sweatshirt. His left hand
holds a rifle propped against his shoulder. The hand and the
sleeve of his sweatshirt are covered with blood. His right

THE LURE OF ANTLERS

hand grips the bull's antlers covered in dark brown velvet. That hand appears to be bandaged across the palm, wrapped round with adhesive tape. The bull's soft, white muzzle rests on the young man's right knee. Its eyes are glazed. Its ears droop. As I study this photo, I feel nostalgia. I would like to be there again.

The other photo is slightly out of focus, a close-up of the young man sitting on a striped couch in a wood-paneled room. Sun streams through an unseen window, backlighting the scene on the couch. There are plants in the room, a free-standing fireplace, a mahogany Gibson guitar leans up in the far corner. The feel of the room is peaceful, pleasant. The young man is looking down at something, exactly what it's hard to tell. His expression is neutral, not smiling, not frown-ing; he appears to just be there, in that moment. Stretched out on his chest, with its back to the viewer, lies a huge gray cat. The cat's ears are cocked off, as if it's purring, and its left paw is stretched up toward the young man's chin, in what seems to be a gesture of affection. In the cradle of the young man's left arm lies a little girl, perhaps two years old. Her soft eyes are cast down toward a blanket that she holds in chubby little hands. She wears a blue sweatshirt, and blue pants with large pink flowers on them. The sun streams through her long blond hair. She is nothing short of angelic, the expres-sion on her face one of contentment, of safety. As I study this photo I feel something entirely more complicated than with the first photo. A sense of loss. A feeling of being out of place. Yet, below it all I feel this surge of love. I would like to hold that small, beautiful child again.

These two pictures say so much to me. In them resides that young man's essential conflict, the choice between the hearth and the wild, between the comfort of family and the lure of freedom. He, as so many men do, suffered with that choice. In the picture with his child, he had come to something deeply gratifying. But his yearning for open country, his childhood experience of family, the cultural messages he inherited, they all demanded something else.

As I study these pictures, I can't help but think about rites of passage. In this culture we really have none. When does an adolescent boy or girl officially become an adult? What ceremony signifies it? When one gets a driver's license? When one can first legally enter a bar and order a drink? When one is old enough to vote or to die for one's country? When a boy kills his first large animal? When a girl begins her menses? In actuality we have no recognized ceremony, no one to lead us, to tell us the true ways of manhood or womanhood, no one to tell us when we've arrived. When I look back at that young man's life I see his confusion. No one ever declared him a man. He felt he had so much to prove. He had to sort through so many cultural messages that said that hardness, toughness, competitiveness, destructiveness were elements of manhood, that when you were good at these things, then you had arrived.

Spring finally came in late April. "Breakup," Alaskans called it. The snow and ice began to melt, and the dirt roads and paths turned knee-deep in mud. Six months' worth of garbage and dog turds turned up in the black slush of backyards. People bought tickets for the Ice Pool, the lottery for when the ice officially moves on the Tanana at the little downriver town of Nenana. The birch and aspen sent out their first tender buds. Waterfowl returned, great honking flocks of geese passed overhead, eager to return to their nesting grounds.

We had made it through our first winter and we were on our way to being real Alaskans. I felt a secret pride in that. There was nothing I wanted more.

But the city had begun to depress us both. Besides, our Arkansas landlady wanted to double our rent. She made no bones about the fact that she liked the idea of Fairbanks becoming a boom town. "Best thing that ever happened here," she said. "Town needs some jobs." When I confronted her about the rent doubling, she made no apologies. "Shoot fire," she said, "I can make a lot more rentin' to construction workers than I can to a coupla' college kids. Take it or leave it."

For both of us it was clear that the particular circumstances of our shelter had to change; we were not experiencing the pristine life I'd promised B before we left the lower 48. We talked it over and made a decision to move.

We scrounged what money we could, and I bought a ten-by-twelve white canvas wall tent and some rough-cut lumber. I loaded the whole works on a pickup that I borrowed from a friend at the university, drove twelve miles out of town, up a rough dirt track a mile or so that led into a large tract of state land. With an ax and a bucksaw I cut a trail a hundred yards through the bush into a nice stand of white birch. There I cleared and leveled a spot, then hauled the lumber in on my back and built a deck and tent frame. With the wall tent up, I built a bed and some rough kitchen counters inside, and a screen door to keep out the mosquitoes. With that I pronounced it home.

We would have to haul water in jerry cans for drinking and cooking. The outhouse was just a hole in the ground, with a pole wired between two trees over it. The cooking facilities consisted of a Coleman stove and a plastic dishpan. I dug a hole down to permafrost and buried an ice chest for a refrigerator. It wasn't what we'd left in the lower 48, but who cared? It was free and we had some room. We were still living the adventure. We moved out with our few possessions the end of May. We figured we were good in the tent for five months at least. We had no winter plan.

We were squatters and we weren't alone. Other young people, caught by the rent gouging in Fairbanks, moved out onto state land all around town. The state didn't know or didn't care. A few squatters seemed insignificant in those vast lands. A week after we moved into our tent, a couple of B's friends from the hospital put up their tent fifty yards away through the trees.

But I couldn't stay. I wanted to be farther out in the bush, farther away from anything to do with civilization, wanted the life I'd come north for. I hired on with the Bureau of Land Management again, this time to ramrod the construction of the first ever recreational trail built in the interior of Alaska. With neighbors close I didn't feel so bad about leaving B behind to fend for herself for the summer.

She seemed to take it well, seemed happy for me. She only expressed one concern. "What am I going to do if I get a bear in here?" she asked.

"Don't worry about bears," I said. "They won't bother you."

It was the same thing I'd said coming up the Alcan, when we were camped one night in a campground along the highway, and on her way to the outhouse she'd been startled by a bear coming out of the woods. And the same thing I'd told her on our honeymoon, our second day married, camped in the mountains of southern Colorado. Earlier in the day some people we had run into had spotted a black bear crossing a creek bottom just below us. That night she was scared, worried about the bear coming into our camp. I tried to comfort her by minimizing her fears, by denying her feelings. I wanted her to be brave, wanted the city girl I'd married to be an instant outdoor woman, even if she didn't feel that way.

Early summer found me up in the Crazy Mountains, a jumble of bald and rocky hills southeast of the big bend of the Yukon. Despite a summer fire fighting and surviving a tough winter, I was still way green, at least in contrast to my crew of Yupik Eskimos, who had come to the Alaskan mainland from the windswept bleakness of Saint Lawrence Island. Saint Lawrence Island is a hard refuge of rock and tundra, one of the most remote places on the planet, lying far out in the storm-thrashed Bering Sea, closer to Siberia than Alaska. It's a place that gives grudgingly, an arduous and tenuous existence that makes for tough and seriously capable people. Those men I worked with could travel by dog team for miles over a frozen sea, using only the forms of drifted snow for a compass. They knew how to sit patiently for hours over a seal's breathing hole, completely still and Zen-like, waiting for a kill. After days out on the ice they could unerringly find their way home, through a winter darkness so complete it holds the world for months at a time. Back they would come to a village lost in an eternal white expanse, a group of tiny plywood shacks huddled against the harsh Arctic wind.

For the Yupik, compared to their lives on the island, trail building was a picnic, a cakewalk. For me, though, it was serious work. I was twenty-four years old and proud that I'd been given so much responsibility, despite the fact that my foremanship was one of those easy assumptions made by a dominant culture. Since I was the only white on the crew, could write tolerably well, spoke English with a midwestern accent, and had some experience with the government way of doing things, it was naturally assumed by the bosses back in Fairbanks that I would be the foreman. I know now that those Yupik men could have resented me for my enthusiasm, for my youth and inexperience, for my race. But in truth they never displayed such sentiments. They were always kind to me.

I took to the work, loved it. At the time I could not imagine anything fitting me any better. We set up our first camp by helicopter, twelve miles off the road. After that we packed in huge loads of supplies, the Eskimos putting me to shame with what they could carry. Sometimes I would stop and watch them move up a mountainside, loaded high with cartons of water and food and trail-building tools, a single set of bowed legs protruding from beneath a load big enough for an ox. I envied their toughness, the way they took everything that came their way with such equanimity. I wanted to learn from them, to understand their ways. But too often I was incapable of settling inside myself enough to match their quietness. What I observed mostly is that there are other ways of being in the world, ways that are quieter and more connected than the white man's way. I learned, too, that those ways are not always easy to emulate.

We all worked hard, searching out routes, cutting sidehills and switchbacks, building cairns. We went weeks without any fresh meat or produce, subsisting mainly on macaroni, canned beans, corned beef, and Hershey bars. Everyone tired of the diet, though I did more than my crew, because every day they managed to supplement the store-bought fare with birds' eggs and greens and who knew what else they gathered off the tundra. The Eskimos got a big kick out of offering me the more questionable morsels. "You want this egg?" one would say. "It's got a little bird growing in it."

"It's all yours," I'd say. "I'm not all that much into little birds."

"Okay," he'd say, "but you don't know what you're missin'."

"I'm sure of that," I'd say.

Or when we'd catch some grayling: "You want this little fish head?"

"No, thanks."

"The eyes, they's the best part, you know?"

"No thanks, I'll stick with the worst parts."

"Okay, suit yourself." And then he'd make a big show of tipping his head back and dropping the fish head between parted teeth. He'd chew with exaggerated pleasure, eyes half closed. When he was done he'd shake his head in mock concern. "You white guys sure don't know much about eatin'. Kinda worries me."

While I was in the mountains with the Yupik, B was getting up every morning, putting on a white uniform, and driving twelve miles over dusty roads to her job at the hospital. Off work, she would spend most of her time at the tent, reading, tending a small garden, visiting neighbors. On two occasions she had to scare off a black bear by banging on a pot with a wooden spoon. She never talked about giving it up, though, of moving back to town; I think she still wanted so badly to meet my expectations.

I came into town once in June, a couple of times in July, for fresh supplies, and for my crew to take on a little of Fairbanks, which meant mostly hanging out in the bars on Second Avenue. The visits were short, only a couple of days, and even then I was restless; I wanted to get back to the bush.

B seemed to be doing okay. She didn't complain much about anything, about the hardship of living out there without running water, or of needing to commute to work every day over dusty roads in a white uniform. She told me about the bears, was proud of herself for handling them. I was proud of her, too. It was imperceptible to either of us at the time, but I came to see later it was that summer that our paths began to take different turns. It was only a small opening for her, her first hint to herself that she had more abilities than she ever imagined, that she could be more than a woman who defined herself in relationship to a man.

Early August I brought the crew into town again. B and I were glad to see each other. We spent two days together, picking cranberries and blueberries, connecting again after so much time apart. Both mornings, though, she was sick, nauseous, had to get up and go outside to vomit. When she came back inside, she was pale and drawn and refused food, saying she hadn't been eating breakfast lately.

"Maybe you got the flu," I said.

"I don't think so," she replied.

That Sunday night, both of us set to return to work the next morning, we lay spooned together on the narrow mattress. With the nights coming dark again, a candle burned close to the bed, flickering exaggerated shadows on the tent's walls.

She pulled away, turned over, and faced me. "You're probably going to be mad," she whispered.

"Why?" I asked.

"You just are."

"Well, if I am," I said, "I'd like to know why."

She was quiet a moment. Then the words came out in a rush. "I'm pregnant."

I was stunned. "How?" I said. "How? You're using birth control?"

"It doesn't always work," she said. "Sometimes it doesn't. That's just the way it is." She paused. Then quietly. "I know you don't want a child, but I do. And nothing you can say will change my mind."

I didn't say anything more to her. There was nothing I could think of to say. A thing that was not supposed to happen had, and I was unprepared to deal with it. I held her again, but as I did I felt myself pull away from her. I felt myself blame her. She'd slipped up. Betrayed me. I hated thinking it, but it was there in my mind: perhaps she'd gotten pregnant on purpose.

I slept little that night. The next morning I got up early and returned to the hills. The days that followed, as I worked, as I cooked meals, before I fell asleep exhausted, the questions just kept running over and over in my mind. What will it mean to be a father? How was it going to change my life? How would it change us together? I had never even entertained the idea of children. Children did not fit my image of myself. I felt my world closing in, felt all that freedom I had sensed when we came north just slipping away. All I knew how to do was react. React, and pull away.

One evening, late August, the high country turning red and gold, a small herd of caribou came down off the mountain above us and literally walked through camp. The season was open. The limit at that time, south of the Yukon, was three per person. I had my 30:06 along, so I leaped out of my tent and shot fast, dropping three: two bulls and a yearling female.

The survivors wheeled and ran back in the direction they'd come from, mouths agape, eyes white with fright. They disappeared fast over the ridge. I walked up to the larger bull lying in the tundra, its eyes already filming. Looking down at it I felt a pulsing of my blood, a raw and primitive triumph. I wanted to shout, but the Eskimos were close so instead I did my best to appear casual and calm, like this was something I did every day. Beneath my elation was also a twinge of regret, some sense that this thing I'd done was inevitable, but a part of me wished it could be different. As usual I pushed these feelings away and pulled out my knife.

The Eskimos were delighted to have fresh meat, and got right to work butchering. They had two of the caribou skinned and quartered, and the head of the yearling boiling in a five-gallon Blazo can, before I managed to get the skin all the way off my bull. The old man of the crew came over to help me finish up. He shook his head when he saw that I'd cut off the skin on the legs halfway between the elbows and wrists. "You sure messed up a coupla' pretty good mukluk tops," he said.

"I didn't know," I replied.

"Yeah," the old man said, "I guess that's right."

What *did* I know? After all, I'd killed them, and those Eskimos wanted me to know how to make mukluks, too? Besides, I was more interested in the antlers than any mukluks. I sawed them off the heads of the two bulls, and indicated I was intending to pack them out. The Eskimos were astounded. "You can't eat them things, you know," one of them said. "They ain't even gonna make no soup."

To the Eskimos, keeping antlers was on par with holding onto the price tag from a cellophane-wrapped beefsteak. That is, unless you needed antlers for tools or carving or ceremony, which wasn't the case. But in the way of tolerant people, they accepted my strange white man notions, my ignorance of the practicalities of life. They even helped me pack the antlers to the road, and stayed mum about the fact that we transported them in a U.S. government vehicle, a big violation of the federal employee code.

The next day for lunch the Eskimos offered me the eyes and cheek muscles from the yearling's head, delicacies, honoring my taking of meat. I ate the cheek muscles but declined the eyes. It was the antlers that meant the most to me. They were my symbols. I believed that in taking them I was one step closer to becoming an Alaskan, a real man. But I could not say any of this to the Eskimos, or tell them that the caribou were the first big animals I'd killed in Alaska. I had to keep up the appearances of a leader, couldn't let on that I had experienced so damn little. Nor could I tell them that I was about to be a father, that I was scared out of my wits, that I had no idea how to be tough and soft at the same time.

Not that the Yupik were fooled by much. I know they saw through me. But in the way of secure men, if they had any critical thoughts they kept them to themselves. It's a given that white men are odd. It does no good to call them on it. Tolerate that their minds work differently. Endure their impatience and loudness and clumsiness with feelings.

One of my main reasons for going to Alaska was to kill wild things, to hook fish, to spend my life in the wilds trapping and adventuring. That's what real men did. Instead of reading the pages of *Outdoor Life* or *Field and Stream*, I wanted to live them.

It was to the tattered farm fields and green-algaed ponds of Indiana that I escaped as a kid. Always in my mind, though, I was inhabiting another place where fish and game were abundant. As soon as I was able I was going to go to a place where a fellow could fish and hunt year-round.

It's an ironic thing, but somehow the blood sports, killing, gave me an outlet, a taste of a bigger freedom. My heart hurts today for children I see languishing in the insipid suburbs and hard cities of America, who suffer so from a media-driven material culture that insists they will never have enough or be enough. I see them slouch, empty-eyed and bored, through the potted trees and fake flowers of suburban malls. The sterile worlds they inhabit make the lackluster fields of my childhood look close to paradise.

The years that followed the killing of those first caribou, I killed moose and bears, dall sheep, and more caribou. In the Arctic I've felt killing caribou come too easy at times. I've glassed dozens of bulls at once, taking my time, looking for the largest antlers. I've often thought I might have some sense of what the old-time bison hunters must have felt—limitlessness, the blood instinct rising up from the offer of sheer numbers.

The blood instinct. I remember being in high school, walking beneath leaden skies through a bare-branched oak and maple wood. I had my first shotgun cradled in my arms, a single-shot, chrome-plated Harrington and Richardson. With the impulsive reflexes of youth, I pulled up and shot at the whisper flight of a large bird passing close overhead. The bird crumpled and tumbled, badly broken, into the yellow duff of newly fallen leaves. I approached it, a great horned owl, still alive, struggling to prop itself up on one broken and bloody wing. That magnificent bird made no attempt to escape. It just turned its head and followed me with unblinking yellow eyes, as if accusing me of great stupidity. I stared down at it and as I did I felt something strange and new come over me, that this living thing was possessed of a deeper knowing than I was capable of. My awareness made me feel small and ignorant. I stood there and regretted deeply taking the life from something so beautiful and mysterious, for ending flight, for destroying a symbol of the same freedom that I longed for myself.

One of the courses I teach at the college here in Arizona is environmental ethics. Every year I assign a paper asking students to revisit their lives to try to identify a moment when they began to think about responsibility to the natural world. I define that moment as "deontic," in the Latin as a God awakening, a sudden awareness relating to duty and obligation as an ethical concept, a moment containing an epiphany, an awakening, coming suddenly to a new understanding in life. Always, one or more of the young men write of cruelly killing some living thing, of blowing up a frog with a firecracker, of shooting a beautiful songbird with a BB gun or setting one on fire, of hanging a cat, of catching a fish, killing it, and suddenly realizing that a fish is also a living being. Always the act they admit to, and their attendant sorrow for it, is a moving experience for the class. The young women shake their heads in dismay and bewilderment, though most of them have known brothers or cousins or boyfriends who have done similar things. Other young men in the class are then moved to recall their own cruelties. We then talk about what it might be in the male gender that elicits such things. We ask if it's simply cultural identity, or might it be that cru-

THE LURE OF ANTLERS

elty and carelessness come with the territory, men are simply hardwired to do destructive things? If so, then why do some men begin to see themselves, begin to question their destructiveness and cruelty? There never seems to be easy answers. But there is an agreement among the students that if young men are indeed hardwired, then we live in a culture that does little to encourage them to own it. In fact, many of the messages encourage just the opposite.

That day, a boy standing under the autumn skies in an Indiana woodlot, I know that I experienced an opening, a budding recognition that perhaps I was not cut out to kill wantonly. I shot the owl again. I had no choice. I sprayed its wild essence across the autumn leaves. But I regretted what I had done. It was not enough regret, though, to stop me from hunting. For the vast majority of human history men have been hunters, and despite the distance from the natural world created by our technological addictions, the call of the hunt still courses in men's veins; the instinct for it can run deeper than what the logical mind might refute. No, it would be some years before I even began to ask any questions at all about sport hunting, that there may be more to it than I imagined.

In Native American cultures an owl appearing in someone's life was once (and may still be) viewed as an omen of something significant coming, perhaps death or a difficult transition. In most ways my last years in Indiana were a symbolic death, a painful, wallowing transition from adolescence into a long period of something else, perhaps best defined as limbo, neither adolescence nor manhood. Perhaps that owl, as it flew over me, was bearing a message of things to come. But I was not capable of knowing it wanted to speak to me. Instead I killed it, took its freedom, and in my culturally deaf ignorance I may have silenced the message bearer. Or there's another possibility: it *presented* itself to me. It allowed itself to be killed so that I might begin the process of learning some things. This is the version I prefer.

When the trail work ended I found myself back in Fairbanks, where BLM offered me a winter job. I took it, deciding not to return to college. I figured with a baby coming it would be best to save up some money.

Come October we abandoned the tent camp and moved into a little 12-by-24, two-room wanigan on the outskirts of Fairbanks. The word *wanigan* comes from the Canadian Cree, their word for lean-to or shelter. In Alaska, *wanigan* usually refers to an add-on for a mobile home. But the wanigan we moved into had no mobile home attached to it. The guy we rented it from had moved the mobile home down to the Kenai Peninsula. "You want the wanigan," he said over the phone, "you can have it for a hundred twenty-five a month. You want a wanigan with a trailer, you're going to have to buy your own trailer. Don't call me if anything goes wrong. It's your baby." I remember thinking at the time, If the guy only knew.

B and I were both dedicated to simple living. The wanigan had no running water. But we were used to hauling water, and we both could shower at the university. We did have electricity, which was more than a lot of the other back-to-the-landers had. The heat for it, instead of oil, came from a propane-fired heater, which was an entirely expensive way to warm a house in Alaska at the time.

The toilet, which sat in a corner of the tiny bedroom, had been liberated from a sailboat somewhere. Pour in a little water and pump a foot pedal and things were supposed to disappear straight down. To conserve water we flushed only when the smell of the contents began to dominate both rooms. The toilet dumped into a shallow, cribbed cesspool just outside, which froze solid by the middle of December.

With no outhouse, we had to do our affairs in plastic bags stretched over the toilet. When the bags got full we would tie them up and stick them outside the front door to freeze. When we got a dozen or so bags stacked up, I would haul them to the Fairbanks dump. "Poopsicles," we called them.

Our second winter was another cold one. B, very pregnant now, drove off to work each day through the ice-fog and darkness. I sold the Land Cruiser, intent upon buying her a car that would start in the cold. The Germans make the best, I reasoned. So I bought her a VW Bug, which would start, but was the most miserable vehicle imaginable in the cold, even with a gas heater in it. I taped up all the air vents so the thing would run as hot as possible. But it didn't help much; she had to drive with an ice scraper in her left hand, working furiously at the frost building inside on the windshield.

The idea of fatherhood still seemed so abstract to me. I tried to imagine what it would be like, but I couldn't get a picture of it. At night, though, my dreams revealed my truth. I dreamed of wild horses trapped in corrals, of being caught in swift rivers, fighting to stay afloat, of sinking and drowning. Some nights I would wake in a sweat, enveloped in a cloud of despair.

B went to work the first day of March, worked her whole shift at the hospital, came home that evening, and changed clothes. "It's time," she said. "The baby's coming." An hour later I took her back to the hospital.

From her first days at St. Joseph, she'd pushed for the rights of pregnant women. During her pregnancy she had helped teach a class on the Lamaze technique of childbirth, the first alternative birth method ever taught in Fairbanks. She was determined to have her baby this new way.

But for all her preparation, her labor was a long and hard one. Thirty years later I find it difficult to recall much of it. All I can remember is that it was a gray day, flurries of snow scudding along icy streets. And I seem to recall the labor room as dark. I can remember her lying there, trying so hard to be calm, looking flushed and beautiful. She asked me to sit on her left side, because she was so totally left-handed she preferred holding hands that way. I sat with her, and did my best to help her with her breathing. But I knew little of the techniques; I had been absent for the Lamaze training. In time a nurse friend of hers came and took over the breathing chores. I sat to the side and waited.

I stuck with her until she went into the delivery room, or at least until the nurse on duty asked me to leave. I can't remember what I did after I left her. Did I sit in the waiting room? Or maybe I went to a bar across the street from the hospital, the old International Hotel. Some part of me thinks I went back to the wanigan and returned later, after B delivered. But I can't recall.

All I know is that I didn't go into the delivery room with her. She asked me to, and I could have. Not that the doctors in Fairbanks at that time approved much of a father being in there. But she was well enough thought of at the hospital, despite her heretical notions of childbirth, that her doctor said he'd make an exception for me. But I said I didn't want to be an exception. The truth was I didn't go into the delivery room because I was scared. Try as I might, I could not find a connection to this baby that was about to be born. I felt that my life had veered out of control. I was lost, unsure of what I was supposed to become, how I was supposed to behave.

Cara Nicole was born the afternoon of March 2, a sweet, healthy baby, after the long labor. I first saw her through the window of the maternity ward. That moment is from the movies. A nurse holds her up, all bundled in white. I stand on the other side of the glass, awkward and unsure of myself. The baby is a prune, a red-faced, miniature Winston Churchill. The nurse opens the blanket. The baby's hands are tiny and delicate, the fingernails miniature. It strikes me then that her fingers are the most beautiful things imaginable. Although a part of me softens at the sight of her, mostly all I feel is bewilderment. How did this happen? I know that my life has just changed radically. One way or the other, things are never going to be the same.

Today I have to ask myself if I have any definite regrets in my life. Not that it does any good, but I have a couple. One that stands out: that I didn't find a way into the delivery room on that gray afternoon in early March. Later, many times I would look at my child and wish that I could have seen her come into the world. If only I could have known her at the moment of her entry, if I could have embraced her beginning, then in some way I might have been able to better embrace being a father.

Prior to Cara's birth we had acquired a big mottled-gray tomcat we named Schultz. Schultz was a charmer of a cat, affectionate, smart, an instant hit in our household. But when we brought Cara home we worried that the cat might not take to her. We need not have worried, though. Schultz seemed to sense immediately that the new addition was important. In fact, he actually appeared protective of her, though I dismissed this possibility at first. That is, until one night Schultz woke me from a deep sleep. He was mewing frantically and kneading my chest with his paws. I struggled awake, and as I did I heard strangling noises from our daughter's crib. I jumped out of bed, turned on the light in her room, discovered that her blanket was wrapped around her throat and she was rapidly turning blue. There's no doubt in my mind that Schultz saved her life.

Cara was two years old when one of the neighbor's sled dogs chased Schultz up a tree and held him there for most of a day. By the time I rescued him his kidneys had backed up and he was in tough shape. I took Schultz to the vet, but there wasn't much the vet could do. I brought my cat home and sat with him as he died. This is silly, I scolded myself, a damn cat and I'm all attached to it. Caring about a cat didn't fit the image of a hard hunter. But I couldn't leave. Finally, with a last soft whisper, Schultz quit breathing.

I carried him out into the woods that night. A full moon howled overhead. I dug a hole and buried him, then sat down in the moss next to the grave. I began to cry. The death of that cat opened up some part of me that desperately wanted out. I cared for Schultz. But I knew even then that the tears were for a lot more. They had to do with a recognition, however unconscious it might have been at the time, of the final loss of boyhood, whether I liked it or not, of a forced march into the complex world of adulthood. Despite my resistance to it, two years into parenthood I imagined myself taking on my father's life, the silent disappointment of it, a victim of circumstances that were outside my control. It took a cat dying to open me to the grief of that possibility.

7

dogs

It is easy to forget that in the main we die only seven times
more slowly than our dogs.

JIM HARRISON, *The Road Home*

I've always been drawn to dogs. Here in my study, as I write
this, two dogs lie close to my feet. They wait patiently for
their afternoon walk, or for whatever I have in mind, for that
matter. They are unconditional in their enthusiasm for my life.

I grew up with dogs. When I was a kid on the farm we had
a collie named Sandy, a dog I can barely remember. My dad
gave him away to a neighbor when we moved. The neighbor
reported years later that Sandy spent most of his last days
waiting at the edge of the driveway for us to return. Shortly
after we moved to Indiana, we got another collie, a pup—I
can't remember its name—that immediately got hit by a
speeding truck. I saw it happen. The dog crashed under the
front bumper, rolled and thumped under and out the back,
apparently dead. Crying, I pulled him to the roadside and sat

down by him. My dad came with a shovel, picked up the dog like a sack by its hind feet, and carried it out behind the house. He started digging a hole to bury it. As he did the dog slowly came back to life. It shook its head dazedly, stood and staggered off to the garage. That dog recovered, only to get hit and killed by a car a year later.

Then there was the peeing cocker spaniel that my dad hit with the claw hammer. I can't recall exactly, but I think it also got killed by a car. Next came Sparky, a little black-and-white terrier mix. I found him as a stray and brought him home. My mother surprised me and agreed I could keep him. Sparky was a rambler and, surprisingly, a great hunter. Quail, pheasants, rabbits, coons, whatever you wanted him to hunt he'd go for it and most times find it. On rabbits, though, he was too fast. Instead of bringing them around to the shotgun he would more often than not just run them down. That is, until he went off on one of his amorous adventures and came home a few days later dragging a mangled hind leg. Sparky was in shock, trembling, flinching at the slightest noise, his eyes wide with terror. We took him to the vet and the vet removed a .22 bullet from the bone, tried to pin the shattered leg together. For days after the shooting, Sparky lay in a box by my bed. Still in shock, he rarely slept. The pin protruded from the top of his hip and it worried him; finally he pulled it out with his teeth and we left it that way. The leg healed with a big lump of hard gristle at the break and was useless. The lower half just flopped around like a puppet's arm.

Three legs instead of four, though, turned out to be a bonus. Sparky would still hunt, but with his bad leg flapping out behind him like a wind sock, he slowed down just enough to make a fine rabbit dog. He was kind of an emotional mess, though, after the shooting. The shock never really left him. He gave up on love (I suppose there's a metaphor in this) and he started to bite people. I was the only human he appeared to care anything about. He tolerated my parents. When I left for Denver, Sparky was tied out behind the house. My dad threw him some food regularly. To this day I feel bad about leaving him there all alone. At the time it never occurred to me that I had a responsibility to that dog. It was probably a year after I left home that my parents took him to the vet and had him put to sleep. I remember them calling me, saying what they'd done. I hung up the phone, went out, and got drunk.

Dogs were always around and I remember always wishing I could have more. There's one story with this that replayed itself plenty of times later. My dad and I got into a big argument over me wanting to get another dog, a black-and-tan coonhound that I wanted to order from Arkansas. We sparred over the issue for a while, and then he put an end to the discussion. "One dog's enough," he said, "and that's it. We're not having another dog around here."

Of course, I had to get in my last jab. "Someday, when I get out of here, I'm going to have all the dogs I want."

He looked at me, smiled. "You say that now. But I suspect you'll grow out of it."

I can't say I intended to take up racing sled dogs when I got to Alaska. The dream I carried with me up the highway in 1968 was eventually to get a few dogs for running a trapline in the winter. I had the Jack London notion of life in the north: a little log cabin in the bush, thirty or forty miles of trapline through pure wild country. I'd trap marten, mink, wolf, wolverine for the cash we'd need. Hunt moose and caribou for meat. Snow-machines were still fairly unreliable affairs back in the sixties, so I figured I'd do it the old way. Dogs wouldn't break down; they could do the work of pulling me from set to set. I'd feed them the carcasses of the animals I trapped, something you couldn't do with a snow-machine. Life would be good.

But my first taste of Alaska sled dogs was a little different from my notions of how it would be. Our neighbor next door to the wanigan had a few malamutes, big, slow-footed, heavy-browed, black-and-white brutes, bred more for the AKA show rings of New York and Los Angeles than for anything useful. We could always tell when he was about to take them for a run; bedlam reigned in the neighborhood. Those mala-mutes would set to moaning and screaming, beside them-selves over the possibility of an alternative from the boredom of life on their chains. The neighbor would hook one dog all slobbering and eager. Then he'd bring up the second, hook it, and get right into the business of beating the two of them with a length of garden hose filled with lead shot, just to keep them from killing each other. By the time he had four or five of them hooked up he'd broken up at least a half-dozen fights, was down to his shirtsleeves, his parka and hat stripped off and thrown in the snow, too sweated up and beat himself to enjoy driving them all that much.

That first winter in the wanigan he took me for a couple of rides. I stood and watched while he went through the usual hook-up routine, flailing and hollering, the dogs barking frantically. Finally he got the last one hooked. With a split-second lull in the action he yelled for me to get into the sled. I leaped in and he handed me the garden hose. "When they start to fight, just jump out and whale the tar out of them!" With that he pulled the tie rope and we careened out of the yard. We made it to the river, a distance of no more than half a mile, before the wheel dogs got into it. I leaped out and beat on them and they gave up pretty quick. But that didn't keep the swing dogs from going at it next. I worked on the swings for a while, my neighbor yelling all the time, "Lay it across their noses! Their noses! That's what gets to 'em!"

It took a couple of more stops before those malamutes finally settled down into a lazy trot, tails up in the air, looking like nothing at all had ever happened. I knew after the first ride that I wasn't much interested in owning malamutes. I failed to see the romance in that kind of dog mushing; it looked like a lot of unnecessary work. Still, though, I carried the notion of a trapline with me.

Later that winter I went to one of the races put on by the Alaska Dog Mushers Association in Fairbanks. Trucks with dog boxes built on the back were lined up around a half oval of tie-off posts that were set behind the start/finish chutes. Mushers unloaded dogs and tied them around their trucks. I was surprised at the size and the looks of the dogs there—rangy, wiry, light-framed little things, many of them more houndy-looking than how I thought a husky was supposed to look. And there was every possible color—reds, whites, blacks, black and whites, grays, very few of them with the white masks I thought real huskies were supposed to have. Another thing I noticed: there must have been close to three hundred dogs there, pure bedlam, dogs barking everywhere, yet I never witnessed a single fight. All these dogs wanted to do was run. They were crazy to run. I thought to myself, Now maybe I could get into that.

That spring we bought the wanigan and the lot it was on for $4,300, only to discover that the back half of our new home was sitting on the neighbor's lot. It needed to be moved. Late May I got an old-timer to move it, a fellow who had moved a lot of houses around Fairbanks. He jacked the wanigan up and backed an old Army trailer under it. The timbers on the trailer looked weak, splintered away by the gooseneck. "You sure this thing will hold my house?" I asked him.

"No problem," he said. "I've moved a heck of a lot bigger houses than this on it."

"Okay, you're the expert."

I watched the old-timer lower the wanigan onto the trailer. The weight was almost off the jacks when suddenly there came a loud splintering noise and the wanigan crashed to the ground.

"It broke," I said.

"I'll be damned if it didn't," the old-timer agreed.

The wanigan was leaning at a crazy angle. I forced open the only door and crawled inside. Nothing appeared to be much damaged. "Can you pick this thing up again?" I called out to him.

"Don't know why not," he said.

It took him an extra day of jacking and blocking. He replaced the timbers on the trailer, set the wanigan on it again, and this time moved it to its new location on the front center of our lot.

I built a foundation out of treated timbers under the wanigan, then lowered it carefully. Off one side and across the back, I added more foundation for additions: two little bedrooms, and rooms in back for a utility and bath. By late spring I had the deck and walls framed up, but could take it no further, because I had to go to the bush again. This time BLM wanted me to lay out a trail into the White Mountains north of Fairbanks.

That summer in the White Mountains, my boss in Fairbanks agreed to my proposal that we try a string of pack horses instead of helicopters for moving camps. I argued that horses would be cheaper. I hired a packer with a string of seven horses. My crew was mixed, Indian and white. We laid out close to thirty miles of trail that summer. Only a couple of times did the bears run our horses off; it took us most of the day to find them. The first three-week hitch it rained twenty out of twenty-one days. The packer had forgotten my sleeping bag, so I slept in wet saddle blankets and don't recall sleeping warm once the entire three weeks. The tents leaked and the ground was so wet, most nights I'd awake from fitful sleep with water puddled around my hips and shoulders. Even though it was a wet, miserable time, I still liked the work, liked feeling I was tough enough to handle about anything. The last day, approaching the road, the sun came out. Sun or not, I was ready to go back to Fairbanks. It was the first time since I'd begun working in the bush that I felt glad about heading home, anxious to see my daughter.

Come fall I decided to return to the university, figuring since I was a family man now I'd better get something more substantial than BLM going in my life. But distractions from that possibility abounded. I decided I would get some dogs for recreation, something to give me a break from the rigors of the university. One Saturday, late October, I saw an ad in the *Fairbanks Daily News Miner:* "Junior dog team," it said. "Good honest race dogs. Will sell cheap." There was an address listed.

I got in my pickup and drove to one of the better residential areas in Fairbanks. The house was a big log affair, set nicely back off a street that ran along the Chena River. I knocked and a man came to the door. I explained to him what I was there for. "They're my daughter's dogs," he said. "She's been racing the junior races the last couple of years, but she's lost interest in dogs. More into boys now." He pulled on his parka and we walked around behind the house. Five dogs were tied along the riverbank, all typical racing huskies. They ran circles on their chains, excited, except for a black one, more squat than the others, scarred and gray at the muzzle. He just stood there at the end of his chain, eyeing us steadily.

"That one." The man pointed at a nicely built blond male. "He's young, but shows good promise as a leader. We call him Swede. The other one there"—he nodded at the silent black dog—"he's a good leader, a fine gee-haw dog. We bought him in an Indian village up on the Yukon. Name's Blackie."

The grizzled dog's ears perked up, attentive to his name.

"I'll be right up front with you, though," the man continued. "You have to watch him. The Indians used him to hunt moose. He sees anything that looks like a moose, he's off the trail and after it." He shook his head. "My daughter was driving the team on a new trail, and they came up on a horse standing out in a field. That little black son-of-a-bitch bolted off the trail, took after that horse, led the whole damn dog team under the fence and out across the field. Brushed her off on the way. The horse went through the fence on the far side. It's the God's truth, he had the whole works halfway through that fence before the sled got tangled up enough to stop the team." He stepped over to the black dog, reached down, and scratched his ears. Blackie wagged his tail. "When you drive him, you just have to stay alert for anything big, that's all."

I eyed the other dogs, asked a couple of questions about them. They all looked pretty good to me, though I wasn't all that sure what I was supposed to be looking for. "They're an honest bunch," he said, "but I'm tired of feeding them for her. You take the whole works today, I'll let you have them cheap."

I paid $250 for the five, which even then was a lot less than you'd pay for just an average retired gee-haw race leader. I gave him another $50 for the doghouses and chains, tied the dogs in the back of my pickup, told him I'd be back for the houses. I took my new dogs home. B greeted me at the back door, Cara in her arms.

"I got some dogs," I said.

"Great," she said. "So now what are you going to do?"

"Start driving them," I said.

At that point B was still one to go along with most of my schemes. She had a damn practical streak in her, though.

"Don't you need a sled, and some towlines and harnesses to do that?"

I thought about it. "I guess I do. I'll build the sled and tow-lines, you sew some harnesses."

In the backyard I built five little bonfires, thawed through the frost layer, then drove heavy rebar, for tie-up stakes, down through the thawed spots. B set to work making some harnesses out of nylon webbing. Evenings after school I worked on the sled in the living room, Cara crawling nearby. I'd taken a pattern off my neighbor's freight sled, just scaled it down to what I thought might be race-sled size. Only I figured I would build a new, improved model out of plywood. None of that traditional bent oak, ash, or birch for me. I was going to set some trends.

The sled when finished weighed about eighty pounds (contrasted to an actual race sled, which weighed twenty-five) and had runners, glued and laminated out of plywood, with about as much flex as railroad ties. I couldn't wait to put it into action. The next day I hooked my five dogs—Blackie in single lead, Swede and a fine little brown female named Lena in swing, at wheel a white dog named Karo (slow as syrup) and another brown dog by the name of Brother.

Brother was one of a kind, a character with one blue eye, one brown. Everything he did was sneaky. And he had a rare talent. Anybody walked into my dog yard and got close to Brother, he would wait until absolutely the most opportune moment, then lift his leg and pee on him. He later distinguished himself greatly by peeing on Don Young, Alaska's strident anti-environment, pro-development congressman, who was then making his first run for the U.S. House. I was out in the dog yard. A good friend, who was managing Don Young's campaign in Fairbanks, brought the candidate by to ask me if I'd be willing to pose in a picture with him. The deal was that I'd crawl up on a little John Deere dozer I had at the house and my friend would snap a couple of shots. I'd met Don Young once fighting fires. I wasn't terribly impressed by him at the time, only recall thinking the guy wasn't any great intellect. For the picture, I thought, what the heck, I could do a favor for my friend. The three of us stood talking in the dog yard, Don working me hard for my vote. He had his back to Brother, and that's when Brother struck. I saw it happen but didn't say anything. I was a little embarrassed. We then went over and I got on the dozer.

I still have the campaign brochure. It's a testimony to the naiveté of my politics in those days. Inside the brochure is a picture of me sitting on the dozer. I'm clean shaven, baseball cap, white T-shirt, Levi's torn at the knee. I'm looking down at the levers and I'm laughing. Don Young stands on the ground beside the dozer. He's wearing a short-sleeved white dress shirt, bolo tie, and polyester pants. It looks like he might have one of those plastic penholders in his shirt pocket. He's got a hammer in his hands and he's laughing with me. The caption below the picture: "Don Young is a man who knows the Alaska working man. He knows how to work and work for you."

Brother wasn't much of a dog otherwise. His other great talent, once I learned what a real working dog looked like, was making it look like he was working furiously, when in reality he was keeping his backline just tight enough to create the illusion of work. This talent ultimately earned him a transfer to another kennel.

I got my dogs hooked that first day, and we blasted out of the yard. My plan was to head down to the river, where we could run for miles. We were approaching the turn that would take us to the river, and I started relaxing a bit, congratulating myself on the fine sled I'd built. Although it didn't steer all that well, it seemed pretty sturdy. I leaned back a little, testing the plywood driving bow, the arc of wood at the back of the sled that serves as a handlebar. The sled hit a bump and the driving bow cracked off cleanly in my hands. I staggered backward, landed on my butt, and watched my dog team disappear into the distance, past the river turn, heading toward town.

It's a sinking feeling watching your dogs escape. All I could imagine was the pile of hair and blood I was going to find if I finally caught up with them. And I was seriously humbled, because even then I knew the first rule of driving race dogs: never, under any possible circumstance—blood, broken bones, concussion—do you let go of the sled. If you set the snow hook to go up and work on a dog, or untangle, you move quickly, move close to the sled, close to the team. So if they pull the snow hook you can fall on something and act as a drag—the sled, the towline, a dog, anything attached to the main operation. Whatever happens, you don't let go.

I can't name the number of times, later in my dog-mushing career, that I careened down the trail on my stomach, holding onto the gangline or the tie-up rope. Or other times—not that many, thankfully—that I had to walk home and get the snow-machine and look for a lost dog team, because I did the unthinkable, I let go. Sometimes you couldn't help it. Once, years after my first team, I was out with a big race string and they were cruising. On a long straight stretch of trail, I turned around on the runners to study some of my pups that were chasing the team. (This was a technique that I used, once we moved out to the river, to sort through pups. Turn a bunch loose to chase the big dogs, watch their gaits, watch which ones had the determination to keep up, which ones lagged behind, which ones tried to run up there with the leaders. Those were the best. It was a technique that made for seriously tough and confident pups. By the time you were ready to hook them, they had the experience of a couple of hundred miles on the trail.) We were probably running a fair training speed, sixteen to seventeen miles an hour. I turned back around to my main dogs and *whack!* I got knocked over like a bowling pin by a tree branch overhanging the trail. When I came to, my dog team was gone and I wasn't all that sure where I was. My eyes were full of blood and I had a bad headache. A couple of the pups had stopped with me. They milled around on the trail close to me, worried. I climbed groggily onto my feet and started walking, the pups following. It's the worst feeling, thinking of your dogs lost and tangled. Maybe some dog could get strangled. Or the whole team gets crippled up from running crazy. Most any race team I've ever seen that's worth anything delights in leaving the driver behind. It's like they whisper among themselves, *If the big guy falls off, we're outta here!* They're bred to want to go, not to stop.

That day, after what seemed like hours, I found the team, off the trail in a swamp, tangled and scared. Scared because the fun was over and the reality was sinking in: they'd left behind the man, the alpha male, the guy who called all the shots, the fellow who fed them. That was part of the strategy for developing a race team. Get them to where the sun rises and sets from your hand and no other.

But I knew none of this with that first runaway team. It took me an hour or more of walking, tracking, cursing, knocking on doors in a subdivision and asking people if they'd seen a loose dog team. Finally I found them, tangled up and happy as truant children in somebody's backyard. Blackie was still trying to go. I untangled them and drove them home minus the driving bow, runners scraping down bare gravel subdivision streets, finally out onto the packed snow of the home trail. I stood hunched over holding onto the side rails. Blackie took every gee-haw command like the veteran he was. It was clear he knew a whole lot more about driving dogs than I did.

After my grand mushing debut I invested in a used racing sled, and shortly after that acquired two more dogs. One I found at the Army dog pound, a bald-faced, blue-eyed, de-barked male named Zero. When he attempted to bark he sounded like he had a terminal case of laryngitis. And his name came pretty close to summing up his abilities as a sled dog. I learned later that he had been used in some laboratory experiment by the Army, thus the de-barking operation. The other dog was a supremely psychotic gray male named Boo. Boo came from a hard-case dog musher, a red-eyed, bulb-nosed man convicted of manslaughter in a barroom fight. He was no kinder to dogs than he was to humans. Boo grew up a pup in his yard, and apparently nowhere in that experience did he garner any evidence that humans were anything but bad news. If anyone tried to get close to him he would des-perately throw himself against the end of his chain, lunging over and over, eyes rolling white, saliva flying. He was an amazingly strong dog, made even more so by the adrenaline that pumped almost constantly through his veins. More than once as I led Boo to hook him to the sled he would panic and tow me across the kennel, shaking against his collar, choking himself to the point of suffocation.

Once you got him hooked, though, he was a dream, an in-credible worker, completely dedicated to getting away from the human standing on the sled behind. Boo quickly put all the other dogs' working abilities into clear perspective, par-ticularly Brother. But the routine of getting Boo hooked got to be too much. Or if I had to get off the sled to work in the team he would spook and try to pull the whole works off the trail, anything to get away from that damn human. I made up my mind to gentle him. Every morning, first thing after wak-ing, I would go out and get hold of his chain and pull him to me. Boo would resist every inch of the way, trembling like he was palsied. When I finally got him up close I would sit on his doghouse and pull his head over my legs and run my free hand all over his body. He got where he'd tolerate it, but whenever I'd lift my hand, then touch him again, he'd flinch like he'd been hit with a cattle prod. Quietly, over and over, I'd say to him, "Boo, it's okay." For a half hour or more every morning I would sit with him. By the end of that winter Boo got to where he'd tolerate being handled that way, but there was no friendliness in him. He could still panic and drag you all over the place.

I began to get the hang of riding a sled. I started hooking Swede up in lead with Blackie, using the old veteran to teach the young one commands. Swede took to commands fairly quickly, though he had a stubborn streak in him; sometimes he just decided it was not in his best interest to follow my directions. Then it got down to a test of wills between us. I usually won, but Swede never made it easy. He was hardheaded, but so was I. Swede was the first dog I whipped hard. The whip, that's the way most fellows drove dogs then. I had no notion that there was any other way to go about it. If it took the whip, then I wanted to get good at using it.

It took a lot of work that first winter with dogs to keep the dog trails open and packed. The interior of Alaska is essentially a semiarid climate. Still, most winters there's a fair amount of snow because what falls never melts; by spring there's usually a couple of feet accumulated. The winter of 1970/71, though, it started snowing in October and never stopped until early December. By mid-December we entered the wanigan through a sloping tunnel, and I had to dig down to the tops of the windows to let in what little light there was. On my dog trail in places the side berms were up above my shoulders. Open places the wind would blow the snow up in big drifts and beat the surface into a hard crust. Where it had drifted a lot, you never knew how deep it might be. Once in the open field behind the house I stopped the team and hooked down, intending to go up and untangle a dog. But I miscalculated the edge of the trail, stepped off too far to one side, and instantly disappeared into snow over my head. I could see the sled up above me. I struggled, wallowing and packing the snow beneath me, until I could reach up and get hold of a sled runner. With the runner spreading my weight across the trail, I pulled myself up and onto the sled, relieved and thankful that my dogs hadn't pulled the hook.

The snow got so deep that winter that the moose couldn't negotiate it. Hundreds out in the bush died of starvation. Dozens more died on the railroad tracks. Others came into town, seeking plowed roads, hard-packed trails, parking lots, anything that allowed them to move more freely. Hungry moose were everywhere. Drive along a plowed road and you were likely to encounter a moose that refused to yield right-of-way. Children waiting for the school bus had to be on the lookout for irritable ones. A page-one picture in the *News Miner* showed a woman feeding a moose pancakes through her kitchen window. Every day there were articles of some confrontation somewhere, or of some act of humanity toward starving animals. Blackie, true to his obsession with big animals, was close to apoplectic that first winter. It got so that he was so often off the trail that I had to start running him wheel, back where he couldn't pull the whole team off with him.

Swede took over in single lead. Because I was at the university during the day, I had to do most of my training at night. After a day of classes I looked forward to going out into the darkness, loved the escape of it: the large silence of dogs moving quickly along the trail, their breath rising in great white clouds, the moon a cold light in a raven sky. I would ride and imagine a day that would come when I'd be free of school and could live wilder with dogs, when I could immerse myself in the beat of winter.

One moonlit night, moderately cold, maybe twenty below, I hooked my seven dogs. Swede had been showing signs of tiring of single lead, so at the last minute I hooked Blackie up there with him, figuring I'd take my chances. We left the yard and crossed the field behind the house at a good pace. The trail entered the woods on the far side of the field. There we dropped down a sharp incline, into a stretch where snow-laden willows arched over the trail. I put my arm up in front of my face to ward them off. The dogs speeded up. We're going to have a good run, I thought to myself. We broke through the willows, just in time for me to look up and see my leaders about to have a collision with a moose standing head down and spraddle-legged on the trail ahead of us.

There in the pale moonlight, everything silhouetted in dark shadow, I watched helplessly as Blackie, baying like a coonhound, leaped for the moose's head. Swede and the swings joined him. The moose, with its ears laid back flat against its head, struck hard with both front feet. The neckline joining Blackie and Swede snapped and Swede went spinning. Blackie leaped again. The moose struck again. This time one of the swings screamed in pain, sending Blackie into even more of a frenzy.

I leaped off the sled with my whip in my hand, ran up, and began flailing at the moose, trying to turn it away from the dogs and up the trail. But all I succeeded in doing was turning its attention to me. The moose shook the dogs off and lunged. I dove sideways, pivoted, and ran back the way I'd just come, laboring hard in my winter gear. As I stumbled along I could hear the moose panting behind me.

Because I could stay on top the trail, and the moose punched through the crust, I just managed to outrun it. After twenty yards or so it gave up, turned around, and went back to the dogs, now badly tangled. Blackie was still willing, though, still trying to haul the whole tangle with him to get back into the fray. Boo, on the other hand, was doing his best to go the other way, and Boo, larger and even more frantic than Blackie, seemed to be the one winning.

The moose stepped back into the tangle. I could hear loud pops, what I thought were bones breaking. At one point the moose grabbed a dog up in its mouth, by the back skin, and threw it down hard. If I hadn't seen it with my own eyes I wouldn't have believed a moose would use its mouth that way.

I came back with the whip. The moose was visibly tiring by now, its back legs collapsing under it. Blackie managed to grab it by the nose again, jerking and snarling. Just as I reached them the moose's front legs buckled and it went down in the snow. Blackie dove for its throat. "Enough, you little son-of-a-bitch!" I yelled. I took the butt of my whip and beat Blackie over the head with it, hammered him, until finally he went limp. Then I grabbed him by the collar and threw him off in the deep snow on the other side of the trail, hoping he'd act as sort of an anchor in case any of the other dogs still had any desire to attack.

Boo, thankfully, was still doing his best to pull the whole works back toward home. The moose struggled up on all fours again, panting and weaving. I took the whip and drove him a short distance up the trail. Then I hurried back to the sled, grabbed handfuls of harness and towline and pulled the sled around. Blackie came to, shook his head a couple of times, and started for the moose again. I lunged for him, unhooked him, and loaded him in the sled, where I took the neckline dangling from his collar and tied him to the back stanchions as best I could.

With quick glances back over my shoulder, I set to work untangling the rest of the dogs. Amazingly enough, they all seemed capable of movement. But they seemed pretty subdued, ready to go home. Except Blackie. He still struggled to get off the sled.

We got going, headed home. From what I could make out in the dark, there were no serious injuries. Back at the kennel I set the snow hook and went in the house without unhitching. I called to B from the back entry.

She flicked on the light, took one look at me. "What happened? You look like you've been in a fight." She stepped closer. "You've got blood and hair all over you."

"Moose," I said.

That was all she needed to know. We went out and unhooked. In the beam of a flashlight we examined each dog. They were stiff and bruised, a few cuts here and there, but as far as we could tell there were no broken bones. Blackie was recovering quickly. For him it was just another day in the life of a sled and hunting dog. The best I could figure, the popping noises I'd heard when the moose struck were the sounds of dogs punching through the crust of the snow.

The next day another musher who lived close called me. "I was out on that trail that leads up to your place," he said. "It looks like somebody had a hell of a tangle with a moose up there. There's blood all over the place."

"You got that right," I said.

The rest of the winter driving dogs was a nerve-wracking experience. I took to carrying a rifle strapped in a scabbard in the basket of my sled. Several other mushers who got into scrapes with moose ended up having to shoot them. I knew one woman musher who spent the better part of an hour under her sled while a moose raised havoc with her team, killing a couple of dogs. Nerve-wracking or not, for me the whole thing was still one big adventure. Sure, I thought about what a shame it was that moose already fighting for survival had just another stress put on them by mushers out there recreating. But I was hooked on driving dogs. I wasn't going to stop.

On a whim, figuring I had nothing better to do, later that winter I entered an amateur seven-dog race put on by the Alaska Dog Mushers Association. Swede and Blackie in double lead. The whole team was fired up to be doing something besides driving the home trail, even Brother. To my amazement we won. I entered a few other amateur races that winter, won another one and placed high in the others. I was beginning to feel pretty cocky.

That spring, with all the snow gone, I staked Boo in the side yard, out of sight of the other dogs. "Boo," I said, "you're going to learn to trust me if it kills you." My intended strategy was to become the only living presence in his life, to get him to accept me on my terms out of sheer loneliness.

Come evening I threw an old Army mattress in his chain circle, rolled up on it in my sleeping bag, and talked to Boo until I fell asleep. I talked to him when I woke in the middle of the night, with the sun just barely below the horizon. Talked to him before breakfast.

B was impressed by my dedication. "You sure know how to win a dog's heart." In her words, though, I suspect resided the opinion that I might not have been doing much for winning hers.

The first couple of nights I doubt if Boo slept at all. He just lay at the end of his chain, hind legs coiled up under him, front legs pointed straight out at me, alert, his eyes fully attentive to my every move. By the third night he might have dozed off a couple of times. The fourth night I woke and Boo was asleep, his head down between his front legs, a little slack in his chain. The next night he wagged his tail when he saw me come out of the house. When I walked into his chain circle he stepped toward me tentatively, then backed quickly away. "That's okay," I said to him, "you're getting better."

It took two more nights sleeping with him before he finally gave in. I came out of the house and he ran a little excited circle on his chain. "So you're glad to see me," I said. He wagged his tail. I knelt and held out my hand. He came to me, let me frisk his ears a bit before he pulled away. I felt a great deal of satisfaction in that moment.

My patience with Boo was one side of my way with dogs. I loved working with them, and I felt I had a talent for it, could just kind of sense them in some way that wasn't easy to describe. The whole idea of racing sled dogs appealed to me: being outdoors, working with animals, competition, a sport that required a broad knowledge. I felt for the first time in my life that I had found something that fit me perfectly. But my love of dogs was a strangely mixed one; it was not always about patience. Mostly it was about control. I gave up any notion of wanting to trap with dogs, decided I wanted to focus on racing instead, get some more dogs, just see how it went.

I told B this. She had been out on the sled with me several times and had driven a couple of small teams. She had the bug, too, the "dog-drivin' disease," as other mushers called it. She agreed. I know, though, knew it then, that it was more my dream than hers.

In the glow of my amateur success, I secretly figured there was nothing to this racing business; it was just a matter of a couple of years, get enough dogs to get into the unlimited, professional class, and I'd win races there, too. Little did I know how very much more I had to learn.

8

the undoing of place

One of the peculiarities of the white race's presence in America is how little intention has been applied to it. . . . Once the unknown of geography was mapped, the industrial marketplace became the new frontier, and we continued, with largely the same motives and with increasing haste and anxiety, to displace ourselves—no longer with unity of direction, like a migrant flock, but like the refugees from a broken anthill.

WENDELL BERRY, *The Unsettling of America*

The qualities that make a place are something indefinable, an intricate interweaving of tangibles and intangibles that makes each place feel its own unique way. You know it when you experience it the first time, coming into a new locus—be it someone's home, a city, a rural corner, a region, another country. How it turns some screw in your awareness. Either it opens you, expands you, or it closes you down. Either you feel safe or you don't. You may grasp the meaning of that place— sense some essential familiarity with it, which may feel more like a knowing from another life than anything you've experienced in this lifetime—or the meaning eludes you. The one thing I've come to know all too well is that the feel of a place can change overnight; with our obsession for economic growth, for so-called progress, the soul of a place, the quiet whisper of it that attracts us, can be squandered all too easily.

I'm studying another picture, another hunt. In the background, tufts of golden sedge are scattered randomly over a steep gray talus slope. Close up, the young man again. He sports a sparse beard and his lower lip is pouched full of snoose. A camouflage hunting cap shades his eyes. He's wearing a tan work shirt, Levi's, and a green down vest. His right leg is draped over a beautiful white ram, a Dall sheep lying stone dead. Between his legs, his rifle is propped at an angle. In each hand he grasps a horn. The horns are remarkable, full curl, completely intact. I count the growth rings—the ram died in its twelfth year. Both of the young man's hands are covered in blood. There's blood, too, all over the sheep—its horns and head, the cape of its chest, a big red patch on its shoulder where the bullet exited. The sheep's lower jaw is skewed off to the right, broken in the fall after the shot. The young man is looking straight into the camera, with no hint of a smile. There's a hard challenge in his eyes, in the line of his jaw, as if he's reckoning with important things.

We made a life for ourselves in Fairbanks in the little wanigan house the next four years. Cara grew into such a sweet child. Blonde, green-eyed. Even at two years she had the easiest disposition imaginable, a lovable child in every way. There were times I felt the pleasure of being a father, times I could sense my heart open and a new way of feeling take the place of the fear that usually traveled with me. But those times were often short-lived.

My father and mother both retired early at age sixty-two, a big decision for them, one that surprised me. It never occurred to me that they could spring away from the safety of Indiana, that they might begin enjoying life on their own terms. Their first act, they bought a travel trailer and a pickup to pull it, then headed for Alaska. Three summers in a row they came north. They pulled their trailer into our driveway and camped there, close to their granddaughter. Those were good summers. I couldn't help but witness my father softening and my mother slowing down. They both seemed happier than I'd ever seen them. Alaska did them good.

The first summer they came north my father took a great deal of pleasure in finishing the wanigan house while I was off working in the bush. He closed in the rooms, built a roof over the whole works, handcrafted beautiful kitchen cupboards out of tongue-and-groove pine. He just kept working on it until the little wanigan house was a full-fledged home. And for three summers he built doghouses. The man who told me I'd grow out of wanting dogs clearly took satisfaction in my growing kennel. By the third summer that he came north, with pups I had over thirty racing huskies tied on the back half of our tiny city lot.

My folks came north during a crazy time. Fairbanks was definitely not the quiet little town that they'd left behind in Indiana. Things were changing fast. Oil was the word. Petroleum development. Money! The *News Miner* headlines shouted it every day. It was just a matter of weeks, at the most months, before work could begin on the pipeline, the biggest construction project ever attempted anywhere. The *News Miner* and Alaska politicians told us it was a wonderful thing. Eight hundred miles of pipe. Drama! Jobs! Humans against the forces of nature. Get that baby going, and then the money would really begin to flow. We'd all be rich.

The word was out. Fairbanks was filling up even more with boomers eager to get to work on the pipeline. Pimps circled the downtown blocks in big cruisemobiles. Prostitutes openly solicited in the bars and streets. Every sleazeball construction vagrant and coke dealer who could afford the price of a one-way fare came north like a fly drawn to a corpse. They teamed up with the Chamber of Commerce sharpies and the big construction companies and oil corporations, and got right down to the business of turning a quiet little town in the middle of nowhere into a den of thieves.

Many of the city police quit and took jobs for more money up on the North Slope. Law and order took a backseat to runaway commerce, to greed. By the winter of 1972 Fairbanks had gone from being a town of one or two murders a year to a place where somebody got fatally shot or stabbed every week or so. Old-time residents who had never locked a door in their lives lined up at Samson's Hardware to buy dead-bolts and padlocks. Fairbanks no longer felt like a hometown, but instead a frenzied, testosterone-poisoned construction camp, a crazy and dangerous place to raise a child. For most of us who had been there awhile the simple tasks of the seasons became more complicated, and life took on the rhythms of a surreal and clumsy dance. It was boom time.

But the *News Miner* and the promoters ignored most of the negatives. This boom was good for Alaska, they said. It was going to turn us into a state to be reckoned with. That is, unless this ignorant bunch of posy-sniffing environmentalists and Natives got in the way. No, not everybody was going along with the rhetoric. There were some old-time Alaskans who had seen it all before, who knew the reality of Alaska's boom-and-bust history, a few souls who were brave enough to speak out. And some of my own contemporaries who had come north in the sixties, incurable idealists, were also taking a different stand. They said some other things needed to be considered first, like where the pipeline was routed and how it was engineered. It wasn't something that you could just throw down through earthquake country, across miles and miles of permafrost, over hundreds of rivers and streams, through thousands of acres of wetlands, over the Brooks Range and the Alaska Range. What happens if the thing breaks? And the Natives, they were standing firm. There was the matter of their pending land claims. The state and federal governments had never officially reckoned with them for the theft of their lands. The Natives wanted things settled before any pipeline could be built.

Most of us, though, went the other way. We opted for the money. Those with environmental concerns, people who had a different vision for Alaska, were characterized in the *News Miner* (and sadly, still are) as outside meddlers and troublemakers, obstructionists who just didn't understand the way things needed to be. Washington, the dreaded federal government, the Democratic Congress and Jimmy Carter, that communist-leaning bastard, were the biggest villains, though. Washington agreed with the Natives and the tree-huggers, and they were going to hold things up. Of course, the *News Miner* never made any mention of Alaska's two-handed contradiction: one hand reaching eagerly for all the federal handouts, like military bases and federal agencies and highway funds, while the other pushed the federal government away when some development project was at stake or a regulation was proposed that attempted to moderate greed and recklessness.

I was conflicted. I didn't like what was happening to Alaska, but I didn't figure I could do a lot about it. And we needed oil, didn't we? Secretly, I sided more with the tree-huggers. But in public I certainly didn't want to be perceived as a sissy environmentalist. In a convoluted bit of rationalization, I still saw myself resisting authority. No, I reasoned, I was no joiner. I couldn't see, though, that I was resisting nothing, that my silence put me in fact in supreme compliance with the promoters of Alaska's demise.

Come summer, I decided that I wanted to work for myself. I was tired of the government way of doing things, the waste and the bureaucratic paper-shuffling. Besides, with a boom on, there was a lot more money to be made in construction. A friend from the university and I decided we'd give log-home building a try. Not that either of us had much of clue how to build with logs. But we were not derailed by such an insignificant detail. We studied several log houses, how they were put together. Then we read a book on log building. We figured we were ready. We put out the word that we were available. Our first summer we got contracts to build three cabins. We took our time and did some nice work. By the next summer we had more log work than we could handle, and on the side I was picking up some little jobs for a big construction company that was gearing up to build the pipeline. I really didn't like the work, didn't feel called to do construction, felt confined by it. But I was making a lot of money at it, more money than I ever imagined I could. And money meant dogs.

A couple of years into the boom, B and I began to talk about what we might want next, decided we should begin to look for another place to live, somewhere truly out of town. My craving for the wild places hadn't diminished. In fact, it seemed to be growing, gnawing inside me like a caged animal. If we weren't ready to live out in the bush, at least I needed to go there once in a while.

A friend of mine who worked for Alaska Fish and Game told me about a lake that he'd flown over once, up on the south side of the Brooks Range. He said the mountains around that lake were heavily populated with Dall sheep. The lake was very remote and high, marginal altitude for a float-plane to take off.

I wanted to go there. I'd heard about a bush pilot up in Bettles, a fellow who was supposedly one of the best around. I called Paul Shanahan via radio phone, described the country I wanted to get into, the lake. "Yeah," he said, "I've been over that lake a couple of times. There're some sheep in there, that's for sure. Nobody I know of has ever gone in there, though."

"You willing to give it a try?" I asked.

Shanahan considered it. "We won't have any problem get-ting in. It's the getting out with a load that's going to be the challenge." The phone crackled with static while he consid-ered it. "Hell, we'll give it a try. Might mean we have to ferry you out one at a time to a lower lake or something. But I think we can pull it off."

A friend by the name of Murry, an Army veterinarian at Fort Wainwright, and I caught a ride on the mail plane up to Bet-tles, a remote outpost of a few log cabins, a tiny post office, and a lodge, clustered at the end of a gravel strip. Shanahan met us at the plane, wearing khakis and running shoes, a red-headed wisp of a man who looked like he weighed about ninety pounds, nobody's image of how a bush pilot was sup-posed to look. We threw our gear in an old pickup and hauled it down to a Cessna 185 tied on the river. As soon as we tax-ied out into the current of the Koyukuk there was no mistak-ing why Shanahan was somewhat of a legend in that part of the Arctic. He just had that casual, calm skill that defines whether or not some bush pilots live longer lives than others.

On a later occasion I flew with Shanahan on the North Slope, and he told me then how he'd once been flying an old Twin Beech on the mail run between Fairbanks and Barrow, and both engines on the Beech quit at the same time. As he related it: "Without engines those things glide about as good as a goddamn cement block. All I could do was take her into a lake and try for the shallow end, so she wouldn't sink to the bottom and drown me." Which is what he managed to accomplish, only he broke an arm and a collarbone in the process. And both doors got jammed, so he couldn't crawl out and wade to land. Somehow he managed to struggle into a sleeping bag he had with him. There he sat in freezing water up past his waist for over twenty-four hours, before the Civil Air Patrol located him by his emergency beacon.

We flew east and north. The country spread out below us, green and mottled with lakes and streams, miles and miles and miles of untracked wilderness. To the north, the southern foothills of the Brooks Range climbed up into what looked like an endless mass of high gray peaks. Even though I'd already flown over a lot of country in Alaska, I'd never felt anything like this before. It was as if we had penetrated another dimension, a step back into something entirely primal. Shanahan looked over at me and he must have seen my awe. Over the clatter of the engine he yelled, "Ain't a bad piece of country, is it?" I nodded, and felt such great joy for my life right then. Joy, because I was entering a wilder place than I'd ever been before. And because I was still caught in the fantasy, the idea that it was all out there just for me. At that moment I was not in an airplane flying through the twentieth century, but was eddying backward in time, seized by the sensual excitement of a man about to enter virgin territory.

We flew up into the southern foothills of the Brooks Range, banked, and twisted north into a narrow valley with a frothing stream plunging from it. As we broke over a low ridge, there below us was the lake, a long narrow jewel of water surrounded by steep mountains of gray talus and pale green tundra. Shanahan dropped quickly, nosed into the close end of the lake, and landed. We skimmed across the water's surface, slowed, and settled to a stop on the far end. "Here's where I leave you," he said. "Weather depending, I'll be back in a week."

Murry and I waded ashore with our gear. We stood there and watched the Cessna take off. The engine's roar beat against the mountains. Water sprayed white and charged from its floats. It gained speed. One float tipped up, then the other, and then the plane was off, disappearing quickly over the ridge at the west end of the lake. I felt it then, and have many times since, the mix of joy and vulnerability of a bush pilot leaving you in some remote place. Your lifeline, only one person alive who knows for sure exactly where you're at. Pray that nothing happens to the pilot. Pray for good weather the day of his scheduled return.

It was (and still is) against the law to shoot sheep the same day you fly, so we couldn't hunt that day. We took our time setting up camp at the edge of the lake. As we did we spotted sheep all around us. Once the camp was together, we glassed the steep slopes. In the space of an hour, we counted over twenty legal rams. We walked the lake shores. There were no signs that any other humans had ever been there before, though we both speculated that at one time or another an occasional Eskimo must have wandered through, looking for game.

The next morning we got up early, ate a quick breakfast, then climbed a mountain at the head of the valley. Within a half hour of climbing we came up on a fine, full-curl ram. He stood staring at us less than a hundred yards away, white and muscular, horns perfectly formed and unbroomed. He was alert but not particularly afraid of us. Murry wanted to take only a record-book sheep; if he couldn't kill big, he said, he wouldn't kill at all. He told me to go ahead and shoot. I crept forward a few more yards, dropped down into a sitting position, and shot. The ram hunched, then launched itself forward into space. He landed hard on rocks thirty feet below and tumbled sickeningly, over and over, down the mountain. I felt my stomach grip as we watched the fall, scared that I'd lose him in some crevice or his horns would be damaged. Finally his descent slowed and he came to a shuddering stop on a rocky outcrop just above the valley floor.

Murry slapped me on the back. "Good job," he said. We climbed down to the ram and I touched him. He was a beautiful animal, his horns miraculously undamaged from the fall. I felt a wave of affection for the animal, an appreciation for it. I asked Murry to take the pictures, then we skinned and caped the sheep, cut it into quarters, and packed it back to camp.

That night we fried back-strap on the camp stove. There's no better wild meat that I know of. A fat bull caribou, taken before the rut, is wonderful. A dry cow moose can be superb. Elk is almost always good. But a wild sheep, it's as if the essence of the mountains is concentrated in the flesh. On your tongue is the taste of pure wild.

The next day we walked around the end of the lake and climbed a high mountain. It was slow going, but we were in no hurry. It was late afternoon before we finally made the top of the ridge. There in a little bowl below us, no more than fifty feet away, stood thirteen legal rams. Two of them were a curl and a quarter, one even larger. They just looked at us, curious, not at all afraid.

"Shoot the big one," I whispered.

Murry thought about it. "No," he said, "it's too late in the day." We did have a long way to go back down to our camp. If we had to deal with a dead sheep, it would be dark by the time we made it to the lake. The mountainside was no place to be moving then. I urged him to shoot anyway, figuring if we had to we could hunker down on the mountain and wait for first light. But Murry declined. "We can come back tomorrow," he said. That's how confident he was of taking a big sheep there.

This account may not mean much to nonhunters. For a hunter, though, in the last half of the twentieth century, sheep hunting is not supposed to be as easy as it was for us in those mountains. It's virtually unheard of to have that many rams to pick from. The sheep we stalked had never seen humans before. They saw no threat in these clumsy, slow, two-legged creatures. We experienced something that's impossible to know today in Alaska, or likely anywhere else in the world.

Murry and I agreed we would get up early and climb hard the next day, no messing around. We'd get up to those rams and kill one and get it out long before dark. But the next morning we woke to the tent sagging in our faces. True to the unpredictability of weather in the Arctic in mid-August, a foot of snow had fallen during the night. There was no way we could climb in those conditions, so we spent the rest of the week camp-bound and never saw another sheep.

The day that Shanahan was due to pick us up, the sun came out and the snow began to melt. Around noon we heard a plane approaching. The Cessna landed, taxied close to our pile of gear on the lakeshore. We loaded up and took off. I'll come back, I vowed as we cleared the ridge and dropped down into the valley below. Little did I know what was in store for that country.

Years later I ran into Shanahan up on the North Slope, and he told me that after he flew us in there the pilots up in that country had taken to calling the lake Brunk Lake, because as he said then, "No one else was ever crazy enough to want to go in there before you came along."

Several years later the state of Alaska pushed a haul road through the Brooks Range to the North Slope, the first road ever in those mountains. Today I'm not exactly sure where that lake is; I can't pinpoint it on a map. The best I can figure it, though, is that the haul road comes within a few miles of it. A year or so after the road was built, I talked to my friend at Alaska Fish and Game who had told me about the lake. I asked him if he knew anything about the sheep in those mountains. He told me that the road came close enough to the lake that hunters could pack into it fairly easily. He thought the sheep had mostly been shot out the years immediately following the road's construction. I felt something go cold inside me. I felt anger and regret. It was as if a sense of ownership had been violated; that was my country. I knew that my experience there was going to be difficult to have again, anywhere; Murry and I had experienced one of the last untouched places of the last frontier.

The construction of the road north through the Brooks Range—the Dalton Highway—was like a slash across the face of the Mona Lisa. I've seen it so many times since, how the promoters get their way and a road is pushed into a place, and as soon as it is something terribly vital, a crucial spirit is sucked from the country. The sellers of Alaska, sellers the world over, push for more access, more roads, talk about the economic necessity of them. Beneath the obvious economic grab, I suppose some promoters and engineers and construction workers believe they're doing something useful and good, that somehow they're advancing the cause of mankind. But what they won't see, can't see in their blind greed, is that every mile built is one more nail in the heart of the natural world. It's happening planet-wide: in the Amazon, Canada's wildlands, Siberia, in America's National Forests (which have over 375,000 miles of roads already—eight times the total of the interstate highways—and over 500,000 more miles planned).

Today, I'm well aware of the paradox of my own special privilege in entering that country when I did. I could afford to use an airplane, so the argument could be made, and is, that without roads, access into wild country is left to only an elite few. In the scheme of the American class system, though, I'm anything but elite. The point is, I made it my priority to go there, and I wouldn't today if I could access it by road, because the place wouldn't be the same. The qualities I desire to experience would be gone. Certainly, though, I must take some responsibility for being part of the place's demise. It's not lost on me that my entry, to be the first to kill a sheep there, was a violation of sorts, a very small act, comparatively, in a much larger, destructive drama that's been going on for several centuries now. The central issue, then, is not whether by road or airplane, but about all the destructive things and attitudes we bring with us, the mentality that builds roads and hunts areas to extinction. This is what's ultimately destroying the biosphere that we all depend upon for life.

The year after Brunk Lake, late June, I flew with another friend up to Deadhorse, the staging center for the Prudhoe Bay petroleum development. This was my first introduction to what was actually happening in the Arctic. What I saw shocked me. Drilling rigs, ten stories high, towered above a flat, treeless world. The tundra for miles around was cut with roads and scarred with the never-healing tracks of winter exploration vehicles. Deadhorse itself was a boom camp, acres of trailers and rough plywood buildings, equipment, and pipe yards. Everything looked like it had been thrown together in a big hurry, a graphic and ugly contrast to the clean tundra world of lakes and ponds that spread beyond the development. I could not shake the reality that just five years earlier nothing had been there; it had been purely wild country. I couldn't know it at the time that what I was witnessing around Deadhorse was only the most minute beginnings of what Alaska's central Arctic plain would come to look like. I didn't know then that I would return years later a number of times to work there, and see petroleum development spread like a cancer beyond the horizons.

I couldn't wait to get out of Deadhorse. We hired a bush pilot to fly us into country that, only a few years earlier, had been designated by the federal government as the Arctic Wildlife Range (known today as the Arctic National Wildlife Refuge). We lifted off the strip at Deadhorse, banked east, and soon left the scars of oil development behind. As we flew farther east, the flanks of the Brooks Range curved north to meet us. Closer and closer to the mountains we came. We crossed the Canning River, and as we did I felt like a space traveler who had broken through a time barrier and returned to a primal planet.

I would guess the visibility was close to fifty miles in any direction that day, maybe more. From the air we could see the whole of it. To the south, the high peaks of the Brooks Range, snow covered and sharply sculpted, reared up into a white cumulous sky. At a distance the lower slopes, gray talus broken by the browns and greens of spring tundra, looked stark yet at the same time alive and alluring. In the foreground, steep brown foothills dropped abruptly to a flat, yellow-green coastal plain. Scattered bands of caribou moved over the plain. Rivers running from the mountains fanned out across the plain to flow into the ice-choked Arctic Ocean to the north. The mountains and the plain and the ocean all came together in a visually contained ecosystem that was unlike anything I'd ever experienced. All the elements of landscape came together in a complex and integrated whole, an exaggerated abundance of beauty.

Our pilot flew us up into a broad valley lined with low peaks, and landed on a gravel bar of a river. I can't remember its name, if it even had one then. He agreed to come back and pick us up in ten days. It's almost inconceivable now, but for those ten days we may have been the only human beings in the Wildlife Range, an area the size of the state of South Carolina.

We were not there to hunt, only to try to witness the summer migration of the porcupine caribou herd—and, truth be known, to check it out for hunting later, maybe locate our own private reserve. As we made camp, a few scattered caribou bands moved quickly across the hills around us, pushed by the black clouds of mosquitoes that boiled up from the wet tundra. We went to bed with the midnight sun hanging low and red on the north horizon.

Sometime during the night we woke to grunting noises outside our tent. We crawled out to behold thousands of caribou around our camp: cows with knobby-kneed little calves at their sides; gangly yearlings; big, fat, slick-sided bulls, their antlers covered in brown velvet, all of them restless and moving, the sesamoid bones in their feet clicking like muffled castanets. This was an entirely different experience for me from those first caribou I'd shot up in the Crazy Mountains. The scale of life was beyond understanding, stunning enough that, for once, wishing for my rifle was not my initial reaction.

We saw grizzlies and wolves, Dall sheep, and a lone wolverine during those ten days. I did not want to leave. When the plane came winging in, settled, and rattled onto the gravel bar, like Brunk Lake it was another place I vowed I would return to.

I only wanted more after those two trips up into the Arctic. I did not know then that my return to the Arctic Refuge would be years away and under entirely different circumstances. I don't recall seeing, or perhaps more accurately acknowledging, the storm gathering to undo that place.

9

thirty mile

I went to the woods because I wished to live deliberately, to
front only the essential facts of life, and see if I could not
learn what it had to teach, and not, when I came to die, discover that I had not lived.

HENRY DAVID THOREAU, *Walden*

Despite the way I might have wanted the world to be, even
then reality lurked at the edge of my desire. I had some
understanding of what was happening in Alaska. I knew at
some level that I was witnessing the last gasp of America's
three-hundred-year push to tame and develop a whole continent, to turn it all toward economic ends. I could not extend
myself fully into all the philosophical notions of it at that point
in my life, but I understood enough to know that "the last
frontier" the promoters championed so exhaustively was
about to end. I had some comprehension that America stood
at the apex of something that had defined it since the beginning. Where I got lost in my thinking was in my own resist-

ance to the idea of anything changing. I wanted frontier, desired to live in a place that had no limits, where constraint and consideration were not requirements for good citizenship. I was still caught in the myth of the American West, wanted to believe in it. The thought of inhabiting a place without the frontier stamp on it held little invitation for me.

But it was all changing so fast. Construction of the Trans-Alaska Pipeline was about to begin. Jimmy Carter's administration had settled the Natives' land claims, and now the feds were dealing with what was known as the Alaska National Interest Land Claims Act. All over the state, scientists and bureaucrats were attempting to identify lands of great public value. The big, wide-open, free Alaska that I had come to love was about to be carved up into Native lands, National Parks and Wildlife Refuges, petroleum reserves, National Forests. But not until the state of Alaska got its own share, places picked mostly for their oil and mineral potential. Not until the state map resembled a patchwork quilt of arbitrary and artificial boundaries that changed everyone's lives.

In Fairbanks land prices were shooting up astronomically. Tracts of shoddily built houses sprouted like thistles over land that had months before been spruce forest, houses that would not have done well in California, let alone a place just 125 miles south of the Arctic Circle. A Fairbanks developer, who was also a state senator, bought the homestead fields behind our house, built a mini-mall and several dozen condominiums, then paved a big parking lot. With that the dog-training trails out of the wanigan house became an obstacle course that took some real skill to negotiate. On the Chena River floodplain below us, the same developer used his political influence, conveniently sidestepped the Fairbanks zoning ordinances (what few there were), and put in a park for several hundred mobile homes, cutting off our trail access to the river.

B and I agreed it was time to move. In my mind it had been time to move for a long while. This time, though, I was determined to go for the dream.

I was only months away from graduating from the university. I had no plans for using my degree. What I was most interested in was driving dogs. Whenever there were a few extra dollars in the bank account I would talk B into spending it on something related to dogs: another brood bitch, a new leader, a sled. She usually went along with me. She would come home evenings after work and help me with the training. And she even entered several women's races. Dogs were my obsession, though. For her, I think, it was more a desire to be part of something with me. She was trying to find a common denominator in our marriage, which meant mostly seeing things my way.

And my way, it was clear, was that as soon as I got out of school we were going to make a break for it. Homesteading had been closed since the summer of 1969, our second in Alaska, so that was no option. If you wanted to get somewhere far out of town, out in the bush, then you had to find something that had already been homesteaded and patented.

A dog-musher friend named Denis told me about some land, a patented homestead, he'd found out of town on the Tanana River. The land was a couple of miles off the Alaska Highway at the thirty-mile marker. He'd bought forty acres of it and was building a cabin there. He thought the old fellow he'd bought it from still had 120 acres left. Denis said he'd sure like to see some other dog mushers settle out there. There was no road access to the land. To get there you had to take a boat across the Piledriver Slough, then travel a footpath for about a mile. Or you could take a boat down the slough and out onto the main river. It was ideal dog-training country, Denis said, flat, with lots of winter trails on both sides of the river.

It sounded good to me.

1973. Summer again, the world coming alive, green and rich. I launched my canoe on the Piledriver Slough, floated down it to the wide, rough-charging Tanana River. I had a USGS map draped over my knees, with the approximate location of the land marked on it. As I held the canoe steady in the quick current, I studied the map, all the bends and forms along the river. The summer sun circled the sky, striking the water, glistening, a diffuse, hard, angled light. Before long I passed a new cabin nestled back among the trees on the north bank. I figured it was Denis's; I knew I had to be getting close. At the far outside of a long bend I steered into a low-cut bank, steadied the canoe, and stepped ashore. Mature white spruce spread along the river, the finest cabin logs imaginable. Mixed among the spruce a few mature white birch stood bent and gnarled as old men. Beneath the trees, prickly wild rosebushes, cranberries, and willows spread over a yellow-green sponge of moss. There were no signs of any human activity there, recently or in the past. It was as fine a piece of virgin river bottom as one could imagine.

I walked along the river's edge, then cut inland. Shortly I came upon a place where a moose had bedded down in a little moss-filled depression. From that spot I could see off in the distance, across the river on the south horizon, the great white peaks of the Alaska Range thrusting up high into an azure sky. I stood there and knew this was it, the land I desired. The dream of my childhood—a log cabin on a river, a dog team, hunting and fishing and living off the land—after years of waiting was about to begin. The front door of the cabin would go where the moose had bedded. A good omen, I reasoned. Home.

The land I stood on was part of an original 160-acre homestead that had been acquired in 1924 by a fellow by the last name of Wallace. It was the law back then that you had to clear ten acres and plant a crop to "prove up," as they called it. But the reality of homesteading in Alaska in those days was that it was pretty much a federal giveaway. Often all a home-steader did was stake a claim and wait the required time; the government never got around to inspecting to see if land had been cleared and a crop planted. The government just handed over the patent, as the deed was called, when the time was up.

There was no indication anywhere that Wallace had ever lived on any of the land, no old cabin, no stumps, no sign of a clearing. In 1932 Wallace traded it to a Fairbanks grocer named Busby for a winter grubstake. Busby never lived there either, and ten years later he turned it over to a fellow named Joe Kaeger, who still lived in Fairbanks. Their deal was that Kaeger would build him a cabin in town in return for the land.

It was late June when I looked up Joe Kaeger in his cabin in downtown Fairbanks. Full summer, it was still a bit cold from a rainstorm that was moving through. I knocked and he hollered for me to come in. The shades on the cabin windows were all drawn. I walked into the living room, where Joe sat in a worn red easy chair, about four feet away from a lit oil stove. I guess like a lot of the old-timers he'd had his fill of cold and was suspicious of getting too involved with summer, because everybody knows it's too damned short-lived to trust much. Joe Kaeger was a wiry-looking old man, a life-long bachelor, thin and dried out as kindling. He'd been in Alaska over sixty years. The lines of his face all turned up-ward like he'd spent all sixty of those years smiling and be-ing agreeable.

I took a seat on a yellow plaid couch across from him. We made some small talk. I hoped I was giving him some sense of who I was, that I wasn't some real estate agent or something. Finally, he looked at me and smiled. "What can I do you for?"

"Would you be interested in selling that land you have out on the Tanana?" I asked him.

Joe considered it a moment, then shifted a little closer to the stove. "I suppose I would. I got no use for it. Hell, last time I was out there was 1952. No, maybe it was '51. Don't matter. I know it's been at least twenty years anyway. Then all I did was go out there and cut a cord o' wood. Brought it back into town and sold it." He chuckled. "I wasn't even sure I was cuttin' on my land. Course it didn't matter back then. Times was different."

"So you'd sell it?" I said.

"Sure," he said, "but I ain't gonna sell it for what these real estate fellas are gettin' for land around here. It's ridiculous what they're askin'." He paused and looked me in the eye. "I ain't gonna charge what they're askin'. I'm only gonna ask what's fair."

I did my best to appear casual. With the oil boom under way, land around Fairbanks was going for anywhere from $1,000 to $3,000 an acre. Not river land either, but just raw land, no easy water, maybe permafrost on it, certainly no good timber. Land like that out on the Tanana was virtually impossible to find.

"What do you figure you'd have to have for it?" I asked.

"Well," he said, "I'm thinkin' two hundred an acre. You figure that'd be too much? You do, I'd be willing to negotiate."

"That seems like a pretty fair price," I said, barely able to contain myself. "You take payments on it?"

"Sure," he said. "What can you afford?"

We agreed on a couple of thousand down, payments of two hundred a month, no interest. I told him I had in mind getting a couple of friends of mine to buy the two quarter sections back off the river. I'd keep the forty acres on the water. He agreed with that. In my mind I was working the numbers. I figured it would be no time at all until the land was paid off.

Joe stood and hobbled with me to the door. We shook hands on the deal. "It's good to see some young fellas take over up here," he said. "I'd be out there with you, too, if I could manage it."

When I graduated from the university the spring of 1974, I had already made a commitment to give sled-dog racing all I had, to turn professional, and in my secret heart to become the best at it. We had close to forty dogs now, counting pups. Blackie and Brother were gone, too old, too slow, sold to a recreational musher. I'd bought a young leader by the name of Annie, a real character of a dog, in ways more human in her qualities than dog. I started running her up there with Swede, and right off the bat she began pushing him in every way. Swede and Boo were the last of those first dogs. It had become increasingly clear that Swede didn't have the same speed as the new young dogs I was raising. He needed to go. I sold him to a fellow training for a new distance race called the Iditarod. I kept Boo more out of sentiment than any practicality.

B and I agreed that it was time to move to the river. I'm not sure what she imagined for herself. My own fantasy was to stay out there, train what I had, raise a lot of pups, and then in a few years show up in Fairbanks with a top dog team. The wunderkind from the bush was how I figured it. I knew by then, though, that to make the top I still had a lot to learn.

Earlier that spring, with the sap full up in the trees, my building partner and I went out to river property. Thirty Mile, we called it. We cut forty-four good house logs: fine, straight-grained, hundred-and-fifty-year-old white spruce, all within fifty yards of where the moose had bedded. Then we stripped the logs with peeling spuds made from the leaf springs of an old pickup. We laid the bark out in long, white,

pitchy strips right where the trees had fallen. Then I got Denis to come down with his horse and skid them up in a pile
next to the house site. There we ricked them up. I asked Denis if he'd turn them with a peavey now and then through the
summer, so they'd dry nice and straight.

B and I decided we'd move out to the river by the end of
summer, depending upon whether or not I could get a cabin
built before winter, which might be a challenge.

Just before I graduated I'd heard about a job up on the
Charlie River, running a riverboat and outfitting a camp for a
group of scientists studying the Charlie for National Wild and
Scenic River status. I left the first of June, ran a riverboat full
of gear and supplies up the Yukon and into the lower Charlie, where I set up a big camp. The Charlie was a fine, wild
river then, running clear out of a low range of mountains on
the south side of the Yukon, midway between the villages of
Eagle and Circle. In high water I would take the scientists upriver in the boat, through duff-colored rocky bluffs that
pitched straight up off the water. We'd travel far up into the
headwaters. There the slope of the river ran downhill like a
chute. Sometimes wolves would lope off gravel bars ahead of
us, or white Dall sheep would scramble up the cliffs above.
When I think back on it, that was about as fine a summer as
one could imagine. But I've heard the Charlie's changed now
that it's been designated Wild and Scenic. Like so many
places that have been *officially* designated wild, it's become a
recreation destination and the wild's being sucked from it. I
don't know if I could stand to go back.

I figured to stay with the job as long as I could, so I knew
it would be a push to get a cabin up on the Tanana before
winter set in. The first month up on the Charlie I only made
it once into Fairbanks to see B and Cara. Then in July I got
a radio message that said my mother had had a major heart
attack; she was in critical condition in a hospital in Cleveland,

Ohio. She might not live. I fired up the riverboat in the middle of the night, ran down the broad, silty Yukon with the midnight sun full over my right shoulder, the sixty miles to Circle. I tied the boat and climbed the riverbank there, got in my pickup, and drove fast over the Steese Highway, two hundred miles of gravel road to Fairbanks. It was early morning when I pulled up in front of the wanigan house. B met me at the door. "You've got less than an hour to get cleaned up," she said. "I've got a ticket for you. Your plane will make Cleveland late tonight."

It was past midnight when I arrived at the Cleveland airport. I took a train downtown to a huge, empty station. I hailed a taxi, told the driver I needed to go to the Cleveland Clinic. "Nobody goes in there in the middle of the night," he said.

"That's where I need to go."

"Okay," he said, "but I drop you off at the hotel there, you stay inside. Don't go anywhere."

From the Charlie River to Cleveland, Ohio, in less than twenty-four hours. The shock of the contrast was palpable, hard, jangling to all my senses. The Cleveland Clinic was located in a ghetto, a shrine to urban decay and blight. Shadowy figures moved among vacant buildings, along dark streets and into alleys. I checked into the hotel and the clerk told me the same thing, don't go anywhere. But I had to. The hospital was just across the street. What could go wrong with it that close? I took my bags up to my room, then came down and crossed the street, walked up a short stretch of sidewalk toward the closest building. I'd just about made the entrance when suddenly two German shepherds burst around the corner of the building, snarling and barking. They pinned me up against the door. "Freeze, fucker!" somebody yelled. Two cops followed the dogs, guns drawn and pointed at me.

I threw up my hands. "I'm here to see my mother," I hollered.

The cops closed in on me. "Don't move, don't do anything." They got close, and one shined a flashlight in my face. "He's a white guy," he said.

They called off their dogs then and interrogated me. "Nobody white comes here in the middle of the night. What the hell are you doing here?"

I told them I'd come from Alaska, that my mother was in serious condition; she might die. I needed to see her.

With their dogs pacing close, the cops accompanied me to the entrance of my mother's building. "Don't come outside until full daylight," one of them said.

I took the elevator up to the fifth floor, where I found my mother still alive, attached by tubes to machines and bags of fluid, her breath coming in ragged gulps. She'd had emergency open-heart surgery and a tough time of it. I pulled a chair up by her bed and waited. It was mid-morning before she finally opened her eyes and looked at me. "You're here," she whispered. "I'm so glad you came."

I spent a week with her and my father, waited until it was clear that she was going to make it. But being in the Midwest again, I felt all the old restlessness come up, felt the place closing in on me. Even though it was my mother I'd come for, I still felt the urge to leave as soon as I could. Damn it, I'd say to myself, why can't you just be here, it's your mother. But talking to myself did no good. I knew I'd done the right thing in coming, but all I could think about was getting back. I wanted to get the work on the Charlie done and get to building the cabin. In many ways Alaska's hold on my young man's heart was stronger than my mother's.

I'm not proud, today, that I found it so hard to be there. But I know this: to this day when I return to the Midwest, I still feel the same stifling confinement that I felt as a boy. I don't suppose that will ever change.

It was the middle of July when I flew back to Alaska. When I stepped off the plane in Fairbanks it was like coming home after years away. B met me at the gate. "Welcome home," she said.

"It's good to be back," I said. We embraced. I spoke softly in her ear. "If I ever go outside again, it'll be too soon."

I spent the night in town. The next morning I got up early and headed back up to the Charlie. It felt good to be on the Yukon again, back in the wild. But I was anxious for the summer to end; I wanted to get started on that cabin. It was the end of August before we finished and I pulled the camps, and I made my last trip down the Yukon, headed home.

I figured I had six weeks, seven at the most, to get a dog yard cleared and the cabin up before the first heavy snows came. A couple of young fellows who had worked for me up on the Charlie volunteered to help. We packed the floor joist and plywood decking in on our backs. Fourteen hours a day we worked. We set the pilings, notched and squared and set deck logs, and nailed up the deck in three days. With me doing the notching and fitting and my helpers the grunt work, we made a round of logs a day on the walls. Nine rounds, nine days. Another four days for the gables, ridgepole, and purlins. It looked like we were going to make it before winter.

Denis offered us a little cabin to stay in, the one he'd built before he built his main cabin on the river. One night the boys I had helping me headed into town to drink. I stayed there. I had a dog with me, a neurotic half-Siberian I was keeping for a friend. Also along were some pups just weaned from one of my best bitches. I had the pups with me so they could run loose in the bush, to gain confidence about things.

The sun no longer ruled; the nights were turning dark by ten or ten-thirty. I was exhausted from a long day setting logs, so I ate a quick meal of peanut butter and pilot bread and crawled into bed. Sometime later I came up through a deep sleep to the pups whining and the Siberian *whoofing* scared off in the trees. I lay still and listened. The head of my bed was only a couple of feet from the door. I heard something move outside. Suddenly, whatever it was hit the cabin door, rattling it like a sheet of paper. Then came a low, insistent growl, a terrifying sound with enough big creature in it to send adrenaline pumping through my veins.

I sat up quickly, shucked my arms out of my sleeping bag, and reached for my rifle leaning between the bed and the door. I pushed the safety off and jacked the bolt and felt it miss the shell. The animal outside the door snuffled and growled low, then hit the door another hard wallop. I jacked the bolt and felt it miss again. I pushed out of my sleeping bag and swung my feet to the floor. "Get out of here!" I yelled. I stood and stumbled over to the table, stopped, and listened, feeling helpless and scared. Whatever it was was still out there, snuffling close to the door. "Get out of here!" I hollered again, feeling around at the same time for the lantern that was supposed to be hanging from a purlin.

I found it, then felt across the surface of the table for the box of kitchen matches. I fumbled a match out of the box and struck it. The cabin flared into feeble light. I put the match to the lantern, cracked the valve. The lantern hissed to life.

I grabbed my rifle again. I had carried that rifle all summer with the clip full, hadn't given a thought to the fact that the clip spring might fatigue enough for the bolt to miss the rim of the shell. I snapped out the clip, pulled out a shell, and slipped it into the chamber. With the rifle held on the door, I waited.

There was nothing now, no sound except one of the pups whimpering under the cabin. I waited several more minutes. Nothing. And then a rifle shot crashed through the stillness, reverberating through the trees. I must have waited ten minutes or more, expecting another shot, but none followed.

With my rifle held ready I opened the door. On the trail to the river I spotted two lights coming toward me, swinging wide arcs across the trail, playing off the trees in exaggerated shadows. Denis shouted, "Stay in your cabin, there's a wounded bear on the loose!" His wife was with him. They were both armed.

Denis had come to Alaska from Minnesota. He stood at least six foot five, and weighed over two-fifty. Big as he was he still moved light on his feet, athletic and easy, so easy at times that he appeared almost dainty. I know if he was alive today he wouldn't like me saying so. Denis was younger than most anybody else in the community, but was already an infamous legend. He worked hard at being bigger than life, would kill just about anything he could get his sights on, damn the seasons, the species, or any ethics that might be involved.

He and his wife came inside and described how their dogs had started baying and then they'd heard their horse running wild in the corral. Denis leaped out of bed, naked as a tortellini. From his front porch he shot at a hazy black silhouette. The silhouette bolted off into the woods, leaving a blood trail and large tracks in the silt. "It's a damn big bear," Denis said. "We have to go look for it. It's too dangerous to leave it out there wounded."

I fiddled with the clip, pushed it back into my rifle, hoping this time it might work. I grabbed my lantern. The three of us walked out into the night, a quarter-mile upriver where another couple were staying in a cabin. We told them the story, suggested they stay alert. Denis's wife was reluctant, but Denis insisted that we go back to the river and pick up the blood trail. "We can't leave a wounded bear out there," he said. Poisoned with testosterone and adrenaline, I agreed.

Through the moonless night we stumbled, in the frail, hissing light of Coleman lanterns, following a spattered blood trail, accompanied here and there by the unmistakable prints of a large grizzly. We followed the trail a hundred yards upriver before it cut into the woods. There it was harder to follow, but with careful study we managed. We'd made about fifty yards when the world suddenly erupted. Agonized, angry roars beat against the darkness like the devil's own voice—*Waaargh!*—over and over again. Trees rattled and snapped. We held our rifles ready for the charge, for a snarling fury to erupt through our pale circle of light. But none came. And then as suddenly as it had begun the roaring ended. The dark woods around us were completely still.

Denis's wife finally broke the silence. "This is stupid," she said, a voice of badly needed reason. "I think we should wait for morning, when we can see what's going on out here."

"Maybe we should," Denis agreed. He was scared, I could tell, an emotion that in time I came to know about him, that his big-man bluster often covered a terrified boy. As far as I can recall, though, that was the only time I ever heard his wife, before or after, publicly disagree with him about anything. Denis was one of those men who insisted on being in charge, at least in public.

We retreated to our respective cabins. The next morning we got up and picked up the trail again. When we approached the spot where we'd heard the roaring, the ground all around was gouged and ripped, small trees scarred and broken. We held our firearms ready, but there was no need for that. At the base of a big spruce we found him, an old boar grizzly, shot hard, up high and behind the lungs, stretched full out on his stomach, his head twisted grotesquely off to his right and up under his leg. Blood froth rimmed his mouth. His canines were broken and dangling from their roots. The bear had clearly died in great agony. I remember thinking, the way his head was twisted off like that, it looked like he had been ashamed to die the way he had.

He was a big bear, record book, but old and thin, missing back teeth; there was no way he would have made the winter. He was also missing the outside toes on his right front foot, the sure signature of a bear that had raided cabins along the Salcha River for years. Glad as I was that he hadn't come into the cabin with me, I was awash with sadness; I wished him a better death. The case could be made that he would have died anyway. But there seemed so little dignity in going the way he had. I couldn't express that to anyone then, particularly to Denis, who was quite proud that he'd killed a grizzly.

I try now to recall how I felt standing there in the dark that night with that bear roaring. It's strange, but I don't recall feeling any fear. I felt fear in the cabin, I guess, because I felt so helpless. But in the woods, all I can remember is a calmness, a feeling of being exactly where I wanted to be. Mixed with it, too, was a sense of exhilaration. This same mix of feelings I've experienced other times, always when I've been in the most danger. There may be some grand psychological explanation for it. If I had to label it, though, I'd call it a swift, exacting moment when my life finally comes to some essential connection, some place where the dread of my own mortality is temporarily exorcised. I would say that this place is something that our ancestors, in less predictable and less insulated-from-nature times, must have felt often. I would guess, for the most part, their lives were a good deal richer for it.

I went back to work on my cabin that same day. As I worked I felt a continuing sadness for the bear. But at the same time, mixed with it, I felt a joy for living, for the privilege of being in a place where grizzly bears still roamed, where there were things big enough to eat you, where life was a bit unpredictable. I felt alive, very alive.

10

dog man

I thought my whole life had changed, and my basic understanding of values had changed, that I wasn't sure if I would
ever recover, that I had seen god and he was a dog-man and
that nothing, ever, would be the same for me again.

GARY PAULSEN, *Winterdance*

We hauled the roof boards and rafters in by boat, put the roof boards up in a September snowstorm, set the rafters and insulated the next day. I put up aluminum roofing, taken by a fit of practicality. "Aluminum will last forever," I said, damning the aesthetics. By the sixth day of October I had the windows in, and I'd built and hung exterior doors. The day the cabin was finally closed in, it was just six years and five months from the day B and I had first arrived in Fairbanks. We were both twenty-nine years old and we had a new home in the bush, a 26-by-32, trapper-style log cabin, low walls and an open ceiling, and a fine loafing porch on the front. We had no elec-tricity. Propane lights instead. No running water. Just a pitcher pump in the kitchen. No interior walls. That first winter the three of us lived in one big room with a barrel stove in the middle, a good enough place to be. Mid-October, B and I moved the dogs in by boat, twenty-some adults and a dozen pups, chained along the sides. They stood eager and quivering, their noses lifted high, sifting the rich river smells. When we nudged up against the bank in front of the cabin, the dogs pulled hard at their collars, eager to be ashore, as eager as I was, it seemed, to take on this new life. We led them up one at a time, tied them in the new dog yard. With the last one tied we stood back and watched them sniff out their new territory.

"They're home," Cara said.

B said, "We are too."

Life on the river quickly took on seasonal rhythms. One day it was fall, and the next winter, that time of long, dark, brutally cold nights, when the air stabbed at your face and the northern lights danced holy across the sky. We settled in.

There was a little community of dog mushers who lived in the vicinity, most of them up along the Alaska Highway, six or seven couples total, all of us in our mid- to late twenties. With so much work to do in the summer, there was little time for us to socialize then. But winter, that was our time to come together. Many nights we would hook dog teams or take skis, travel moonlit trails to gather in one cabin or another for potlucks and saunas.

All of us, I believe, were imagining another time, a time of our great-grandparents. The women would collect off in their own corner and talk recipes and baking, canning meat, summer gardens, children. We men, holding to the roles we had defined for ourselves, would talk of our own things: hunting, fishing, log building, boats. Whatever our conversation was, though, without exception it would always eventually turn to dogs. Dogs ruled us.

Once our first winter, B suggested that she and I begin socializing with a new couple she'd met in Fairbanks. "Do they talk dogs?" I asked her.

"They don't have any dogs," she said. "They're just normal people."

"I'm not interested in normal people," I said. "I've got nothing to talk about with them." And that was it for me and any socializing with regular people.

Outside our dog circle, ruled by the single-mindedness of the born-again zealot, what a bore I must have been. Even before coming to the river, dogs had become my identity. We talked and talked and talked. Of sleds and gear, of the right kind of food, of medicines and veterinarians, of breeding, of lead dogs. We talked about what it took to make a top dog, that certain combination of desire, athletic ability, and speed that showed up in maybe one out of ten, or twenty, or even a hundred for the very best. I suppose I had the dog disease worse than others. There was something about the sport that seemed to meet so much of me. I took it on like a noble cause. There was something deep and crazy in it, the mystical pull of addiction. A couple of months ago I read Gary Paulsen's wonderful book *Winterdance*, about his experience running the Iditarod. Even though, like the recovering alcoholic, I know it's not something I can ever do again, I caught myself scheming how I might be able to put together another dog team and run that race. Just once more, I told myself. Then you can let it go. It took a week or two after finishing the book for my dreams to quit being about dogs.

We talked of "jumps," the way a good one strides full out and eats up the distance. That long, loose-jointed, almost reckless reach. It's a way of moving that no other animal on earth can duplicate over distance. None. A cheetah, the fastest animal living, could outdistance a top dog team three-to-one for the first hundred yards or so, but be left behind, exhausted, in a half mile. A fast thoroughbred horse might stay with a sprint team two miles, at the best three. Six or seven miles and everything in the animal world is left behind, and that's just when racing huskies are warming up, settling into their full stride, down into that rhythmic, hypnotic pace that's like poetry. I can think of few things more beautiful. It's still that way for me, and it's been twenty years now since I drove that last fine team, the one that Jenny led.

We talked of the whip, too. How to put the edge of fear into a good dog, that extra drive that's instilled by pain. Beyond the quality of the individual dog, beyond the point of desire and toughness, it gets down to who's driving them. Good dogs can be made either better or worse by the musher. It's a delicate balance. The highest compliment you could pay someone then was to say he was a good dog man, even if that someone was a she. A good dog man meant that musher could communicate with dogs, could get all they had to give. In those days, at least that's what I told myself, it usually meant the person had learned to use the whip efficiently. I suppose it's still that way for some driving dogs. But I'm glad to hear some things have changed. People who win now, I'm told, have figured out another way.

It was that first winter on the river that I learned the fine points of whipping from Denis. Denis started driving dogs when he lived in Minnesota. But like most mushers outside, he knew Alaska was the center of the universe, the place with the best dogs and dog men. So shortly after getting out of the Army he came north. Those of us in our community were all fairly accomplished Alaskans, experienced at a lot of things that had to do with living in the bush. Denis, though, the youngest of us all, was the resident expert on everything; he worked hard at out-manning us. In just a few years in Alaska he had gained a reputation as a tough dog man. But then Denis was good at most anything he undertook. Anything, that is, except hold a job. He hated working for anybody else, so schemed every possible way to avoid it. Dogs were one of his schemes. Raise a lot of pups. Cull ruthlessly. Prove out the best ones and sell them for big money. No attachment. No sentimentality.

It was just the two of us in his cabin that night. The propane lights cast a soft yellow glow against the log walls. Denis sat in his big red recliner chair, in a green plaid shirt, down vest, red wool stocking cap, and Sorels. He stood up. As he strode to the center of the room he reached into his vest pocket and pulled out a shot-loaded whip made of braided kangaroo hide. A signal whip, it was called. "I'm never without this," he said. "I'd feel undressed without it." He balanced the whip in the palm of his hand for a second. "A three-footer like this is best; you can work them over close." He took hold of the butt end, circled it once at his side, then with a quick flick of his wrist he cracked it. It sounded like a rifle shot. "You got to put the fear into 'em." As he spoke he reached down and pantomimed the act. "Pull 'em to you by their backlines with one hand and jerk hard. As you jerk, whip 'em with the other till they scream and struggle to get away." He put it to his imaginary dog a few strokes, then straightened and looked at me hard-eyed. "If they lie down and give up, then you know they haven't got it; they're bullet bait. You want the ones that'll go through the front of the harness to get away from you."

Denis was harder than most; he drove dogs with the cold intensity of a samurai, like they were the enemy. He had a reputation for producing tough-minded dogs. They had to be tough to survive his training. Maybe they weren't all that happy—"sour," we called them—but as Bernie Turner, a dog sage who lived up the highway, said, "Those sons-a-bitches that old Denis turns out can sure eat up the ground when you pull the leather."

The next day after Denis's demonstration, I took a ten-dog team out on a training run, a bunch I'd picked out that I thought needed a tune-up. I drove them past the turn-around and headed for home. A couple of miles to go, I called for more speed, the coming home drive that a good dog team needed to have. They gave me a little, but I wanted more. I stopped them, drove the snow hook in where I knew it would hold well, pulled the whip from the pocket of my parka, and moved quickly. I grabbed backlines and jerked each dog to me, worked my way from the wheel dogs to the leaders, cutting each one rhythmically with the whip, hollering loud at the same time "Aw right!" in what we called a fear voice. The whole team began screaming and lunging just like Denis said they should. I ran back to the sled and pulled the hook and hollered "Aw right!" The whole team put their heads down and ran hard for home.

I'd whipped before, but had never given much attention to the fine points of it, to the psychology of twisting a dog's mind into terror. In societies of wealth, where we have the luxury of owning them as pets or as competitive objects, I believe dogs and horses reflect back to us some primary and instinctual world that we yearn to connect with again. In our hyper-domestication we turn to domestic animals for a way back to something. They offer us a reciprocal relationship, a cooperative kinship. We humans, though, rarely honor the reciprocity of that agreement. Instead we often demand that they give us more and more. And most of the time they oblige. When they don't, they usually pay a grim price.

Denis also instructed me on how to kill what we called culls, the ones that were too slow or stubborn, or had some defect like not being able to handle what we asked of them. "Hold them headfirst between your legs," he said. "Draw an imaginary X between their eyes and their ears, put the muzzle right there where the X crosses, and pull the trigger. They never know what hit 'em."

One out of four pups made it for him. The rest he killed and piled on the river ice in front of his cabin, to wait for spring breakup to sweep them away. Sometimes I would think of Denis's pile, imagine it spinning on an ice cake after spring breakup, passing Indian villages along the way, twisting and tumbling along the Tanana, out to the Yukon, and along the Yukon until it entered the Bering Sea. There some Eskimo in a kayak would spot it on an ice floe, a gruesome testimony to some human run amuck.

Those first years on the river I raised my own pups and acquired more adult dogs, and I made my own pile. The ones I deemed not good enough, I drew the imaginary Xs on their heads and pulled the trigger, and watched them quiver into death. If a pup showed a weakness of any kind I killed it.

If killing and whipping were any measure of a dog man, by that first spring on the river I was a card-carrying member. I too had begun to learn how to turn out tough-minded dogs. I learned to strike and yell and flail until they pulled away from me in open-eyed terror, until sometimes flecks of blood spit like fire from their nostrils. I could holler a command and watch fourteen dogs drop their heads and tails, bow their backs, and scramble for life. There was something so powerful about it, so addictive, about the feel of the driving bow jerking alive in my hands.

How easily we take on the sins of our fathers. I know as a young man I carried a hard anger, though I know, too, that anger did not always define me. I've thought about it a great deal, and I can say now that the violence of whipping dogs was not my instinctual way. It was my inordinate desire to succeed at the sport, my early frustration of falling short, that too often spilled over into rage. It was then, particularly my first years driving dogs, that my animals suffered the most. Most of all, it was the ego-driven part of me that was willing to do whatever I perceived was needed to win.

But thank God there are other parts of us. There was another voice in me, a quiet observer who was disturbed at what he saw, who didn't like the dog man I'd become, who doubted the legitimacy of needing to be cruel in order to be the best. That voice whispered the name of my father to me, cautioned me about taking on his rage. But for a long time I managed to push it aside, because a louder, more determined voice prodded me on.

These things I've just written about I'm not proud to recount. Will someone judge me harshly today for the things I did then? I find it easier to recall a gentler part of my life on the river. In my memory certain things from those days hold as much sway now as dogs did then. Like Christmas. A week or so before the big day I would hook a few dogs to a freight sled and take Cara out along the river sloughs to look for a tree. "That one, Dad." She'd point at the first big one we'd come to.

"No," I cautioned her, "let's keep looking. You never know what you might find if you keep looking."

"That one." She'd repeat it a dozen times before we'd finally make a selection. I would saw down the tree and tie it on the sled. B would be waiting with hot chocolate when we got back, and of course she'd make a big fuss over the tree, even though the trees we cut were always sparsely branched, typical subarctic spruce.

But I had a solution for a thin tree. Once I got it inside the cabin I would take a hand drill and bore holes in the trunk, add branches from another tree until it looked as full as any commercial tree you could buy off a lot in town. We would make ornaments and string popcorn, and once we had it decorated I would add a set of tin candleholders that had come from Germany. Neighbors would come from all over for our candle-lighting ceremony. I would play guitar and we would all sing carols. Denis, who would never sing, who could be counted on to say "Games are for cripples and old people," would sit close to the tree with a fire extinguisher at hand. "Can't be too careful with fire in the bush," he'd always say. "Nothing worse than getting burned out the middle of winter."

We made presents for one another. One Christmas, Cara, taken by my carpentry skills, wanted a toolbox. I made her a wooden one with her name burned in the side, and filled it full of tools. Another Christmas I made her a little scaled-down racing sled. We had an old, retired leader named Bubbles, a tub of a dog who had charmed her way into living in the house. Bubbles loved heat. Once the weather turned even slightly bitter, she would install herself so close to the wood-stove that every now and then we'd get a whiff of hair scorching. When we told her to move, Bubbles would look at us in disgust, then reluctantly drag her body only a foot or two away from the stove. She hated going outside under any circumstances. Her only legitimate sled-dog job was to take Cara up to the school bus, which stopped a mile from the house up at the boat landing.

School mornings in the winter I would drag Bubbles out of the house and hook her up to Cara's little sled. Cara would come out of the house, all bundled up in her green winter parka, wolf ruff up around her face, with mittens that a neighbor had knitted for her, the right one with "gee" (for turn right) embroidered on it, the left with "haw" (for turn left.) She would step on her sled. "Don't let this dog buffalo you," I'd say to her.

In her tiny voice she'd yell, "Get up, Bubbles!" Bubbles would make a big show of pulling her down the trail and out of my sight. At which point, too often, she would try to turn around and make a run back to the stove. But Cara, true to her training, would hop off the sled and smack her on the nose and pull her around. "No, Bubbles!" Eventually Bubbles would get Cara to the bus stop. There they would both wait. When the bus came, Cara would turn Bubbles and the sled loose, and Bubbles would double-time it for home, eager to get back to the fire, the little sled careening along behind.

Our first winter on the river passed quickly. By the middle of March it was evident the sun was truly going to reign again. The days turned warm and brilliantly clear. I took to spending long hours out with the young dogs, putting them through all kinds of terrain, searching out new situations—standing water, glare ice, steep hills, even traffic up along the Alaska Highway—to get them bold, so by the time they were old enough to race there'd be nothing that would spook them.

By the middle of April the river ice began to rot. The water rose; the ice began to break into huge chunks, shifting and stirring in the current. Soon the whole river audibly groaned, as if reluctantly letting go of something important. Then, like a huge serpent stirring awake, the great body of ice began to move. Gigantic slabs collided and ground into one another, shattering into smaller chunks as the current ate away beneath. The three of us—B, Cara, and I—stood together on the bank, witnessing the awesome spectacle of spring breakup, the symbol throughout the north of winter officially giving way to the sun. We listened to the grinding and cracking of ice, the thrash of water. There we stood as a family, united by the recognition of our insignificance in the face of such power. I remember that first spring on the river, that I had indeed come to some frail sense of family. Even though other desires still pulled so strongly, there were also the delicate edges of some awkward peace growing in me.

Within days of breakup, the first Canada geese came honking into the islands and sandbars. They built nests there, relatively safe from the predation of foxes. A pair of bald eagles, which I had first observed when I was building the cabin, returned and reinhabited their huge stick nest in a cottonwood snag on the far side of the river. Soon the whine of mosquitoes was ever-present, and thrushes—varied, gray-cheeked, hermit, Swainson's—began trilling in the woods. A pair of elegant little kestrels built a nest at the edge of the clearing. Huge psychedelic-green dragonflies clacked through the air. Violet-green swallows flitted up under the eaves of the cabin, where soon their young were hatched. The world was alive once more, the sun again a round-the-clock resident.

That first summer on the river, I reluctantly went back to doing carpentry, this time working on the pipeline. It took a lot of money to support a family, a growing kennel, and to continue to develop the homestead. Construction was the most lucrative seasonal thing I could do. In a few short summer months I could make enough for us to live on the rest of the year, leaving the winters free to drive dogs. Construction, though, became a joyless affair for me, nothing like the excitement of my early years working out in the bush. Summers became drudgery, something to get through, a season to endure until winter came again. But I wanted my dog dream badly enough to work even at something that brought me little enjoyment.

One late-May day, early morning, I was about to head in for union call. Which meant a mile walk, a canoe ride across the slough, and then a thirty-mile drive into town. Cara had a school friend visiting, a little girl who lived up on the Alaska Highway. I'd brought her in by riverboat the evening before. That morning B was at the stove making French toast for the two girls, who sat at the kitchen table under a low window. I was gathering some gear in the back of the cabin when I heard Cara call quietly, "Dad, there's a bear looking in the window."

I hurried into the kitchen area, dressed only in my under-wear, and sure enough there was a full-grown black bear reared up on its hind legs, peering in the window. It'd been some time since we'd had any fresh meat, and besides, I didn't want a bear hanging around the house. I hustled across the living room and grabbed my rifle from its stand by the front door. As I did the bear dropped down from the win-dow and ambled a short ways off into the woods. I went out the back door. The bear just stood there and eyed me, not afraid, apparently unfamiliar with humans. I pulled up quick and shot it in the neck. It dropped like a stone.

B came out of the house, eyed me standing there with rifle in hands, clad only in my jockey shorts. "Why'd you do that in front of the girls?"

I looked up at the kitchen window. The two girls stood watching, wide-eyed, their noses pressed against the glass. "We needed meat," I said.

"We didn't need it that bad. You didn't need to kill it in front of them."

"They should see it," I said. "They should know how they eat." She turned away to go back into the house. I called af-ter her. "I have to get to work. I don't have time to take care of this bear. You'll have to."

She turned back. "I've never skinned a bear."

"It's no big deal," I said. "It's just like taking the suit off a man."

Indeed, bears with their hides removed look eerily like hu-mans. B, though, as game as she was about most things, was not too excited about taking on the chore of skinning her first one without me there, particularly given the circumstances of the killing. I rolled the bear over on its back and showed her where to cut up the belly and the legs, how to run a knife blade back and forth along the underside of the skin to peel it off in one piece. "Once you've got it skinned," I said, "it's all just anatomy after that."

I told her to use an ax, cut it up into four quarters and two rib sections, hang it all up in the shed. "I'll cut it up smaller, and salt and stretch the hide when I get back tonight," I said.

B looked at me, exasperated. But I paid her little attention, got dressed and hustled off to town. That night when I got back, she had the meat hanging in the shed, and the hide all fleshed out ready for stretching. She was proud of herself, told me she had been well into the job when a pair of super-dedicated Jehovah's Witnesses showed up. How they found us there, across the slough and way back through the woods, is anybody's guess. But they did, and when the dogs barked, B came around the side of the cabin, knife in hand and blood up above her elbows, to see who was coming to visit. The Jehovah's Witnesses took one look at this wild woman, blurted what they had to say, then beat a hasty retreat. "I liked having that kind of effect on them," B said.

I was proud of her. She was turning into a regular bush woman. What more could a dog man ask for?

II

a pipeline to build

But it should be noted that what is crucial to your survival as a race is not the redistribution of power and wealth within the prison but rather the destruction of the prison itself.

DANIEL QUINN, *Ishmael*

I wouldn't do it again, sell myself to the bastards who ruined Alaska. I say this, and as I do I hear myself, the anger and disappointment. I know it's all too easy, simpleminded, to suggest that the loss of a way of life, of a last best place, can be attributed to just one thing. I know it's much more complicated than this, that the greed that afflicted Alaska during those pipeline years is only symptomatic of a larger dysfunction that modern cultures live by, a way of viewing the world that doesn't work, that never has, that today has the whole planet in a downward spiral. But who was I to complain? I took their money. I did whatever it took to have dogs and my life on the river.

Our first summer on the river I gave in and officially joined something. To work on the pipeline you had to be in a union. I became a member of Carpenters' Local 1243. I told myself there was just too much money to be made not to. I took a job at pump station number eight, just twelve miles from our boat landing. B and Cara stayed home to take care of the dogs and the garden. There were thousands of men working on the line then, a thrashing sea of frustrated testosterone. The work was mindless. The contracts to the big corporate construction companies building the pipeline had mostly been let out on what was called "cost-plus," a guaranteed percentage of profit over costs. In short, it meant that the more money the construction companies spent, the more they made. I learned quickly what cost-plus meant for a union man.

My first day on the job the carpenter foreman instructed me to look as busy as I could but do as little work as possible. "That's what management wants," he said. The idea was to stretch the job, to make as much money as we could for the company and ourselves, yet not to get anything done too fast.

I didn't really like the notion of just looking busy, but I thought if that's what they want, then I'll give it my best shot. My first day I went to work laying out some concrete forms, took my time at it. I figured I was being pretty successful at doing as little as possible, that I was hitting somewhere in the range of half effort, maybe even a little less. Around noon the union steward strolled up to me. He was a tall, lanky man from Missouri or somewhere like that. He got close to me but wouldn't look me in the eye, talked slow out of the corner of his mouth. "The boys are sayin' you're pace settin'."

I thought that he was complimenting me. "Well thanks," I said.

"No," he said, "you don't get it. The boys are complaining that you're working too damn hard. You're makin' 'em look bad."

I thought he was joking. "I'm not sure I can work much slower without coming to a full stop," I told him.

"This ain't funny," he said. "You'd better try slowin' down, or you're gonna lose your job."

Later I watched one of the carpenters, an absolute master at nonproduction, spend the better part of a morning carrying a single two-by-four around on his shoulder from one job site to the next. He, like me, was clearing $1,200 a week.

I worked at slowing down, but I never did get the real hang of it. A week later the same steward came up to me again. "Let me see your hammer," he said. I handed it to him. He pulled out his measuring tape and measured the handle. "Just what I thought, this here handle's too damn long."

"What?" I said.

He not-so-patiently explained to me that my hammer handle was longer than the union agreement warranted. The reasoning went, the longer the hammer handle, the faster I could drive nails, thus I'd set a precedent that other carpenters would have to match. That wasn't good for the brotherhood. I had to quit using that hammer, buy another one that the union approved of.

I hated pipeline work. I detested the good-ol'-boy mentality, the mindless push for money. The idea of working less yet trying to look busy went against all my instincts. The union workers were like spoiled children; they all fought among themselves over work that none of them really wanted to do in the first place. Steelworkers fought with carpenters, plumbers with electricians. Teamsters argued with laborers. Once I had to make a couple of power-saw cuts and my cord wouldn't reach the "satellite," a portable electrical plug-in terminal that weighed about twenty pounds and was about the size of a beach ball. I figured instead of going off to find an extension cord I'd just move the satellite close enough to reach. I was just finishing my cuts when this time the carpenter steward showed up with the electrical workers steward, a huge shovel-handed guy who looked like he'd spent most of his life on a sausage and pancake diet. His belly hung out below his T-shirt and he was known all over the construction site as an inveterate whiner. The carpenter steward spoke first. "You ain't supposed to be moving them satellites, you know. That's electrician work."

"I only moved it from there to here," I said. "Like twelve feet."

"Don't matter," the carpenter steward said.

"Yeah," the electrician steward chimed in. "Satellites are 'lectrical. Anything 'lectrical, that's 'lectrician's work. You move one again and we'll be shutting this job down tighter than a bull's ass in fly season, and you'll be down the road, boy."

I learned that if you needed a satellite moved, sometimes you'd wait idly by for an hour or more until an electrician showed up to do it for you.

When the unions weren't fighting with each other, they fought with management. They would threaten to "wobble" at the slightest infraction of what were perceived as their union rights. Once the carpenters threatened to strike because the doughnuts a Teamster brought us for coffee break were stale. The union men complained incessantly of what work they had to do, even though they were making take-home pay of anywhere from $1,000 to $1,800 a week. The whole system was one big ridiculous, boys-will-be-boys pissing match.

The pipe welders were the worst. From a union based in Tulsa, Oklahoma, most of the pipeliners were hard-shell Okies or southerners. Some of them came out of the Oklahoma state prison's welding rehab program. They were hard-drinking, coke-snorting, wild bullies, particularly when there was more than one of them gathered in one place. Talk of their exploits ran up and down the pipeline. Stories of refusing to ride in a bus driven by a black Teamster, then beating him near to death. Stories of knifings. Stories of harassing the few women who worked in the unions.

Miraculously enough, the pipeline was still getting built, but a lot slower and a lot more expensively than the original projection had it. It was easy to see why the costs were escalating. Yet the oil companies blamed it mostly on the environmental restrictions they had to meet.

I was beginning to see that the whole mess was a reflection of a shallow, greed-filled mentality that had taken over Alaska. And there I was taking part in it, prostituting myself for the money. I was just another cog in the wheel that was turning Alaska into an industrial colony. All I wanted to do was quit and drive dogs. "The first snow that hits the ground," I said to my coworkers, "I'm out of here, I'm gone to drive dogs." The irony was that with me saying I was about to quit, the company offered me a foreman's job to try to get me to stay. "You're a hell of a worker," the superintendent said to me. "We could use a few more like you."

That fall the first snow came early September. True to my word, I quit. The snow melted a day later, and it was another six weeks before we had enough snow to drive dogs. If I remember correctly, B reminded me several times that winter that we could have used that extra six weeks of pay, as things got pretty slim for us by spring. But who could complain? It was September, autumn, a fine time of year to be alive in Alaska.

Yes, no matter what I was working at in the summer, in the back of my mind I was thinking about autumn, waiting for the aspen and birch on the south slopes to turn yellow and the nights to come dark again. I waited expectantly to hear the first *kah-lah-aluck* cries of migrating white-fronted geese making their way south. And sometimes, more rarely, tundra swans winging overhead in high, ragged Vs, gracing those of us living along the river with their high-pitched yodeling. Those were the first signals that fall had come, that the brutal twelve- to sixteen-hour workdays were about to end. Autumn, time to hunt winter meat, to kill the berry-fattened black bears, geese and ducks, and huge black hulks of moose standing out among the willow thickets. I had come to anticipate the excitement of putting the crosshairs on a shoulder and squeezing slow. And if the shot was right, watching the moose's legs buckle beneath him. You knew then that you had winter meat, and that was a good feeling.

But things change. One particular moose hunt comes to mind the fall that I quit the pipeline early. I flew with Jerry, a pilot friend, in his Piper Super Cub over the Tanana River flats south of Fairbanks. Jerry and I were meat hunting, flying and looking for our winter fare, not particularly interested in antlers. It was still legal then to fly, spot moose from the air, land, and shoot. (Today regulations require hunters to spend one night on the ground before they shoot. "Fair chase," it's called. But we weren't all that interested in fair chase; we just wanted meat.)

After a half hour in the air we spotted three big bulls standing black against the rust-reds and yellows of a large swampy opening. Their antlers, bloodstained, recently rubbed free of velvet, shone faintly pink in the late-afternoon sun.

Jerry bounced the Cub in on a gravel bar. We crawled out, loaded our rifles, then cut through the fringe of alders at the edge of the river. On the ground things take on a scale entirely different from when you're airborne. What looks like a breeze of a walk from the air can turn into a trail of frustration on the ground, particularly in the humpy and wet torture of Alaska muskeg.

We slogged our way toward where we thought the bulls were, until we came upon a small hump of dry land that held a grove of birch. I suggested that I climb a tree for a better look. I handed Jerry my rifle and angled across the grove, looking for the best possibility. Eyes upward, paying little attention to the ground, I stumbled and fell face-forward into a hole. As I untangled and hoisted myself out I looked up. There, several yards off, staring sourly at me, was one of the largest black bears I've ever seen in the interior of Alaska. I'd fallen into its freshly dug den.

I kept my eyes on him. "Easy," I said. Then as calmly as I could I called, "Ah, Jerry, we got a bear here."

Jerry came up quickly, his rifle ready. The bear just stood there, unafraid, clearly considering us intruders in his business. "Should I shoot him?" Jerry asked. His reaction was not one of fear, but one of the meat hunter.

"No," I said, "let's not take a chance on scaring those bulls."

The bear stood there a few moments longer before he swung his head in disgust, turned, and casually ambled off. Just before he disappeared into the willows he stopped, looked back over his shoulder, and fired us one last irritated glance.

I shinnied up the tree then and spotted the bulls a short ways off, looking as unconcerned and docile as cattle in a pasture. The wind, what there was of it, was in our favor, so we cut directly toward them. Within a few minutes we caught sight of them through a screen of willows, less than fifty yards off. It was my turn to shoot. I crept forward a few paces, stopped, and instinctively put the crosshairs on the shoulder of the bull with the largest antlers. Meat hunting or not, my instinct was to kill the bull with the biggest. I squeezed the trigger and the bull's legs buckled beneath him. He fell as if he'd been driven into the ground.

The other two bulls ran off. Jerry and I approached with our rifles ready in case the one down was still living. But there was no life there. We stood over its immense and once-powerful bulk. Blood oozed from the hole where the bullet had entered. The bull's head was twisted up and toward us, eyes staring blankly, its heavy antlers spreading well over five feet. They were not record-book antlers, but big enough that once I would have been elated by them.

This was certainly not my first moose. It was the one, though, that seemed to bring to the surface something that had been pushing at me for a long time. I turned away from Jerry, still fully taken by the notion that grown men don't cry. But I remember this: I wanted to.

I wondered at the time if I was the only one who had ever felt sadness with killing. None of the men I hunted with ever mentioned it. In fact, nobody seemed to show much emotion at all. Was I just a wimp when it came to killing? I never asked anyone else how he felt about it. Perhaps it was just my weakness, I reasoned. That's how I thought of it then, a weakness.

That moment on the flats south of the Tanana River had to do with more than killing a moose. It had to do with the perfection of the day and the encounter with the bear, with the way the sun touched and intensified the fall colors. It had to do with the collective killing that I'd done over the years—dogs and bears and sheep and caribou and moose—with a budding awareness that blood was staining me in unseen ways.

But something was turning in me. The twinge of regret that had always followed killing had grown larger. There was no great awakening with it; I could not put it together then. But I know now that I was being called to approach hunting differently. And hunting was only a symbol of something more, the need to begin to approach a lot of things in my life differently. I had never given much thought to the circle of life and death, to the collection of sacrifices and suffering that accompany survival. I just followed my passions, whatever the cost, wherever they took me. But my passion for hunting had brought me to a moment of reckoning. The act of killing had become fraught with emotion. A voice deep inside me was demanding to be heard. Change, though, for the most part comes slowly; I could not know then what the voice was asking. All I could do was go on and discover that it would get louder and more insistent, and other events would coalesce into a fist that would eventually pummel my life into consciousness.

Fall, of course, was also harvesttime. Digging potatoes—I loved digging potatoes, pulling back the frost-blackened vines and rolling the soil over with a pitchfork, turning up mounds and mounds of golden brown treasure. And those famous Alaskan cabbages, the smallest the size of basketballs. We wrapped them and the carrots in layers of newspaper and stored them in the root cellar under the cabin. B would also pick wild cranberries and blueberries, buckets full of them, to can into jams and toppings. And then, the last big fall chore, I would spend a week getting in our firewood. It took seven cords to heat the cabin for the winter. A chain saw, a couple of gallons of mixed gas, some chain oil, my labor, were all it took to guarantee warmth for eight months. There was a great deal of satisfaction in cutting wood, in being so directly connected to our survival.

Come late October, with the sun beginning to depart and the nights getting close to zero, it was time for the river to change. The Tanana is a big, brown, turbulent, twisting, silt-laden affair in the summer, one of the siltiest rivers in the world. The silt—rock dust—is produced by the grinding action of glaciers in the headwater mountains. The water is so laden with silt that against the sides of an aluminum boat it sounds like number 60 sandpaper gritting. Late October, though, as the sun loses its power and the weather turns colder, the glaciers at the headwaters stop melting; the discharge of silt ceases. There's a week or two then, the fragile cusp between fall and winter, when the Tanana runs as open and clear as any mountain stream.

But clear water was like a warning, a bell signaling that the thermometer would soon drop dramatically. One day the river began to flow ice. First just tinkling crystals. Then chunks, collecting larger and larger, freezing and coalescing. Finally, one morning I'd wake to a loud silence. The air outside would be still, as if it were holding its breath in expectation. I'd get up and tiptoe across the room, poke my nose up against a frosted window, and squint out. Still too dark to see anything. The cabin would be cold, so I'd throw some spruce chunks in the woodstove, make some coffee, and wait for the sun to poke timidly over the southern horizon. Another hour, gray light, enough to see the river frozen solid bank to bank, a long ribbon of ice and whiteness running from the high St. Elias Mountains on the Canadian border all the way west to the Yukon. The time had come, finally, when almost nothing interfered with driving dogs. Almost nothing.

I never worked on the pipeline again. Still, without my help, close to nine billion dollars spent, it got built. June 20, 1977, the first oil flowed south. Alaska would never be the same again. Millions of dollars of oil revenue began to define all aspects of state government; the politicians went on a spending spree. The profits and the ways it changed all of us were obscene.

The addict holds onto his poison. He resists taking on new behavior. He builds 800 miles of silver pipeline to turn the Arctic wilds to his own means, to keep the petroleum flowing into the veins of an ever-expanding economy, even when he knows that the use of it is ultimately killing him and the planet he lives on. As with any addict—the alcoholic, the drug user—most often his poison leads to demise. But if he can survive the dark night of the soul, in some cases it leads to awakening.

12

a river's force

As you got older and felt yourself to be at the center of your
time, and not at a point in its circumference, as you felt when
you were little, you were seized with a sort of shuddering.

THOMAS HARDY, *Jude the Obscure*

Big northern rivers are dynamic, restless, always probing
and cutting new channels, tearing great swaths of earth
from the banks, sweeping it all downstream to build new
bars and deltas below, always seeking an infinitely complicated balance. Rivers like the Tanana, rivers young in geo-
logic time, driven by huge seasonal loads of water and silt,
are particularly zealous in their destruction and reconstruc-
tion. They have so much work to do.

The first summer that we lived on the Tanana, during
breakup something shifted in the river's upstream course.
Suddenly a greatly increased volume of water was charging
down the channel in front of the cabin. The force of it began
to tear great chunks of earth from the bank. All hours of the

day and night we could hear whole sections splash off into the water. Full-grown spruce would undercut and tip slowly into the current, their roots exposed and broken. They would hang downstream for several days, bobbing in the current, before finally tearing loose and taking even more earth with them. I would come home from days working on the pipeline and feel a growing alarm at how rapidly the land I cherished was disappearing. What had been a safe distance to the river when we first moved there in a short time diminished. When breakup came the second spring, the river groaned under a huge burden of ice. Suddenly it began to move. Across the river's wide expanse, great ice cakes spun crazily, grinding, scouring, crushing, a force that could not be denied. In a couple of days the river cut ninety feet directly toward the cabin. That summer, during a rainy spell, it cut fifty feet more.

I began to have nightmares of the cabin tipping into the river as we slept. In them, B, Cara, and I would struggle frantically in the icy water, gasping for breath, thrashing wildly as the cabin sank to the bottom. I would bolt awake from these nightmares, sweating, a sense of dread roiling inside. I could not escape the sense that something terrible was about to happen in my life.

Through the force of some hard lessons, I've come to accept that the one great inevitability of life is change; the only consistent truth is that things will never remain the same. This, I believe, is true of individual lives and it expands outward into institutions and whole cultures. Yet we resist change so, because for the most part we hope to avoid suffering. With shadowy fantasies of an unknown future prowling our minds, we cling to the status quo. In our fear, we struggle to maintain command of our lives, of our society, of other societies, of nature. The paradox is, it is most often our resistance to change, our dedication to remaining in control—all the war that we make on so many fronts—that causes the most suffering.

I say this, and as I do I'm aware of the frustration I've expressed with the changes that were taking place in Alaska. I've come to believe there are different kinds of change. There's change that follows natural law. Its intention is always toward balance and harmony, *homeostasis,* the ecologists call it. And there's change spawned by humans who are incapable of understanding the infinite complexities of natural law, yet who cling tenaciously to the idea of remaining in control; we do all we can to bend others and nature to our own perceptions of how we imagine things should be. This kind of change can have so many complicated and unbalanced consequences. Ultimately, it always comes eventually to some breakdown for both individuals and cultures, an opening for the natural processes to take us back to balance and renewal.

I suppose river as metaphor for the progression of life is overused, but I can think of no better one to illustrate the changes that came our way.

We lived as a family for close to three years on the river. They were good years. At least that's the way I saw it. Sure, there was some strain between B and me. But wasn't that just the way it was in a marriage? There were times I imagined being single again, felt the pull of it, times I longed for it. I noticed other women, on occasion felt crazy for them. But I never cheated on B. It just never occurred to me that I'd be anything but a married man. Divorce or cheating on her, it was just the wrong thing to do. I guess it could be said that my Mennonite roots thrust a lot deeper than I knew.

The spring of '77, things changed. The details of the moment it began are vague, fuzzy in my mind. It seems like it was midday, and Cara was in school. B and I had just finished lunch, and I was about to go outside to the dogs again, when she stopped me. "Would you sit down please, I need to talk with you." She had that look that I knew well, when she had something to say that wouldn't be easy for me to hear, apology and determination all mixed up in it at once.

I sat with her on the couch in the living room. "Go ahead," I said.

She looked at me earnestly and got right to the point. "I need to do something for myself. I'm tired of so much of our money going for dogs. I want my own money. I'm tired of having to work so hard here."

"Work so hard?" I said. The idea was inconceivable to me, that she wasn't as driven toward things as I.

"Yes," she said, "you don't know how to stop. That's all you do is work. Dogs and work. You don't enjoy life the way you did when we first came north. I need a break from it all."

"So what are you gonna do?"

"I'm going into town and finding a job."

That summer was also the time that the state of Alaska, awash in billions of dollars of oil revenue, in cooperation with the Army Corps of Engineers, decided they needed to dam off the Piledriver Slough for a Fairbanks flood-control project. They did so without consulting anybody along our stretch of the river. They just went ahead with it, then followed it with a gravel causeway across the Piledriver at the boat landing. Again without asking, the state built a new road from the landing, through our property and several miles beyond. Electric and telephone were to follow. It was evident on many fronts, whether I liked it or not, that life along that stretch of the river was changing forever.

The state's idea for the road was to open a big new area for agriculture settlement. Politicians spouted panacean visions of new farms and villages. They spoke of grain fields stretching beyond the horizon. The far north was to be the new bread basket of the world. Of course, nobody bothered to ask if viable grain crops could be grown in a short, ninety-day growing season. Or if they could, would there be any market for the grain? No, the big development minds were on a roll, pushing back the frontier, making a new world out of America's last wilderness. There was all kinds of noble talk about the American dream in their sell of it.

B got a job as a cook for a Bureau of Land Management fire base. Cooking was something she loved. She was good at it, and was excited about giving it a shot on a big scale. She found a woman up on the highway who would take care of our daughter during the day. Since B was going to work long shifts, she figured most of the time she would just stay in town at night. "You're going to have to be responsible for Cara," she said.

"Go," I said. "I'll make out." I felt some relief saying it, because things had gotten increasingly difficult between the two of us. We didn't openly fight, but there was a constant tension between us, a heaviness that seemed only to get deeper and more confused the more we tried to communicate about it.

I must have known at some level that her going was most likely the end of it for us. There was a part of me, the same part that had wanted to run during our wedding ceremony, that welcomed it. And another part, a lonely, scared, confused one, that dreaded it, that could not imagine being alone.

That summer took on its own dance. I was back building log homes, working long hours. I would get up early, water the dogs, then get Cara up and dressed and fed. Breakfast done and the dishes washed, the two of us would hustle down to the boat for the run up to the pickup parked at the landing. I would drop Cara off at the sitter, drive the thirty miles to town, work a ten-hour day, then return in the evening, dead tired. The two of us,

Cara and I, would do the dog chores together, cook a quick dinner—things that B had done before in the summer—then I
would crash in bed. Even though it was hard, I recall enjoying
the routine with Cara; it was really the first significant amount
of time that just she and I had ever had together.

In the meantime, things were getting no better for B and
me. She seldom came back out to the river. I would stop every
few days to see her in town. We seemed to have less and less
to talk about. Early July I stopped to visit her unexpectedly
during the day. She was working in the kitchen. She seemed
distracted, nervous. Finally she said, "I'd like you to come
back here tonight when I get off work. I need to talk to you."

I knew something was up; the rest of the day I felt anxious.
That evening I called the sitter, told her I'd be late. I met B
in her room at the BLM barracks. I sat on her bed. She sat
across from me on a hard-backed chair. I could see that she
was determined to say what she needed to, much like the
time when she told me she was going to have our child.

She began. "You know that I love you, don't you?"

"I guess I do," I said.

"You know that I don't want to hurt you?"

I could feel my anger building. "Just say what you have
to say."

She hesitated, looked at me sadly, then began. "I'm not
happy. I'm tired of living the way we do. I want something
different in my life, and I know I'm not going to get it if I stay
on." She paused, fleetingly looked lost, then determined
again. "I want a divorce."

I'd quit smoking two years earlier, had given it up along
with snoose. "Give me a cigarette," I said. A cigarette was my
first reaction. The second was a sinking despair in my stomach, a hard knot that felt like it might take me to the floor.

"There's something else," she went on. "It's really hard to tell
you this." She hesitated, and then the words came out in a rush.

"I've met another man. I don't know if he's the one for me. But I do know you have to let me go." She looked hard at me then. "When we get this sorted out, I want Cara with me."

She meant all of it. There was a certain way B could say things, not often, but when she did you knew she'd made up her mind and there was little that was going to change it. "I don't know what to do," I said. I felt dazed, overcome. For all the ways that our marriage had been difficult, it had never occurred to me, not once, that divorce was an option. I lived by the code of my upbringing: "till death do us part." Yet the idea of spending the rest of my life in a relationship that had so little soul left in it felt even heavier. I should have welcomed the possibility of divorce, but my first thoughts were of what my parents would think and what it would mean for Cara. Beneath all this, of course, was the outright shock, the hurt and jealousy of having another man involved, and the questions about what it meant to be alone again.

B looked at me. "You have to figure it out," she said. "Because I really am leaving."

It was an unhappy and scared young man who drove the Alaska Highway to the river that evening. I tried to make sense of it. My mind reeled and tripped. What was going to happen to us? Who was this other man? What could he offer her that I couldn't? What about Cara? I wasn't emotionally or spiritually prepared to deal with any of it. I felt forsaken, bottomlessly alone in a way that I'd never felt before. That morning I had had some notions of the future, a recognition of possibilities, however self-centered they might have been. That night I had none.

I don't know who suffered more. How can suffering be quantified, anyway? I suspect that I may have suffered *differently* from B. Because she was the one who made the decision. She finally gained some control of her life and, I believe, she felt good about that. I, on the other hand, felt a complete loss of control. Things were no longer going according to my plan. The complete upset of a life that I had taken for granted plunged me into a deep and terrifying despair. There was no real reason or logic to it. Yet for the first time in my life I came fully face to face with my own vulnerability, had the first tiny glimpse of the extent of my own self-absorption. I was not happy with what I saw, yet had not a clue what to do about it.

As I write these words, over twenty years later, I can still feel the absolute darkness and cloying heaviness of that time. It was the first point in my life that I felt the shock of real despair, the hard claws of a bottomless triste gripping my intestines. A part of me wants to gloss over it, to give it a quick synopsis and move on. But another part of me says go into it, because there may be someone else out there who is confronted with the same depression, someone facing a life involuntarily turning toward a terrifying unknown. What I recall the most, over all the oppressiveness of it, was the feeling that no one else had ever felt what I was feeling. No one else had wandered through this much darkness. Because I had no landmarks, no experience to draw on, I didn't know if survival was possible. I knew nothing then about the quintessential dark night of the soul. I knew nothing of the gift it can be, of the opportunity it is to turn one's life in a new direction, of the possibilities for healing and renewal in it.

Living became a daily suffocating chore. I virtually ceased to function. I turned down log work, just dropped out of doing most everything. Mornings I managed to take Cara up to the woman on the highway. Then I'd come back and wander around the property. Times I would sit at the river's edge and just stare at the mountains in the distance, and not have one sane or soft thought go through my head for the entire day. I quit sleeping and eating, started to lose weight at an alarming rate. Most days it would take me the whole day just to get through my dog chores.

Thoughts of ending my life began to press into my mind. They terrified me. I didn't want them there, but felt helpless against their black power. Once I stumbled down to the river, crying. I slid down the bank and crawled into my riverboat. I sat at the stern and considered ways I could do it. I wouldn't want anyone to find me. Travel upriver, cut into a side slough, and do it there, off alone. Yes, but what about Cara? She'd worry, might never know what happened to me. I couldn't do that to her. Shotgun in the mouth? The thought of the mess it would make repelled me. Truck exhaust? This seemed the most reasonable way. But I didn't want to die at the hand of some damn machine. If I went, I decided, it had to somehow be in the wild, in the fields of my yearning.

Like it or not, I was taken back to my years working at the mental hospital. I wondered if I might be feeling what some of my young charges felt then: reality slipping, a mind that had once been ordered, turning completely jumbled, striking out against itself. I find as I write this I can't adequately describe the feeling of the edges of insanity. The best I can come up with is to say that there was just a complete alienation from some deep, essential part of myself. I lived in darkness. At times the extent of my despair would scare me so much that I would force myself to consciously focus on walking, on literally just putting one foot in front of the other. "One step at a time," I would say to myself. I suppose this is the slim barrier between those who slip into insanity and those who don't: the ability to summon the desire to put one foot in front of the other.

I lived this way for weeks. Not so ironically, it was the ever-present and insistent voice of nature that brought me back. One morning I walked out onto the front porch of my cabin, and realized standing there that I could see the river in a way that I'd never seen it before. There were no trees left in the view. The water was close and getting closer. At the rate it was coming, by the end of the summer the Tanana was going to claim the place. I could no longer afford my self-absorption. I had to pull myself together, at least enough to move the cabin.

I better understand now the retrospective acts of grace that have come to me in dark times. There were probably dozens of them for me that summer. Two, though, were big ones that stand out for me, perhaps big enough to have kept me alive. The necessity to care for my daughter was one. Each evening, each morning, I had to think of her. I did my best, though I know there were many ways she needed more of me than I was capable of giving. The other gift of grace was a cabin to move. In that project I found a glimmer of my old determination; there was no way I was going to lose this place, a centerpoint of the dream that I'd pursued so single-mindedly. I got myself going. I cleared an acre or so behind the cabin— hand-cleared most of it, pushing myself into sheer, stumbling exhaustion. Then, because the state had finished the new road, I could get a fellow from down the highway to bring his D-8 dozer in and berm up the stumps. While he was doing that, I cut two big spruce, cabled them, and had him drag them under the cabin, which was up on pilings. I spread the spruce poles, cross-cabled them, front and back with smaller poles, took my chain saw and cut angles on the butts. When I finished what I had was a big sled built under the cabin.

It took me another day. I jacked the cabin up off the piling, cut them off, then lowered the whole works on the sled. The operator came back, hooked his dozer to the cabin, crawled up in the seat, and poured the coals to it. The dozer bucked, the tracks spinning in the silt for an instant. I had the sinking feeling that the dozer might not be able to pull it. But just then the tracks gripped and the whole works slowly started to move. He pulled it a hundred and fifty yards straight back off the river, over a hole I'd had him blade out for a crawl space. Just as the dozer hit the far edge of the hole, the tracks started slipping again. But it was as far as it needed to go.

There's no doubt that all kinds of metaphors can be made of that summer: the river, the flow and perpetuation of life, cutting into our lives. Seven years earlier I had moved the wanigan in town just after Cara was born and we began our family life. And now with a marriage ending, I was moving another structure, this one the symbol of all my northern dreams. Certainly there's also a good deal of raw irony in it all. Soon, with the road, electricity would come. And with it, a pump and running water. In short, all the conveniences B had been without most of our time in Alaska would be available.

The details of the pain of our separation are the same that so many people experience today, so there's no need to tell all of it. It's enough to say that we all suffered, and that there was some back and forth in it. At my insistence, pleading really, we tried to get together again but it didn't work. By the following spring it was abundantly clear to both of us that we needed to go through with a dissolution of our marriage. We split our property. B took some of the land. I gave her a cash settlement for the cabin and eleven acres it was on. Cara would be in joint custody, though she would live most of the time with B. We also vowed that whatever came between us, we would never use our daughter as a pawn. We did our best with this. It hurts today to hear of children being fought over, one parent refusing to let the other see a child, all out of spite. It's so evident that it's not the parents who suffer most in this scenario. I take some satisfaction in the fact that neither B nor I went that route. I know today that our daughter can share how hard the divorce was for her, how absolutely confusing. Cara can also admit that eventually it became clear to her how right her parents' decision was. Her saying this is about all else that needs to be said. We all survived some turbulent times. Their force, like a river, carried us all to new places.

13

jenny

Living with animals makes us redefine our ideas about intelligence.

GRETEL EHRLICH, *The Solace of Open Spaces*

There was one thing I could cling to to temper the confusion of my life. I stayed on the river and flung myself back into the dog business. No excuses now, there was nobody else but me to please.

Nights alone, feeling my losses, I would lull myself to sleep by imagining the perfect team: the ultimate leader, swings, team dogs, a flawless dog machine with me, the superb athlete, driving them. Other times I'd imagine myself in the final heat of a championship race, closing on the front-runner, kicking, running, pushing my dog team the final miles. I'd see myself closing the gap, winning by seconds.

I knew I had some good animals tied out in the dog yard, some very good ones. But I also had known for some time, all fantasy aside, that without a special front-end dog, a super leader, there wasn't a snowball's chance in hell I was going to make the big time. I had some leaders, but they were all just a notch or two off. They didn't have the drive needed to compete at the championship level, were a little too easily stressed when the pressure was on. I needed that one special dog to pull off the dream of showing up off the river and surprising the racing world. In the long run, it didn't all come down to me, the dog man. It came down to the animals that I was depending upon. Ultimately, it came down to one dog.

I'm studying another picture. Grainy black and white. A city street covered with snow, bermed up on both sides. The snow looks like it's been recently hauled there. Tall, glass-fronted buildings loom in the background. There's an intersection with a stop light, the bottom light lit. A storm fence stretches along the sidewalk, across the intersection and beyond until it fades into the picture. The fence is held up by parking meters. Behind the fence people stand, four and five deep, hundreds of them, cheering a dog team that's charging down the middle of the street. Fourteen dogs, flying, eager, their heads down and working hard. The man on the sled behind looms over them. He's hunched over the driving bow, left foot on the left sled runner, kicking with the right. Long, dark hair flows over his shoulders. He wears dark glasses, a black ear band, and a light down jacket. Over it a racing bib, the number blurred. A moment in time. The dogs, the man, everything about their demeanor speaks of determination. Two leaders, one light-colored one, the other dark. The dark one clearly appears to be in charge. That dog is straining for more, its eyes afire, mouth curved into what has to be a grin of delight.

Jenny. She came to me via a friend the spring that B left for good. I'd sold him a red female—I can't remember her name—a couple of years earlier. The female was not that good, though not a cull either. My friend bred the red female to a male he thought highly of, and out of the breeding got a litter of three pups. The pups were just over a year old when my friend, facing the breakup of his own marriage, came to me.

I poured cups of coffee from the pot that always sat ready on the back of the stove. We pulled up chairs at my kitchen table. My friend was clearly not a happy man. "She's put her foot down," he said. "She says the dogs have to go."

I felt for him. He looked as if most of what mattered to him had been suddenly stolen from him.

"I got three dogs out in the truck that I think will make it for you," he said. "They're all good, but this red one I call Jenny, I think she's pretty special."

We walked out to his truck. He pulled the dogs out and picketed them by short chains to eyebolts drilled into the front bumper of his truck. They were all nicely built and well socialized—happy, not shy or intimidated and wild-eyed the way some of them can be if they aren't handled enough or are handled too rough when they're pups. It didn't take much to guess which was the one he thought most highly of. Jenny was dark red, almost an Irish setter color. She held her head high and smiled a full dog smile. Her movements were quick and springy, athletic. I was struck immediately. Here was a dog that exuded complete confidence in herself, a zest for life.

We came to some agreement on price. I can't remember what, but I know it wasn't much, maybe three hundred dollars for Jenny, and a couple of hundred apiece for the other two. I peeled hundred-dollar bills off the roll I had taken to carrying in my front pocket, handed them over, and then we tied the new dogs in vacant spots in my dog yard. I led Jenny by her collar, reared up on her hind legs and hopping, the way sled dogs do when they're led, always pulling.

My friend paused before he climbed back in his truck. "That red one will make it for you," he said. "I know damn well she will." He slid into the seat and pulled quickly out of the driveway, a man trying to escape something painful.

I stood then and looked over my dog yard: six rows of plywood houses with a water can nailed on the front, ten houses per row, a dog tied to each on a five-foot chain. Sixty dogs—adults, yearlings in training, brood bitches—and another dozen or so pups in a wire pen behind the kennel. An assortment of colors: blacks, black and whites, yellows, grays, a few reds. They all had the classic racing build: fine boned and a little longer along the back than tall, tucked up and waspy at the waist, front legs thin and angled back from the chest, back legs poised and taut as spring steel. I was looking at some top-of-the-line sprint dogs, a long way from my first group of canine sociopaths and misfits.

Jenny leaped on top of her house, stood curious, assaying the whole operation. I called to her. She picked up her head and wagged her tail politely. She already appeared right at home.

Despite my hardheaded will, I was beginning to learn some fundamental things. Like there was a whole lot more to driving race dogs than just knowing how to use the whip. It's a shame it took me so long to understand this; I ruined a couple of promising dogs before I did. I was learning that a good dog, one with full desire, didn't need much fear put in it. A good one was giving it all to you anyway, so you didn't ask for more unless there was a lot at stake. Demand too much and you'd take the desire out of them, break their spirits and they'd never come back from it. There were enough stories of whip men whose teams laid down on them and refused to get up. Or drivers with a hard reputation whose dogs refused to leave the starting chute, or their leaders would bolt into the crowd or duck off the trail the first chance they got. Some of those dogs would rather die than

put up with any more abuse. And some drivers never figured
it out. They couldn't do it any differently; the rage they carried had the upper hand.

Denis was the one who taught me how to "get all they had"
with the whip. But the whip was only one way to drive dogs.
A new type of dog man was breaking onto the scene, mushers with happy, crazy-to-run animals. A couple of mushers
were breeding dogs for attitude and willingness, dogs that
didn't need much or any whip at all. Gareth Wright (who had
been around for a long time) and Harvey Drake, these two
dog men were winning with happy dogs. I liked the idea of
happy dogs. It seemed a more enjoyable way to go about it.
I started breeding for them. By the time that B left, I had a
dozen or so that were just crazy to run. And then Jenny came
along. If I still had any doubts about the power of happy,
Jenny put them to rest. By the end, my own way of driving
dogs softened a lot. More often than not the whip stayed in
my parka pocket. But driving dogs was still all about control.
Control every aspect of their being. Become their god, control when they eat, sleep, run, be happy or unhappy. Break
them down, then build them up.

It was George Attla, an Indian musher, a world champion
many times over, who taught me this last thing. He pulled up
unexpectedly in front of my cabin one evening, the first and
only time he ever visited me. The legendary Attla, Alaska's
number one folk hero. He was a rock-hard driver but a man
who knew secrets about dogs that no one else knew. He had
a stiff leg, fused as a child from TB. And he was blind in one
eye, wore dark glasses day and night. But when the light was
right, and you did see his good eye behind that dark lens, it
held a mystical presence, a tenacity, a driven intensity. Attla
held both people and dogs in his spell.

I knew all about him, knew a visit from Attla meant either
you had something he wanted or you had arrived, were getting

good enough at the game that he saw you as potential competition and wanted to know more about you. I was surprised, honored, and made a little nervous by his presence.

I went out on the front porch to greet him. We exchanged hellos. "Let's have a look at your dogs," he said. I grabbed my parka and we went out to the dog yard. Attla eyed them, said little. But I knew he was calculating everything about them, remembering every detail. He only asked one question. "Where's this new leader I heard you had?"

I showed him Jenny. Attla said nothing. Jenny stood still and studied him. She was subdued, quieter, a way I'd never seen her behave before.

I invited him in the house. He accepted. I pulled out a bottle of whiskey and we sat in my living room. We talked dogs, but superficially at first, the two of us circling each other like prizefighters. And then the whiskey took hold and the conversation loosened. Somewhere in the evening, I asked him what it was, that extra something, that separates a top dog team from all the others. Attla looked at me, smiled slyly. "Most fellas don't know this. To train 'em for the big races, you got to put confidence in 'em, make 'em believe in themselves. To get 'em ready for the Rendezvous or the North American, two, three weeks before, you drive 'em every day. You don't give 'em any days off. Just keep pushin' 'em until they want to quit, and then when they do you have to find some way to keep 'em goin', even if you have to get out there and pull the whole goddamned works yourself."

"Pull them?"

"Yeah," he said. "Make 'em go."

Everything he was saying went against my ideas of driving dogs. When they got tired and bored, you rested them. But this was the champ talking. "Like . . . ?" and I didn't finish it, left the question hanging.

Attla's voice got quieter. "Last year, I got my team to that point. I had to hook my snow machine to 'em and pull 'em out. You got to show 'em they can do things they don't think they can do, get 'em to believe in themselves. You can't do that just by whippin' 'em. You put it back in by showin' 'em you're not all meanness." He took a pull on the bottle, swallowed hard, handed it to me. " Give 'em somethin' to live for. Push 'em over the edge, take it all out of 'em, then put it back in."

I'm reminded now of the way cops on TV work in pairs to interrogate prisoners. One's mean and forceful, the other friendly. The friendly one can get it all, but the mean one has to be there to provide context, to give the friendly one value. What I eventually figured, to drive dogs well, you had to be both, you had to have two personalities, and you had to know how to turn them off and on like a light. You found the balance between fear and friendly. When you did, individual dogs began to rise above themselves. As you molded individuals into a team, they became greater than the sum of the parts.

To this day I don't know what Attla had in mind that night. No doubt he was checking me out. But what else did he have in mind? What did he figure about me? He gave me a gift, intended or not, who knows? Perhaps he figured whatever he gave me, I'd still never beat him. Maybe he speculated I'd likely overdo it—one pill is good, then three must be three times as good—that I'd ruin my dogs; he'd put me out of the competition. Or maybe, just maybe, I got enough whiskey in him that he slipped up, he let go of something that he later regretted. You just never knew what Attla had going on in his mind. The man was a shaman.

I know the distaste some people have for anthropomorphizing animals; they take the scientific view and say animals aren't capable of feeling or reacting the way we do.

They consider animals inferior to humans. Perhaps those people haven't observed animals much or spent any concentrated time with other species, or they're lost in some deeply held cultural perception. If there's a good reason not to assign human qualities to animals, it's because we do more of a disservice to the animals than we do to ourselves. Anybody who ever spent any time around Jenny would not make the mistake of doubting the rare intelligences of other species. From day one she was an amazing presence in the dog yard; she seemed to affect all the other dogs with her enthusiasm. On the trail she learned commands faster and better than any other dog I had ever worked with. By the time she was a year and a half old she was a flawless gee-haw dog. She was everlastingly happy, always ready to run, giddily eager. When I was ready to hook a team I would lay the harnesses out on the towline. Because all of my dogs would come when I called them, hooking up for a training run was easy. I would walk through the kennel and turn a whole team loose, ten or more dogs. They'd mill around, sniffing out other parts of the kennel and pissing on things, until I'd call them up one at a time to be hooked. Jenny was different; she'd never run around. As soon as she was off her chain she'd run directly to the sled and take her position at lead. Sometimes she'd grab her harness in her teeth, shake it back and forth, then throw it up in the air, impatient to hit the trail. I believe if she could have she would have harnessed herself.

With Jenny, even before I raced her, I knew I had a winner.

I started a dog-food business, an all-meat product that a mink food company in Seattle made for me. I shipped it north 40,000 pounds at a time, and it sold well. I was making money. I also had a full-time dog handler now, a fellow who was a hard worker and good with animals. With a handler I had more time to focus on the training, less need to worry about the daily, mundane chores.

I put thirty-two dogs into training in early September. Started them on wheels, a cut-down 1948 Renault with a locking hand brake that I'd rigged up on it. I made short runs—four miles or so—because of the heat. When it cooled off later in the month I moved them up to six. By late October I'd put a hundred wheel miles on them and they were starting to toughen up. Any ten dogs of the thirty-two could lope six miles with the Renault behind like it wasn't even there. Early November it snowed and I went to the sled, ran eight-milers, then tens, then I gave them all a couple of twelves. By mid-December I'd dropped four dogs, sold them—they looked too slow—so was down to twenty-eight that showed top promise. They had over four hundred miles on them when I ran the best twelve in a preliminary race. Jenny ran double lead, her first race, and she performed like she'd always been doing it.

We won, beat some of the best mushers around Fairbanks. I got to thinking maybe this dog team was good enough to take outside. Head south with them, the lower 48. There was more money racing outside in late December and January. But money was not the main reason to take them outside. The idea was to toughen your dogs out there, expose them to all kinds of crazy conditions that they'd never see in Alaska. Then bring them back home in mid-February, savvy and ready for the big championship races.

The day before our departure, my handler and I attended to all the details. Enough frozen meat and dry food to make it to Minnesota (we could get more of whatever we needed there), clean straw in the dog boxes, harnesses and lines all repaired and extras loaded, health certificates for the trip through Canada, four sleds on top of the truck: three racing sleds loaded up on the front rack, and behind, a heavy training sled.

Some friends from town were going to stay in the cabin—it would be kind of a vacation for them—and take care of the dogs I was leaving behind.

Other Alaskans were also getting ready to go outside. They had the same thing in mind, have some fun out there, make a little money, avoid the cold weather in Alaska, come back in the spring for the races that really count. I was excited. I was finally heading into the big time, the dream. Maybe, I thought, I've got a team good enough now to compete with the big boys.

The night before we left it turned cold. I thought I should pull the dog truck into my new shop so there'd be no problem getting it started in the morning. I pulled through the double doors, and just as the cab cleared I heard some loud crunching noises coming from up on top. Instantly I realized that I'd just torn the driving bows off three very expensive race sleds. Stupid was how I felt, humbled, embarrassed. I reminded myself that whenever it comes to dogs, you get too excited, you pay the price. Calm, cool, collected, that's what it takes. Don't give in to the emotions.

I spent the night in the shop of the neighbor who built my racing sleds. The two of us laminated and glued three new hickory driving bows, tied them in with rawhide, slapped on a quick coat of varathane, cranked up the woodstove so they'd dry quick. As I worked, I couldn't help but think of my first sled, the improved plywood model I'd built years earlier; another time a driving bow broke and I felt pretty stupid for it.

I left the next morning with only a couple of hours of sleep. But who cared, I was a dog man and dog men are tough. As my handler and I pulled out the long driveway that paralleled the river, then turned and ran through the woods out to the new road that cut through the heart of my land, I couldn't help but think that this was something that I'd waited to do for a long time. It felt good to be heading out, carrying twenty-eight dogs on the truck, the best I'd ever had. I was a free man now.

My handler drove the first leg while I slept. At Tok Junction, the town where B and I made the decision to continue on to Fairbanks for a shower, he stopped to let the dogs out to pee and stretch. I woke up and crawled out into the cold to help him picket the dogs around the truck. Then I stood there and watched them. I thought about the last ten and a half years. That's how long ago it had been since B and I came north the first time. I thought about what a fluke it was to end up in Fairbanks and how the decision for a shower had brought me to this moment. The little choices that can take a life in such large directions. Had we gone on to, say, some coastal town like Homer or Valdez, I wouldn't be hauling any sled dogs outside right now. I'd probably have ended up a fisherman, be repairing some damn boat over the winter, be thinking about how to make the payments on it. It felt good to be where I was instead.

Early that afternoon, crossing the Alaska/Canada border, the sun setting cold over the St. Elias Mountains to the southwest, I recalled how I had felt so exhilarated entering Alaska the first time. This time I was headed in the opposite direction, and it was curious to me that I felt something similar. Only this time it was like the freedom I had longed for then had finally come to me in some way that mattered more. I was too young to be married then, too young to become a father a year later. It was the first time since B had left that I really felt the rightness of the divorce. It was like my life was starting over, and I was finally at the helm of it.

At Dawson Creek, the town where B and I began our trip up the Alaska Highway, we turned the dog truck east and headed for the first race in Michigan, the state of my birth. Along the way we stopped in Manitoba to train for a couple of days, stayed with some mushers I'd met the year before. I trained on a frozen river, and the dogs just ate up the miles like they were butter.

The plan was to make races in Michigan, Minnesota, Wisconsin, New York, and on the way back home Alberta and the Yukon Territory. The first race in Michigan we won easily. Jenny made a game of it. She loved the competition, delighted in catching and passing other teams. She would speed up going by. Racing outside, most all the racecourses were a confusion of trails. Later, more than once, I wouldn't know which trail to take, and I'd call, "Jenny, take it!" and she would never err. More often than not I would do well in a race just on her ability to decipher trails. On top of that, her eagerness and confidence took the pressure off the dogs I ran with her; they could just concentrate on setting a pace and let Jenny do the rest. It made for a lot of depth at the front end of my team.

But the competition got tougher the next week in Minnesota. Bemidji, two fourteen-mile heats. Most of the other Alaskans had shown up; the stakes were higher now. The first heat my dogs performed flawlessly. When the smoke cleared I was in third place, only three seconds out of first, one position behind the shaman, George Attla. I felt pretty confident I could win the race—my dogs had just cruised the course and they looked practically as fresh at the end as they had at the beginning. They had much more to give.

In races with multiple heats, the first heat you draw for position. The second and following heats, you start in the order that you finished the day before. The next day I watched Attla leave the start line, then moved my dogs up and waited the two-minute interval before it was my time to go. My dogs were eager. They screamed and hit their harnesses hard. Jenny was the cheerleader, leaping and dancing, turning and looking back over her shoulder at the rest of the team, as if saying, okay, get ready to run.

The racecourse in Bemidji followed the perimeter of a large lake, a wide-open, flat, go-for-broke kind of a run. That year, though, there was little snow on the ice, so if you had any trouble, stopping and hooking down definitely promised to be a difficult proposition. But I didn't figure there would be much stopping and hooking down the way my dogs were running.

They left the starting chute that day all business, Jenny stretching them out, going for broke. Halfway into the race I saw that I was fast closing on Attla; he was having trouble with one of his leaders. A remote stretch of the trail, no spectators anywhere, I was within a hundred yards of passing him when he quickly set his ice hook and ran up to the head of his team. I called for trail. My leaders began the pass, Jenny digging hard to pick up speed. Just as we pulled alongside Attla, he jerked his own leaders around in front of mine. My sled brake was useless on the ice; I couldn't stop them. The team dogs instantly overran the front end, balling the whole works into a huge tangle.

Attla looked back at me only once, coldly; he was not the same man who drank whiskey in my living room that night. He quickly unhooked the leader that was giving him trouble, moved it back in the team, then ran past me back to his sled. He called to his dogs. They picked up and began running again, leaving me behind on the ice, working frantically to untangle a bad snarl of dogs.

As I worked on them I knew his was a purposeful action, a clear intention to tangle me. On the race trail Attla was known as a fierce and canny competitor, a fellow often rumored to mess up younger, more inexperienced mushers, just to put them in their place. He amply demonstrated just how canny he was, because he had stopped on a section of the trail that was blown completely free of snow. The snow hook that I carried was useless on ice. In the starting chutes he must have observed my lack of an ice hook. He also knew he was going out with a risky leader, was using this race to test it. He knew that my dogs were running well, that I had a new leader and the word was out that she was good. He knew that I'd catch him if he had any trouble at all with his own leader. Attla had the whole scenario worked out in his mind before he ever left the chutes: teach the young, upstart white boy a lesson.

It took me several seconds to pull my team to a spot where my snow hook held precariously. And another minute, maybe two, to get the whole mess untangled. Races are won or lost by seconds. By the time I was under way again there was little hope of even placing in the race.

But Attla knew me better than I knew myself. The evening he had spent with me he had learned a lot about me. He knew that my desire to win would turn to rage toward him. He must have speculated that I would push my dogs to make up the lost time. This is what he wanted, the absolutely wrong thing for a dog team that was already straining to do its best. And a terribly crazy thing to do so early in the racing season, to risk burning them out when nothing all that big was really at stake.

I was mad. I pulled the whip and drove hard. Two, three, four miles. Within a mile of the finish I began to close on Attla. A half-mile from the finish I came within yards of passing him again, this time with plenty of witnesses along the trail, just in case he tried some other trick. I was just ready to call for trail when one of the dogs in front of wheel began to wobble, making all the signs of a dog that had been pushed too hard and was about to go down. I slowed the team, but it was too late. She toppled over and dragged on her neckline. I stopped and loaded her, not something you should ever have to do in a fourteen-mile heat.

Accumulated time, I finished in third place, virtually an impossible showing given my two stops. Without the tangle, I knew that we could have won the race easily. I was disappointed and angry. When I got back to my truck I told my handler to put the dogs up. I threw my mittens and parka on the sled, then stalked over to Attla's truck. Even with his low showing that day, a crowd of admirers surrounded him. I pushed through them and faced him. He could see my anger. Attla smiled at me, was about to say something, but I didn't give him a chance. "You son of a bitch," I said, "you ever do again what you did to me today, I'm gonna pull my knife and cut your dog team loose, and if there's any chance to do it, I'm gonna cut you, too."

He said nothing, just kept smiling. His admirers looked at me incredulously. They all wanted to believe their hero had done no wrong. That evening at the awards banquet I was still fuming. When Attla got up to accept his check, even though I wanted to stand up and denounce him again, I held my temper. And then he did something no one had ever heard him do before. He apologized. In a voice dripping with contrition: "I messed somebody up today, something I've never done before and I hope I never do again. Those were tough icy conditions out there, but that's no excuse. I messed up Dick Brunk, and I want to apologize to him for that."

He didn't look at me. He turned away from the podium and took his seat, and the crowd broke into wild applause. A public apology. Never once did he apologize to me face to face. Attla was the king of sly. With his public apology he came out looking like the hero, and I was the hot-headed young rookie who, some said, might have actually gotten in his way; Attla, the class act, took the rap.

The top mushers, though, figured the truth. They knew Attla's ways; many of them had also been burned by him. In one way the incident created a new level of acceptance for me. I was willing to take on the champ, tough enough even to threaten him to his face. In their minds, this last one is one of the marks of a dog man. You didn't take shit off anybody.

The real truth of it, though, was that Attla had seen me as a potential new threat to his throne; he manipulated me into taking a lot out of my dogs that day. Enough that for the next several races the team's performance slipped. Perhaps for the whole rest of the season they lost that extra edge that it takes to win the big ones.

Ultimately, though, he gave me another gift. Sure, I fumed over the incident for a while. But it forced me to begin to look honestly at my desire to win, how it blinded me. That single incident shifted my thinking. I learned that driving dogs well is about driving yourself well; it's about having the faith in yourself to believe you can win, but not so much ego that it gets in your way, that it rules your decisions. Slow dawnings. A most basic one: if I wanted to win then I had to restrain my anger, temper my desire. I was coming to learn that so much of driving dogs was about balance.

Another thing I was learning: the importance of details. I should have had both a snow hook and an ice hook with me, just like Attla had. I shouldn't have trusted him so blithely; I knew his reputation. After the tangle, I shouldn't have pushed my dogs so hard. It would have been better to bide my time, wait for him another day when the stakes were higher, when it truly mattered. Attla had come outside for some small-change races. He used them to experiment with new dogs, to give his young dogs experience. The bottom line: he was looking into the future; everything for him pointed toward the championship races in Alaska in the spring. That's when he got serious.

But I didn't need to get more serious. What I needed to learn was what Jenny knew. To find the balance, the joy, the happiness in competition. To revel in the pleasure of passing another team, but not to take it personally if there was no passing to be had. To go out and do your best and find the simple joy in that. I wanted to feel her enthusiasm and willingness, her exuberance. One of the most important things I learned about driving dogs, maybe one of the most important things I've learned about life, I learned from a dog named Jenny.

14

the racing game

Tell me, what else should I have done?
Doesn't everything die at last and too soon?
Tell me, what is it you plan to do
with your one wild and precious life?
MARY OLIVER, "The Summer Day"

You're a full-fledged dog man now. The first winter racing in the lower 48, you win a few races, never place out
of the money in any one you enter, outside or in Canada, or
back in Alaska in the spring. By the end of the season you've
accumulated enough points to win the International Sled
Dog Racing Association bronze medal for the season—the
third highest ranking of all sprint racers. You're making
good money at it now—race winnings, breeding fees, selling
the dogs that are a notch or two off. And the dog food you
designed and market, it's selling well, bringing in more
money, essentially feeding your own dogs for free. You're in
the chips.

You bring them back to Alaska in late February, and you start training for the North American Championship in Fairbanks. Through the winter you've discovered that of the twenty-eight dogs you had on the truck when you left, ten of them are super dogs, the "tens," you call them. They've made every heat of every race you've run. If only you could get twenty as good, you'd win every race you entered. Instead, each race you sort through the other fourteen left, looking for the strongest, the most rested, the healthiest six to go with your ten all-stars.

It's fascinating stuff. The strategy, the training, the breeding, it's so all-consuming. The racing, though, that's where it gets intense. The championship races, they can take you into another dimension.

Imagine it. Race time. The city's hauled in truckload after truckload of snow to cover Second Avenue in downtown Fairbanks. The sidewalks are filled to overflowing—Indians and Eskimos in from the villages, homesteaders from the bush, locals of all descriptions—everyone milling around, greeting each another, going in and out of the bars, some holding children over their heads for a better view of the dogs. It's winter festival time, a celebration of the cold dark time waning and spring just beginning to knock at the door. The dog race is the main event, the dog men the heroes of the day. Photographers everywhere. At the start/finish line, TV cameras. You're part of it, one of the top contenders.

At race time the temperature is a sunny ten above zero, marginally warm for sled-dog racing. But the trail's bullet hard; it's going to be a fast race. You tell yourself, be careful out there. If you're not smart you'll use them up this first day, just hammer them with crippling speed, and not have anything left for the other two heats. This first heat is a twenty-miler, tomorrow another twenty, the third day, the killer, those left standing go thirty.

You're starting with sixteen dogs. Maybe tomorrow you'll have to drop down to twelve, if you're lucky, fourteen. The third day, who knows how many you'll have left? Most likely you'll be down to ten, the same ten that always make it all three heats. Whatever the number, though, they'll be tired, and then you throw an extra ten miles at them. It takes a good dog team to do that third day. It takes a good dog man, too, to get all you can, to push them to the limit without blowing them up.

The teams leave at three-minute intervals. You've drawn the sixth start position. The sixth team of twenty-two. It's a great draw. Just far enough back to run your kind of race: a few teams to chase, but not too many to pass. The trail won't be torn up. Tomorrow you figure you'll be starting higher up.

Your sled is tied to the front bumper of your pickup. The dogs are harnessed and ready, picketed on short chains around the truck. After the second team leaves, you begin to hitch. You've got twelve minutes. You work calmly, methodically, careful not to betray any nervousness or haste. Your handlers work with nervous dogs, keep the lines straight. One holds out the main line. But you do all the hooking. You want the contact, the constant reminder of who's in charge here. You want to touch each dog, to feel their energy, to have them feel yours. A dog every forty seconds, that's the plan. Fourteen dogs, nine and a half minutes. The fifth team left the starting line thirty seconds ago.

Your two leaders go in last. The idea is to give them the least time on the line. Keep the pressure off them as long as you can. You bring them up together, hook them in, then trot easily back to the sled.

These dogs of yours are eager to go, lunging and barking, just crazy to run. Your handlers grab the gangline. You stand on the brake and release the tie-up rope. The dogs surge forward. You've got the brake dragging, scraping through the snow down onto hard pavement. Your handlers pull back on the gangline, all four of them doing their best, and still you're careening down the street; there's just so much damn power out in front of the sled. The sled handlers at the start line are ready for you. They step up and grab the sled, stop it, and hold on for all their worth.

You step off the runners and walk up along the team, checking backlines and necklines, looking close for any signal in a dog that might indicate a weakness, a hesitation, something you hadn't seen back at the truck. You pick up one dog that has gotten over on the left side but runs best on the right, and you drop him over on the right side of the gangline. All the dogs have a paint strip on their right shoulder, to indicate they've been signed into this heat. The race marshal paints them just prior to the start, a different spot for each team, so you can't add new dogs tomorrow or switch dogs with another musher. Over the three days you can drop dogs, but you can't add any.

"Thirty seconds!" the announcer calls over the public address system. You move up to your leaders, stand in front of them. They're screaming to go, lunging, making a big show of it. You call them by name. "Jenny. Heidi." They each acknowledge you with quick flashes of their eyes, then go back to barking, looking straight down the street. "Fifteen seconds!"

On the way back to the sled you plug the earphone in, the one connected to the little portable radio you're carrying in your parka pocket. Halfway there: *five! four! three!*—you run—*two!*—swing onto the runners—*one!*

"All right!" you shout. The sled handlers step back, and you're off, down the middle of Second Avenue, downtown Fairbanks. In your earphone you can hear the radio announcer: "A fine start for the young up-and-coming musher from the Thirty-Mile area out on the Tanana. He leaves today with sixteen . . ."

They start fast. They're stretched out full in front of you, eight tandem pairs, seventy-five feet from where you stand on the sled to the noses of your lead dogs. They're all digging except for a red dog named Rosie, which runs in the middle of the team, and the sour old veteran you bought from Denis, Chicken, in wheel. Both of them bob up high-headed and reluctant, their backlines flopping slack. But you know all there is to know about those two. They always hesitate at the start. That's just the way they are, slow to get into it. You know, also, how the two of them will scramble when you call for it, know how hard they'll come home once you make the turn for the finish.

You can put up with a couple like Rosie and Chicken in a team. Too many like them, though, and you'd never make it off the line. Not making it off the line happens often enough to some of the hard drivers.

You make the end of Second Avenue—twenty-eight seconds running time—and drop down on the Chena River. Ahead there's a short stretch of river, followed by a cut into Noyes Slough, then up over a high bank into a parking lot that leads to the tricky crossing over College Road.

They do it all flawlessly, Jenny bumping Heidi into the turns. At College Road the crossing guards have the traffic stopped. Your two leaders take it effortlessly, blast over the berm on the far side, onto the trail paralleling the railroad tracks. Two hundred yards of railroad right-of-way, then it's a sharp left turn into the bush. Once you make the bush, then you can start breathing a little easier.

They take the left turn, their heads down, all of them running hard, even Chicken and Rosie are starting to get into it—get out there and get it over with. They're all striding, reaching, punishing the distance. A backline or two bob here and there, but mostly those backlines are tight as guitar strings. Yes, that's it, music, all harmony and expression of emotion, sixteen dogs working together, reaching for more ground.

They're all bone-light animals, tucked up in the gut, moving with the grace of harriers. On a good hard-packed trail they'll average twenty miles an hour. Twenty miles in sixty minutes. Places on this trail you'll hit close to thirty miles an hour.

The sled runners have little pads where you plant your feet. You ride with your knees flexed and loose, like a skier. The race sled you ride is twenty-five pounds of bent ash and rawhide, flexible as green willow, half the weight of your biggest dog. On the straightaways your hands grip the driving bow easy. Other times, on the tight corners, it's all white knuckles, a matter of just hanging on and surviving.

You wear a marten fur hat with the ear flaps tied up behind. And a light, powder blue down parka with a wolf ruff on the hood, your racing number over the top, black ski pants, and beaded beaver mitts. Your feet are cased in mukluks made by an old Indian woman you know, light as ballet slippers—smoked moosehide soles, hair-out caribou, bands of red and blue beaded trim at the tops. In the tricky places those mukluks frisk over the trail, skitter quick little steps, then leap for the runners again.

Riding a sled is all about balance and grace, about doing your best not to make your dogs work any harder than they have to. When you steer the sharp curves, you tip the sled up hard, ride it on one runner, so you don't pound your wheel dogs. In the long straightaways and the hills, you stand on one foot and kick with the other. "Pumping," it's called. When you pump you strive for rhythm, for matching the lope of your dogs. Kick. Your leg flies up high and out behind. Kick. The wind cuts cold from the speed you're making. Kick. Your face frosts, a rime of white across your beard and back onto your parka hood. Kick. You can feel it now, what every dog man hopes for and few experience: each dog moving exactly the same way, all driving with the same long, easy, ground-consuming lope. "Cadence," it's called—a melodic or harmonic progression, that rhythm where sixteen individuals become one thing. No, where all seventeen of you become one thing.

It's taken you ten years of breeding and culling, buying and selling, wheeling and dealing, conniving and cajoling, to get dogs this good. Super sleddogs are no different from superhuman athletes. There's something born into them that sets them apart from the average racing husky. The physical ability is a given; they can run faster, jump farther. But it's more than physical; just like in a superhuman athlete, it's some quality of mind. That's what mushers call it, "a good mind." Which means there's no quit in that dog. None, even given the very worst of circumstances. The good minds possess a determination that supersedes any other possibility; it's not a reasonable thing. *Toughness* is another word. So tough that pain, real agony, appears to be only a background noise to them—a nuisance, not a hindrance. The other word used a lot is *desire:* a bred-in willingness to succeed, to compete. An unequaled obsession for running.

You have nothing but words to keep your leaders honest, no reins, no physical control, only *gee* for right turn and *haw* for left, and simple *all right*s and sharp little whistles for more speed, and *easy* and *whoa* for slowing. Not that the good ones are much for whoa; they're bred to run, not to stop.

You don't say much. Driving good dogs means mostly keeping quiet, saying only what needs to be said. Because they're tuned to hair trigger, and talking can just push them over the edge. Your job is to be back there on the sled, shut up and ride as gracefully as possible. Study them, watch for weaknesses, be ready to load a dog if one goes down.

You don't want one to go down, though. Today you're racing the big time. It's what you've trained and raced all year to do. One going down complicates things. You lose time stopping, not to mention the extra weight hauling a dog. No, you just keep quiet, keep pumping, and listen close to the radio announcer for the checkpoint times—both yours and the other teams'. You need to know how you're stacking up with the rest of them. Keep your eyes on your dogs.

You look up along your team and here's what you see. In the wheel, closest to the sled, there's Chicken and Felix. Chicken's a brown dog, the oldest one on the truck. She's the only certified lazy in the bunch, a dog who puts the lie to the notion that the good ones do it all on their own. Anywhere but wheel, Chicken will slack off, screw around, drive you half crazy. She needs to be close to you, close enough she knows you can get to her quick and put the leather on her if need be. You run her today because she's tough as barbed wire; you know she'll never, ever go down, and that she'll make all three days. Certified tough by Denis. They don't get any tougher than that. And you know, too, when you turn the corner for home, or when you need all you can get and you pull the whip, Chicken will scream once, then put her head down and roll; she can move a sled all by herself when she digs in. She's in this race because it's an important one; you know you may need that kind of coming home on the third day.

The other wheeler, Felix, is all toughness, too. That's why he's in the wheel, that and he handles it so well. He anticipates the turns, throws himself against the lines, literally looks like he's on wheels when you take the tight corners. He's totally honest—willing to work, will never try to cheat on you—the antithesis of Chicken. And he glides when he runs, smooth as water-polished stone, a total ten.

In front of the wheelers, that's where you've put your weakest dogs, the question marks. Front of wheel is the least stress, the place for the unproven ones, maybe a new dog you don't know that well, or one coming back from an injury, or a young dog. Today it's a white dog named Frog, a new dog you paid nine hundred dollars for from a guy in Knik, Alaska, and the black dog named Mary. Mary's young, only a year and a half, too young, really, to be running in a big team. But she's got a special edge for a young dog, a total willingness to be there. She's a leader in the making. Even now you know you can move her up front in lead if you have to. But you don't want to have to. You don't want to put that much pressure on her yet. Next year that's where she'll run, up there with Jenny.

The team dogs are next, the reliables, the pick-up-the-lunch-bucket-and-go-to-work-every-day kind of dogs. Six of them, back to front. You try to match them for gait and compatibility. Alex and Coolie run together. One's brown, the other red. They're brothers out of the same litter. They love each other, travel together in the same box, just dig being together. They're the kind of dogs you don't notice that much because they're always doing exactly what they're supposed to be doing; they're not making a big production out of any of it. They're not tens, though, because they come up sore sometimes; they just don't do the speed as easy as they need to. They're what you call two-day dogs; you know they'll make two heats, but are not likely to make a third.

The next pair up are both tens. Doofus is a big rangy black dog that barks the first three or four miles out of the chutes, just out of the sheer joy of running. He's with his son, Jake, out of Chicken, the only male Doofus won't fight with. Jake's a good one, steady, not showy, though he'll lead in a pinch. Doofus and Jake are sired and grandsired by a dog named Junior, owned by a top musher by the name of Harvey Drake. Junior was bred by Steve and Rosie Lasonsky. Drake's whole breeding program turned around when he bought Junior from them. Junior's so crazy to run that when he's left behind in the kennel, sometimes he gets so upset, so screaming crazy and wild about it, that he literally has fits. That's the kind of dog you like to breed, not for the fits but for that kind of desire.

And then there's Adam and Rosie (named for Rosie Lasonsky), both tens. Adam's an entirely consistent gray male, a
no-nonsense worker. Rosie goes out slow, her backline flopping. But you know this dog, you know how she performs.
There seems to be no limit on her speed, or at least you've
never seen her look like whatever's happening is anything
but entirely easy. You can move her up in lead on the way
home if you have to. She's what's called a "coming home
dog," one that just pours on the coal after the turnaround.
Then you'll never see her backline bobble. She's out of
Chicken, the certified lazy in wheel.

Next up there's the two pairs of swings. All four are tens.
They're all dogs unwilling to lead but eager to run just behind the leaders. Swing dogs are the ultimate athletes, combination gymnasts and long-distance track stars. They never
tangle, handle the lines like magicians. If the leaders slack off
and drop their backlines, the swings will spread instantly to
stay out of the way. The leaders pick up their lines, the swings
automatically move back in close so they can get the most
power on their own backlines. Something goes wrong on the
trail, the team starts to ball up, the swings will jitter-step over
the lines, like football players running tire drills. If it's really
bad, they'll twist, dive and hit the ground, roll back up on
their feet, all in one easy motion, just to stay out of a tangle.

Your four swings are all flawless, interchangeable animals,
really. None of them ever has had an off day that you can remember. None of them has ever crippled or even come up
sore. They're "easy keepers," which means they utilize food
efficiently and they never get sick. Lisa and Otter (another
dog from Denis) are a matched female pair, both coal black
and absolutely perfectly gaited. Lisa's blue-eyed, Otter
brown. Both work so hard they have permanent calluses on
their hips, where their harnesses have rubbed off the hair
down to the skin. The other swing pair—Knight, gray and

white, and Jasper, black and white—are both males you bought as young dogs. Both were surprises, really. You don't expect to buy dogs that cheap that would turn out that good. Some of it was just luck. That, and you had a hunch.

Last, the farthest out there, are the leaders. Without the leaders, all the dog power and talent in the world is not going to matter one iota. Leaders make a dog team, take what all the other dogs have to offer individually and turn it into teamwork. There are plenty of dogs that will run lead, but there are few real leaders. Real leaders, super leaders, just demand to run up there. They'll pout if they don't get to. They're competitors.

Heidi, a little blond dog, is a leader, but she's not a dominant dog. She's really as good as she is only because of the dog next to her. Jenny is beyond description. She's the best there is, the one you dreamed about, the one most mushers never get to experience. You platoon other leaders to run with her, a different partner for every heat. You have to, because they can't take the pressure that Jenny puts on. How much do animals understand? You know this: Jenny understands winning. She gloats when you finish first. For her it's all about overtaking teams and passing them, about the giddy joy of racing. Contrary to the romanticized notions of the sled-dog leader, she's not aggressive with other dogs. No, she has a way about her that's not quite aloof but not familiar either. Her talent is more to lead by example, a complete enthusiasm for running, a focused selflessness, that somehow instills in the other dogs the same desire. That deep red color of hers, it has to signify heart. In every heat of every race, Jenny is up in the front. She's that good.

At the fourteen-mile marker, the radio says you're running a tad over forty-three minutes. That's just under twenty miles an hour average. A good fourteen-mile time, but probably not good enough for a first-place finish today. More like third or fourth. But don't think of the finish. Pay attention to this very moment. Not too fast, not too slow, just try to stay in there with the best of them, and hope you have something left for the third day when the chips are down. Just keep quiet and let them do what they're trained to do.

Sometimes all of them look fine, they're all settled in and you're gaining on the finish, and all of a sudden one goes down. This time you've just passed the sixteen-mile marker and you're headed into the homestretch. You're pumping hard, picking them up a little at the end. Suddenly, it's Frog, the new dog in front of wheel, who starts to wobble. Just a little hesitation at first, and then he takes on the motion of a blown tire, wobbling big time. The next thing you know he's down, dragging on his side, like he's been hit in the back of the head with a ballpeen hammer. You drag him on his neckline a ways, just to make sure he's all the way out, so he won't struggle much when you load him.

It's all about speed now.

You hit the brake and in the same motion set the snow hook. You're off the sled running, your knife in your teeth. The dogs still standing start lunging against their lines, thinking they're in trouble. You reach the downed dog. He's trying to stand again, trying to get back on his feet, not wanting to quit, not wanting to risk quitting. You grab your knife, cut the backline, cut the neckline, pick him up, and run for the sled. In one connected motion you throw Frog in the basket, reach down and pull the snow hook, holler "All right," pivot and hit the runners. If you've done it right, it's all fluid, fifteen seconds for the whole operation, start to finish.

The team's slow to gain speed at first, they're tired, and their concentration, the trance of distance, has been broken by the stop. But Jenny's working hard at getting things moving again. She winds them up like a locomotive, climbs up into that rhythm again and settles down. Your only de-

sire now is that you make the finish without any other distractions.

You keep an eye on them as you reach over the driving bow
and tie in the Frog. There was no quit in him, no give up, he
just pushed himself past the point of no return. He wasn't in the
shape that the rest of them are, didn't have the miles on him.
You made a mistake taking him, a new dog, one you didn't
know that much about. The guy you bought him from said he
was good. And you watched the Frog run in the guy's team. He
looked good, in your mind the best one in there. But you
should have known better than to trust a new dog in an important race. It's always ultimately all about you and the decisions you make. It always seems to get down to the old saying:
"Races are won by the dogs you leave at home."

Your policy is if they go down once, that's it for them,
they're sold as soon as you get back to the truck. It's a policy that has its flaws. In early January when you had that
mix-up with Attla, a little black female, a hell of a hard-
working dog, went down in the second heat. You were mad,
driving way too hard. But it was only a fourteen-miler, a
short race, and the black female went down like a stone in
water, a half mile from the finish. You had your policy. You
sold the black female to a fellow from Alberta who had said
to you before the race that he'd take anything you wanted to
get rid of.

You can't win them all. The fellow from Alberta called you
two months after you sold the black bitch to him, said that
she'd been carrying pups. She had three healthy ones four
days after he bought her from you. "She's the best dog I ever
drove," he said. "The pups look good, too."

That's just how hard and tucked up in the belly she was,
how willing she was to run, how tough she was. You lost a
good dog that time, sold her way too cheap. She was a ten,
but you couldn't see it.

If you're driving top dogs, though, and you know them, they don't often go down. To win you have to count on the flawless run. If it's all working the way it's supposed to, you the driver become a part of it. You become the dogs and the dogs become you. You think something, more speed maybe, only think it, and the dog team thinks the same thing. You feel them pick it up. It's not something you can prove. You just know it because you experience it. Because you've put so much of your life into this game, so much energy, spent so much time in the kennel and on the back of a sled, you've become them and they've become you. It's spooky sometimes.

How much did loading Frog hurt you today? In sprint racing, seconds count. Loading and hauling one dog can mean dropping several places in the finishing order. Fifteen seconds it took to load him. But there's always the chance that one of the other front-runners will have trouble, too. Never give up. Never. Just keep pumping, let those dogs of yours know you're working with them. There's still fifteen of them out in front of you, and they're all looking strong. Whistle to them, the sharp little signal for more gas—"Wheet!" That's all it takes. They respond, put their heads down and give you more.

You're closing on the finish now. Keep kicking. The radio announcer says they have you in sight at the College Road crossing. Kick. You're headed home. Call to the leaders as they enter the crossing. " Straight ahead!" But Jenny doesn't need any command. She knows as much as you do.

You're off and running. They cross the street in fine shape. You leap for the runners. Kick. Down the steep bank, onto Noyes Slough. Kick. You notice Doofus falter on the downhill. He's looking tired. But Doofus always looks tired at the end, and he's never gone down. If he did, you would have to break your sell-if-they-go-down policy. If Doofus went down there would have to be something out of the ordinary happening. Speak quietly to him now, assure him: "It's all right, big fella, we're almost home."

You're on the river now, closing fast on the team that started in front of you. Whistle them up—Wheet!—ask them to finish hard. The musher in front is having trouble with one of his swings. It's trying to pull off the trail, a sure sign of a dog that can't take any more pressure. You come closer, and when your leaders are within twenty feet, you call "Trail!" The guy hits his brake, just like the rules call for. Jenny blasts by, passes the team like they're tied to a post. No looking back now, just keep pushing, keep kicking.

You're up the riverbank and making the turn onto Second Avenue. Way down at the end you can see the trucks lined up at the finish. The crowds behind the storm fences see you and begin to cheer. Jenny picks it up; she loves the sound of that cheering. So do you. Kick. Let them know you're serious about this game. Kick. The finish is a hundred yards away.

Off and running, your lungs burn, but you can hear the announcer now: "And here he comes, ladies and gentlemen, a young musher from out there at Thirty Mile on the Tanana, starting in sixth place today, finishing with a fine time that puts him right up there among the leaders . . . "

So you're a dog man now. You know the warm seduction of a crowd cheering. But that's not even close to the main thing you love about driving dogs. What you love is putting together so many disparate elements—diet, medicine, gear, dealing, breeding, developing pups, the psychology of training. You love shaping it all into one thing, the power of that many elements molded together into a single composition, the sheer enjoyment of being the key to the success of it.

You're a hero in the making. You've played the game the way you thought it was supposed to be played. And you're so close now.

15

trophies

So my counsel is: Don't worry about things—food, drink, clothes. For you already have life and a body, and they are far more important than what to eat and what to wear.

JESUS

Some people speak of instant revelations in their lives, burning bushes on the road that are impossible to ignore and lead to simultaneous change. My own progress has rarely been so neat. Most of my changes have been gnawing, chewing, grappling, full of resistance. There have been only a few epiphanies. In this, I suppose, I'm no different from most. We cling to what's familiar. The more tenaciously you're dedicated to having what you perceive you want, the more difficult it is to let go and surrender to what you actually may need.

There was another development in my life. Before I left to go outside to race that first time, I met a woman. She was talented and beautiful. What followed was an addictive, crazy, wild ride for a year and a half, the kind of relationship that must often follow the breakup of a marriage gone stale. She wanted to settle, have children and a home. I couldn't do it again. Perhaps it's enough to say that for years after we ended it I had dreams about her.

What mostly needs to be said about that time is that as my outer life took on more and more the trophies of success—a top dog team, a beautiful woman, money in the bank—my inner life was becoming more and more jumbled. The voice that had begun to speak more insistently during the breakup with B was now whispering questions nonstop. *Does this drive for success have anything to do with the real desires of your life? Isn't there something else that needs doing?*

I bought a couple more key dogs the following summer. And I had another young leader coming up, an amazingly tough little black dog named Mary. Maybe Mary didn't quite have the attitude and confidence of Jenny, but she looked good enough to run up there with her pretty consistently. With both Mary and Jenny, the championship might just be possible in a couple more years.

It was all coming together. But beneath my obsession I was getting uneasy with the sport. The run-in with Attla was just one of many altercations among mushers. So many of the men I knew sacrificed family, relationships, morals for their sport. Too many seemed to delight in the perverse control of their animals, as if compensating for a lack of control or meaning otherwise in their lives. In all these regards I wondered about myself. The voice insisted: *Was I just another misfit, another person who had nothing better to do with his life?*

For all the ways I still worked at it and was fond of dogs, my desire for the sport was waning; a new desire was trying to make itself heard. The most noticeable evidence was the recognition that I didn't want to spend my time talking dogs any longer. I began isolating myself, began avoiding other mushers, quit attending Alaska Dog Musher Association meetings. When I was home I began reading more in the evenings and playing my guitar. Consciously I was beginning to note that something seemed missing in my life. What exactly? I didn't really know. But there was definitely a discomfort building inside me, something that sprang from the black despair that I had experienced with the breakup of my marriage.

The next racing season we went outside again. This time I had a beautiful young woman on my arm. The team was entirely consistent, never placing lower than third in any race we entered, even then no more than a few seconds out of first. But toward the end of the trip the dogs began to show the first signs of boredom and mental fatigue. I knew I was facing the do-or-die point of the season, the place where most drivers decide to rest them and hope they'll recover their enthusiasm. The other choice was to take the shaman's counsel: take it all out of them and put it back in.

This is what I decided to do. I packed them off to western Montana to train in the mountains. It was a tired and bored dog team that I hooked the first day there. The first team left the truck. But if it hadn't been for Jenny, still eager and willing, they might not have. Mary was in the second pair of leaders. The other leader with her didn't want to move. But Mary got the team going, towed the other leader out on its neckline. But I could see that she did it reluctantly; Mary showed all the signs of a dog tired of the routine. Both teams trotted up the hills and loped lazily down. Their fire was gone.

I was worried, not sure that I'd made the right decision about pushing them. But there was no turning back. For four days straight days I made them go out. The fourth day I had to get out in front and pull the team without Jenny in lead, a quarter mile or more to get them started. I had to be more stubborn, more determined for them to go than any combination of them was determined not to. There was no anger, no whipping or shouting on my part. At least I'd come that far.

The fifth day, even Jenny seemed reluctant. She went out looking back at me, like asking, are you sure you know what you're asking? But her habit of going was stronger than any desire not to. It was the same story again with the second team; I had to pull them myself to get them started.

I was about ready to give up. Nights I couldn't sleep, worrying about what I was doing to my dog team. When I went out the first thing in the morning I worked hard at putting on the happy face.

Something shifted on the sixth day. Both teams left the truck on their own, but painfully slow. It was as if it had finally gotten through to them that they had no choice, so okay they'd do it, just get it over with. After the turnaround I noticed a spark of resolve come into them. They picked it up on their own and ran faster for home.

The seventh morning there was a different spirit in them at the start. Not eagerness. No, it was more, we *have* to do this thing, we *know* we can, so let's get out there and get it done with as fast as possible. Both teams ran those Montana hills as if they were flat, cruised them with an ease that I had never seen in a dog team before. The giddy eagerness was gone. In its place was what I'd call a cold professionalism. Get out there, get the job done, bring it on home.

I ran them two more days, and each day they seemed to get more confident. They had reached a threshold of mental pain and had gone past it. They were a different dog team, with a new cohesiveness, beyond anything I'd driven before. Attla, the dog shaman—his advice had proved true.

The next morning we pulled them out of their boxes and watered them. They stood quietly around the truck, ready to be hooked. But this time instead of pulling out the sled and harnesses, we loaded the dogs back in the truck and headed for Alaska. I figured we were ready.

Several days after returning I entered my team in the Anchorage Fur Rendezvous for the first time, the World Championship of sprint racing. Twenty-one teams entered the race. There had been little snow in Anchorage. The trail conditions were terrible: icy and rough, so bad that race officials shortened the course five miles from the normal twenty-five. In the Anchorage paper the day before the first heat, I read an interview with George Attla. He said it was going to be a tough race, one that would take a lot out of dogs. He didn't know what his chances were. Given the trail conditions and the shortened course, someone unexpected might win it.

The first several miles of the Anchorage Fur Rendezvous are a nightmare, a complexity of city streets and road crossings and bike paths and sharp turns and loose dogs and spectators wielding flash cameras. It takes good leaders to make it out of town onto the back trail. We left the starting chutes on Fourth Avenue in downtown Anchorage, all business, Jenny and Heidi in lead. The two of them took every turn, made every road crossing like the pros they were. We were close to making it out to the backtrail, but had one more major obstacle ahead of us—a long tunnel that passed under a busy main street. We approached it fast, a dark cave with a spot of light at the other end. Neither leader had ever been through such a thing before. But they didn't hesitate. They took it on the run. Just as the sled entered the dim light of the tunnel I saw the leaders hesitate. I hit the brake. It caught on something solid. The sled stopped with a shudder and a loud *ping*, then the sound of metal ricocheting against the tunnel walls. Instantly I knew that the locking carabiner that attached the mainline to the sled had broken. My whole team was loose and running from me. They quickly cleared the end of the tunnel and left me standing with only my sled. In that instant I felt all my dreams and hard work plummet into nothingness. I felt the red-faced embarrassment of losing a whole dog team in a championship race. What kind of a dog man did that? I felt all the reminders about the importance of details, details, details flash through my mind. But it was a goddamned carabiner that had been shock-tested to a ton! Mountain climbers trusted their lives to these things!

But then I heard a woman yell, "Grab them!" I pushed my sled as fast as I could through the tunnel and into the light. There fifty yards up the trail stood my team, strung out perfectly, held by a half-dozen spectators. I don't know who it was that yelled, but she knew something about sled dogs. I hope she's reading this, whoever she was, because I never got to personally thank her.

I hustled to them, on the way unclipped a little double brass snap that I carried on the sled for tying in downed dogs. When I got to the team I grabbed the mainline. With that pitifully small and fragile snap I clipped fourteen dogs to the sled.

"Let 'em go," I hollered. The spectators stepped back and the team began running again. I grabbed the sled as it went by, ran with it a ways, then swung quickly, as lightly as I could, onto the runners. We were back in the race.

But we had lost a lot of time, and I had little faith that the snap could hold for the seventeen miles of trail we had yet to go. No way could it. It would probably test to no more than a hundred pounds of shock. But what the hell, I figured. It's a chance, take it. Just keep them running steady. No stops if you can help it. Work hard at keeping the sled directly behind the wheel dogs. Ease your way around the course.

By some miracle we made the turnaround. Shortly after, Heidi began to hold back, showing all the signs of a leader tired of the pressure. I had no choice. I braked them very carefully to a full stop and gently set the ice hook. After sled dogs have run some miles and you stop them, you have a few seconds, maybe twenty, twenty-five at the most, while they grab snow and fuss around, before they start lunging to go again. I knew the snap wouldn't take much lunging. I ran to Rosie, the slow starter, the coming-home dog. My hands fumbled as I unhooked her. I got her free and pulled her up to lead, switched her with Heidi, and pulled Heidi back and hooked her in Rosie's old spot. By the time I made it back to the sled, some of the front-end dogs were just starting to hit their backlines. I pulled the ice hook and called to them. They started moving. As gently as I could I swung aboard.

Rosie put her head down and ran hard, taking over the pace-setting chores from Jenny. Shortly before breaking into the city again we caught another team. I called for trail, held my breath as we began the pass. Rosie and Jenny, all of them, charged by without a glance at the other dogs. We ran a couple of hundred yards before I turned and looked back. The team we had just passed was already fading out of sight.

We took the first street crossing at Tudor Road flawlessly, then traced our way back through all the obstacles of the city. On the dreaded hill on Cordova Street, the spot famous for tired dog teams quitting, not wanting to put any more pressure than necessary on the snap, I ran up the whole thing. I was badly winded at the top. But we'd made it. We finished Cordova and took the haw turn back onto Fourth Avenue on the fly. I could hear the cheers. Don't screw up now, I thought to myself. Don't lose it here in front of all these people. I could see the finish line several blocks down the street, the dog trucks and people, and my handlers waiting there for us. I kicked as hard as I could to keep the sled off the snap. We closed and crossed the finish line and I felt myself breathe again.

There's no way that snap should have held. But it did. For the day, even with the two stops, we finished in second place, thirteen seconds behind the leader. Attla was in third, forty-nine seconds behind me.

The next day I used two clevis bolts to attach the mainline to the sled. We started second, Jenny and Mary in lead. I have few specific memories of the run that day, other than ice crystals glittering like knives on the trail. I don't remember much because I drove a dog team that was so physically tough, so mentally controlled and responsive to my commands, that they ran like a machine. Only once, close to the end, did a dog falter. On Cordova Hill, a little more than a mile from the finish, the wheeler, Felix, started to pull off. He'd had enough. But I talked to him, reassured him, and he picked it up again. We had the first-place musher in sight by then. Through the cheers of people lining Fourth Avenue I closed on him. There, in front of thousands, I played out the dream that I had lulled myself to sleep with many a night.

We crossed the finish line. Cara, just a couple of weeks short of her tenth birthday, waited there with my handlers. "Dad," she yelled, "you did it!" I was too exhausted to say anything back to her. She ran up to the team, grabbed the towline, and helped lead us back to the truck. On the way I noticed that my sled and parka front were spattered with blood from the dogs' feet. Not a good sign, not good at all. But accumulated time for the two heats put me fifty-five seconds in the lead. Attla had dropped to fourth. In a newspaper account of the second heat he called for the end of the race. It was just too much to ask of dogs, he said. And I read my own words: "They're a good dog team. . . . No, I hope I don't have to put them over that trail again. . . . They would go out tomorrow and do the same thing, but I hate to tell them to do something that hurts that much."

After a lengthy debate among the race officials, the third heat was canceled. The trail, they agreed, was too poor to continue. The headlines in the *Anchorage Times* the third day said it all: BRUNK WINS BLOODY ABORTED RACE. A caption below my picture in *The Anchorage News* said: "For Brunk, a 35-year-old Fairbanks musher, the victory came as no big surprise. It was his first Rendezvous race, and he won on a brutal trail against a superb field."

Sunday night at the awards banquet I got up and accepted the World Championship trophy. I gave a little speech, said how humble I felt to be joining the ranks of the great dog men who had gone before me. The crowd applauded warmly. I was the world champion, at least a year ahead of when I thought I could be. But I was not satisfied. Only two days instead of three. A trail five miles shorter than normal. I wanted more. I knew they would have gone another day. I knew, also, that if anything was going to break their spirits, a third day on that trail might have done it. But that was always the dance you did with their minds, to take them too far. Still, I wanted to believe that I could have driven that bunch of dogs through the gates of hell and come out whole again.

But the Rendezvous hurt them badly. I had to lay them off for close to three weeks for their feet to heal. They lost valuable conditioning, weren't ready for the North American Championship in Fairbanks in March, though they still ran well enough there to place fifth. The next race, the Tok Race of Champions, a two-heat affair, they ran third. I was disappointed. If we could have had just one more day, three heats, I felt they could have won it; every time I ran them they just seemed to get tougher. The old team was coming back. But Tok was the last race of the year. The 1979/80 race season was over.

I took my world champion dogs back to the river that spring, tied them out in the dog yard, and settled into an inexplicable depression. I turned down work, ignored my friends. For the better part of the summer I sat in my cabin feeling lost. All I could think of was wanting out, of letting go of it all. None of it made any sense. The dream had come true, and there seemed to be so little to it. My phone rang, people all over the country wanting to buy dogs. Young mushers came to my door, asking my advice on training and breeding. I was the champ, but another part of me, the voice, kept prodding, kept insisting that something else needed doing. Try as I might, though, I could see no alternatives. There was just a mounting and grinding dissatisfaction with my life, and the only thing I could think of doing was the unthinkable: get out of dogs.

I would go out into the kennel and study my dogs, try to look into them and find the old thrill. But it wasn't there. There was none of the old passion, no sense of a future with them. None, even knowing that these dogs were some of the best, that Jenny was just coming into her prime, that I had a number of young dogs coming up that looked even better than the veterans. I debated back and forth: quit now or make one more season? Quit now, or prove beyond a doubt that this dog team is the best one going?

Joseph Campbell describes in *The Hero With a Thousand Faces* three stages of the traditional mythological journey. The first stage he designates "the call to adventure." With the call to adventure, destiny summons a person and shifts his "spiritual center of gravity from within the pale of society to a zone unknown." We are called to venture into the mysteries of our deeper selves, to take up what is most often called the spiritual quest. Of course, we can refuse the call, but not without consequences. Campbell goes on to say, "Refusal of the summons converts the adventure into its negative. Walled in boredom, hard work, or 'culture,' the subject loses the power of significant affirmative action and becomes a victim to be saved. His flowering world becomes a wasteland of dry stones and his life feels meaningless."

Mythology defines metaphorically the fundamental choice that all of us face. We are all called to examine, to explore, to expand, to unfold. We can accept the soul's journey before us and take up the quest. Or we can refuse it. We can languish in the bile of our own fear, remain chained to the thorny illusions of safety and comfort and success.

My own spiritual adventure—the journey of the heart—began, my best guess is, the day I was born into a Mennonite home, to a family that forced me early on to ask questions. The journey of the heart can be aided or hindered by literal journeys, by movement into and through physical landscapes. My literal journey began with my youthful pilgrimage to Alaska. The wilds of Alaska were a spiritual opening for me. The journey of the heart, though, however it is undertaken, is rife with detours and obstacles, particularly when the traveler is one who follows the ego's desires with such rapacity. The path I took in Alaska became obscured in the fog of my nascent desires. It was not boredom that held me captive, but my obsessions and the shackles of culture—the larger culture and my chosen subculture—that Campbell speaks of. Something was missing. The trappings of success were not enough to quiet the voice. Some fundamental ways of being that I carried were beginning to feel like a too-tight set of clothes. I needed to begin shedding them.

I recall well the conversation with a friend in my cabin the night I declared my intention to resume the journey. She was someone who liked serious talk. Late in the evening I expressed my quandary to her. "Of anyone I know, you're someone who always appears to be following your instincts," she said. "So what do they say?"

I'd never thought about it that way. But her question illuminated the truth of my dilemma. "I've quit following my heart," I said. "I've gotten sidetracked."

"How?" she asked.

"I don't really know," I said. "I just know I have. It's so damn hard to admit this"—I choked on the words—"but I need to get out of dogs."

She looked at me, surprised, said nothing for a while. Then: "Do you know what it is you need?"

"I don't know exactly why or what it is. But I know I'm not getting it here, doing what I'm doing. I have to go find it, whatever it is."

"I guess you do," she said.

Many times since I've asked myself, Why did you quit, just when you had so much figured out, when you were at the top? Did you feel you didn't deserve success? Were you afraid of it? The answers are always the same. Success was not the villain. Misappropriated desire was. I lived with an inordinate measure of it. It filled me like a drug, stoned me, and too often shielded me from seeing what needed to be seen. I quit when another part of me began to rule, when I began to sense that I needed to honor something beyond my obsessions. It was a larger desire that pushed at me, larger even than the dogs I drove or the place I lived or the things that I could accomplish. At the root of the decision was the recognition that my original intent, the sheer joy of driving dogs through wild country, of feeling so many things come together in a right way, had been lost to the compulsions of accomplishment and competition. In the pursuit of a goal I had lost touch with the process.

Fall, that cusp of time when the Tanana begins to clear, I picked up the phone and called a dog musher in New York who had said he'd pay top dollar for whatever I had to sell. "Come get the race dogs," I said. "Get them as soon as you can, before I change my mind." That night I told my

handler that I would sell him all the young dogs and whatever gear he needed, cheap. "Just get them out of the yard
before morning," I said.

The fellow from New York arrived at the Fairbanks airport
two days later. I picked him up. We got in my truck and settled into the drive out to the river. He waited until we were
close to the turn off the Alaska Highway before he asked the
big question. "You're really getting out?"

He doubted it, I knew. Lots of dog mushers talked about
quitting, but few did. The addiction of it held most of us too
strongly.

"I am," I said.

"I figured you'd change your mind," he said, "but I thought
I'd better take the chance coming up anyway."

"I told you you could have them."

"Why are you doing it?" he asked. "You've got it all now."

"There's something else I have to do," I said. Fortunately he
was kind enough not to ask what. Because I could not have
told him.

He paid my asking price for the race dogs, my dog truck,
some of the gear. I couldn't help him load the dogs. I walked
through the kennel and said good-bye to them, to Doofus,
Lisa and Otter, Knight and Jasper, Rosie, Mary. I stopped
with Jenny. I kneeled down and took her head in my hands
and looked her in the eyes. She knew something was up. She
just stood there quiet, not at all her usual, eager, squirming
self. "Good-bye," I said. "Give 'em hell." I hugged her and
stood quickly.

Without looking back I walked away from them. I made it
perhaps a half-mile downriver before I sat down on the bank
and cried like a child. I stayed there a long time, looking out
toward the mountains in the distance, gazing down at the
rush of the silty current at my feet. The questions kept running through my mind. What now? Who have I become?

How do I proceed from here? I was a free man. But freedom felt like a huge hole in my life, something that might take a long time to fill.

It was coming dark when I finally got to my feet and made my way back to the cabin. They were all gone, my yard empty and completely silent for the first time since B and I had moved dogs to the river six years earlier. All gone, the dogs, B, Cara. My new love had moved back to town several months earlier. She had had enough of my quandary, of my inability to say yes. I had heard it before: she needed to make a life for herself.

That night I slept fitfully. The next morning I got up, and true to my waking ritual walked through the living room to stand at the front window and look out over the kennel and the river beyond. The view brought me fully into my new reality. There was no movement there, nothing, no sounds, just an empty dog lot. It struck me then that for the first time in years I didn't have to go out and water dogs, didn't have any chores, no feed to cook, no kennels to clean, no pups to socialize, no perfect dog team to fantasize about. What could a man do with so much time on his hands?

I sold my sleds and remaining gear to another racer, turned my dog-food business and my cabin over to a friend for the winter. It took less than a week to get rid of everything. But there were too many stories of dog mushers who got out for a year or two, then started all over again. I knew there was no staying around any place where there might be sled dogs; I too would be at it again. I bought a plane ticket to Fiji, Australia, New Zealand. At least I'd be warm, I figured. For the first time I admitted to myself that I was tired of the cold, fed up with the struggle of Interior Alaska winter. The South Pacific, I figured, was about as far away from Alaska and my old life as I could get. I wanted to be that far away from anything familiar.

Cara, my girlfriend, and I flew to Juneau to spend Thanksgiving with my girlfriend's mother. I can't recall why we did. It seems now like a complicated way to say good-bye. That weekend Cara asked me more than once why I had to go. "I don't know," I said to her. "It's just something I need to do." Children must believe that adults are all set, they won't change and everything is safe. How difficult it must be for a child to come to understand otherwise.

We all flew back to Anchorage together. There we said a tearful good-bye in the airport. I watched them board a plane for Fairbanks. A part of me wanted to run after them, go back to the river, to be a father to my daughter, a partner to this woman. But there was another part of me that wouldn't allow it, that refused to meld. This other part of me pushed harder, determined to take me away from anything comfortable, from anything safe. I had to go.

An hour later I boarded my own plane. I recall the takeoff like it was yesterday: the plane hurtling down the runway, lifting and turning slowly out over the dark waters of Cook Inlet. I opened the journal that Cara had given me at the airport. Inside the cover, written in her child's hand: "Dear Dad, Don't get too homesick, and have a real nice time. I love you. Love, Cara." I looked down at the big white, glaciered mountains of southern Alaska reeling below like a slow-motion movie. I fought back tears that seemed to spring from a bottomless hole in my heart, a hole carved by a great deal of letting go in a very short time. The plane banked and headed south.

initiation

16

simple things

That night, as I lay wondering whether I would get sleep or explosion, I got the idea instead. A man who couldn't make things go right could at least go. He could quit trying to get out of the way of life. Chuck routine. Live the real jeopardy of circumstance. It was a question of dignity.

WILLIAM LEAST HEAT MOON, *Blue Highways*

After a long flight through Hawaii I landed in Nandi, Fiji— the brand-new Fijian International Airport—time-warped from the travel and blue-white from too many Alaska winters. I stepped down the gangway into the glare of the full-on tropics. In the distance, through the heat waves off the runway, coconut palms swayed in the breeze. In less than twenty-four hours I'd come from spruce forests and glaciers to palm trees and white beaches. I could feel my life shifting, sense that regardless of how I might want things to be, I'd let loose my grip of the shore. Where the currents were about to take me was anybody's guess. I stepped onto the tarmac, my first entirely foreign place. An airline worker directed me through an open doorway into the terminal and customs, which I cleared with a desultory inspection and wave of a hand from a large, uniformed Fijian man. I walked outside to the fringes of the airport, where I was immediately mobbed by hordes of East Indian men trying to sell me something or take me somewhere or get something for me, anything to make a Fijian buck. I felt as if I'd been dropped into a surreal world of human birds, their mouths open, all screaming to be fed. A taxi driver, who looked like he might be Omar Sharif's brother, pushed forward. "Ride, you wanna ride? Anywhere you wanna go."

"Downtown," I said.

I rode to town along a road of sugarcane fields and small block and sheet-metal houses. Nandi was a wormhole of a town with the downtrodden, hard-hustling edge that over the next years of traveling I would come to know about ports of entry all over the Third World. I checked into a too-expensive room with white rattan furniture. I put on my shorts, my legs white as Wonder Bread, and started getting tropical.

But it was hard to be there, to feel the rightness of it. The good-bye scene at the Anchorage airport still hovered in my awareness like a scolding finger. You left. Here you are a thirty-five-year-old man, an age when most men are settling into the basic responsibilities of life: a job, a family and a house in the suburbs, a mortgage. But not you. You're headed out into the void like a fugitive.

The questions kept tumbling over and over in my mind. What about the woman I left, would we ever see one another again? And Cara? What does me leaving mean for the two of us? I felt alone and sad. Yet I also felt excited to be on the road, to be out in the world after so many years of work and self-imposed responsibility.

That evening I strolled downtown and found a bar, a regular Hemingway kind of place, with ceiling fans and stained teak tables and a swarthy bartender. I took a table and ordered a beer. A slick-haired Indian fellow came over to my table. "You wanna buy me a beer?" he asked as he sat down. Being the entirely green traveler that I was, not wanting to start my traveling career as an ugly American, I accepted his invitation for me to buy him a beer.

The beers came. He lifted his bottle in salute. "To America?" he said.

"I'm from Alaska," I said.

"Oh, Canada," he said.

"No, Alaska," I said. "It's America but it's different." But as I said it I thought just how undifferent Alaska had become. My infatuation with it had faded, and in its place was a sadness for the loss of something vital there.

We drank a couple of Black Labels, and then he said to me, "You are lucky to be an American."

"Why's that?" I asked.

"Because you are so wealthy. You have so much. Here in Fiji, we Indians have nothing. The Fijians, they have it all, all the land."

It was abundantly clear the guy didn't particularly like me, that he was using me. And I didn't feel particularly warm toward him. But I was trying hard to trust the direction of things, to get into the adventure. Besides, I was an American and most likely I did have a hell of a lot more than he did. After a few more beers I lent him five dollars in response to some story about his mother needing cataract surgery. Shortly after the loan he disappeared to the rest room, never to be seen again.

I wanted to get out of town. After another day dodging the Indian hustlers in Nandi, I boarded a bus, crept past the surly Hindu bus driver, and grabbed a seat toward the back. Next to me sat a handsome young Fijian. As we rattled and swayed along the twisting gravel highway between Nandi and Suva, I tried to make conversation with him. "Where're you from?"

I asked. In mellifluous English he responded with some Fijian name that was immediately lost on me. We rode in silence for maybe a half hour more before my seatmate turned shyly to me and asked, "Are you having a good time in Fiji?"

"I've enjoyed what I've seen so far," I said.

That pleased him and got him talking. He was eager, in a humble kind of way, to share what he knew of the countryside we passed through. We exchanged pleasant banalities for a while and then conversation faded out again. Shortly before his stop he turned to me. "I would be quite pleased if you would visit my village."

Fresh from the human gauntlet in Nandi, I was immediately suspicious of the invite. I hardly knew this guy. What did he want from me? "I'd like to do that," I said, but I didn't figure I would.

He seemed genuinely pleased. "Wonderful," he said. "Very good." He tore a slip of paper off the corner of a newspaper he was carrying and wrote his name and island and village on it. He handed it to me, hesitated, then said, "I must tell you that you cannot come just as my guest. I must share you. You will be the guest of my village."

I was flattered, but the concept of being shared by a whole village kind of jarred me. Where else on earth, at that moment, did a whole community of strangers want to share my company?

Suva, a small, colonial-looking city, the capital of Fiji, the cosmopolitan center of the South Pacific, was a pleasant contrast to Nandi. I spent the night in a rundown hotel near the city center. My journal from that day:

> Fiji is a foreign place—neat, beautiful. Scenes that remain in my mind from the bus trip: An Indian woman, dressed in a gold sari, leans and picks a large red flower

in the morning sun. She straightens, turns smiling, to show it to someone in her house. A group of men sit in the shade of a mango tree on a sugarcaned hillside, their brace of oxen waiting patiently. A little black girl waves to us as we pass. She pivots gracefully on her toes, her white dress swirling round her legs. The bus stop and marketplace in Sigatora—a bustle of activity. Stalls with bananas, papayas, pineapple, other unknown things. It's been a nice day. There's no reason to feel lonely or fear the unknown. Yet I still do. A little.

For a couple of days I toured Suva and the flower-scented countryside beyond. As I did I debated with myself about the propriety of visiting the fellow's village. Did he really mean it, the invite? On the Suva docks I drank some dark, unnamed alcoholic fluid with some hard-eyed Indonesian sailors. Things turned hostile when I refused to lend one some money. Under their glares I excused myself and hustled away. Later in the day I had another beer-drinking bout, this time with some native Fijians in a seaside village pub. They bought the beers. In fact, wouldn't hear of me buying any. "You are our guest," they'd say whenever I tried. And there were no requests for loans for their mother's eye surgery, either. It was the local custom never to let a guest's glass be less than completely full. I'd take a sip, big or small, and one of the lads would immediately top off my glass. They considered it a serious breach of etiquette, the ultimate social *faux pas,* if the bottom of my glass was ever seen.

Needless to say, a custom like this leads to nothing but pain and the loss of untold brain cells. If I remember correctly, one of the lads, a fisherman by trade, helped me back to my hotel and instructed the desk clerk to keep an eye on me, just in case I needed anything. He put me to bed. "American," he said as he tucked me in, "you will be okay now."

It took me a day to recover from my drinking bouts in Suva. The next day I took another bus round to the north side of the main island, where I boarded an interisland boat that took me to a smaller island. My journal page for that day, at the top in large letters: DRUNK! Below that:

> Today I met George and Heather Canuck, the epitome of North American insensitivity and arrogance. As Mark, another Canadian, said, "They aren't really listeners." In John the Aussie's bar I met Bill, the eastern queer aristocrat running away from the reign of Ronald Reagan. He hit on me, and after I went out on the beach to sleep, the Indian cook came out and did the same. This is a crazy place, populated by too many fucked-up expatriates.

That night I slept on the beach in front of the bar. The next morning I woke badly hung over, with sand gritting my teeth. I'd had enough of the alcohol and empty nights for a while. I walked down to the dock and asked around. A couple of hours later I found myself aboard a blue outrigger boat with a forty-horse Evinrude pushing it through water as clear as rain. The deck space I shared with several cases of canned goods, a forty-liter tin of kerosene, a half-dozen yellow chickens trussed up with binder twine, and a bare-chested giant of a boat driver wearing the native *sulu* skirt, his bare feet splayed like snowshoes on the deck. "You sure you know where we're going?" I asked him. He smiled and assured me we were headed for the island written on my slip of newspaper.

The sun crackled. I hunkered down under a piece of woven grass mat and kept watch. Dolphins curved and dove alongside us. I was still full of doubts about what I was doing, going off on an invite from some guy I'd met on a bus ride. Who knew what I was getting myself into? Not to mention that I wasn't feeling all that well, nauseous from the roll of the sea and the accumulated residue of my drinking.

After an hour or so across open water, a small, lush, low-lying island came into view in the distance. We approached the reef. The boat driver nonchalantly caught a wave and surfed the outrigger through a narrow entrance into a crescent-shaped lagoon. Behind a white-sand beach fringed with coconut palms stood a small village of grass huts with palm-frond roofs. I had entered paradise.

The boat driver sent his craft up on the beach and I crawled out with my pack. I asked him where the village of my invite was. With the wave of a huge arm he indicated a single-lane track that led into the jungle. "Some distance," he said.

I plodded through the sand to the edge of the beach. A young man sporting an immense afro stopped me. "Where are you going?" he asked. I showed him my slip of newspaper. "Would you like me to guide you?"

"No thanks," I said. I didn't like thinking it, but I couldn't help imagining that the guy probably wanted to rip me off. I turned away and walked along the track, which was lined with coconut palms and taro patches. In a short time I came upon a crew of children who seemed delighted to see me. But I doubted them, too. Yeah, I caught myself thinking again, just so they can beg something from me.

But my doubts about the kids' motives began to dissolve when I sat beneath a grove of palms to nurse my hangover. One of them came up to me with a green coconut, whacked the top off with a huge machete, and held it out to me. "Here," he said in hesitant English, "for you to drink." Other children gathered around, and soon there was a whole laughing gaggle of them asking me where I was from, what I was doing there, where I was going. I did my best to answer, but the questions came faster than I could handle them.

The village proved to be less than an hour's walk from where the boat had dropped me. I approached looking like the Pied Piper, with a whole entourage of happy, bright-eyed children. The first adult that I came to was a large, middle-aged woman with fuzzy hair, sitting on the ground, weaving a grass mat about the size of a gymnasium floor. I told her my name, that I'd met a man on a bus who'd invited me to this village. "Oh," she said with obvious pleasure, "you are the American Inoke spoke of. He said you would come." She quit her work, heaved herself to her feet, and led me along a beaten path into the village. "This is Inoke's friend," she said to everyone we came upon. "He's come to visit us." Everyone beamed toothy smiles and shook my hand like I was a Hollywood celebrity.

Inoke was a village official of some kind. He traveled often, was off on an errand to another village and wasn't expected back until the next day. But his absence didn't seem to matter much when it came to the village taking me in. Everyone was clearly, genuinely happy to have me there; they got right down to the business of sharing me, treating me like I was the best thing since the invention of the machete. It was not a forced, obligated, awe-of-the-white-man kind of treatment, but an unconditional, joyful, I was the-best-thing-that-ever-stepped-into-their-lives kind of giving.

In the evening the village women laid out a huge feast on a white sheet spread on the floor of one of the main huts. Breadfruit, fish, taro, yams, foods I'd never seen before, all spread out like a Fijian Thanksgiving. The women motioned for me to sit down. I sat, waited, figuring that some of them would join me. But no, they motioned for me to start eating. So I dug in.

About half the village was gathered around watching me make a glutton of myself. I figured that if I didn't do my absolute omnivorous best I might offend them, so I ate way more than I wanted. Finally, stuffed, I said, "No more, I can't hold another bite." The women all smiled and nodded and a couple of children helped me to my feet. As soon as I stood, everyone else in the hut made a dive for the food that I'd left. I felt like such a fool; they'd given me the chair of honor and were just waiting for me to get done so they could eat themselves.

Alaska was far away. That night I slept on a grass mat in a small hut with half a dozen kids who just happened to wander by and fall asleep where they were. The next morning I got up at dawn and walked with a couple of men up to a waterfall above the village. They treated me with respect, were interested in my life. I told them what I could about it, though I wasn't sure at all what it had come to or who I was any longer. Inoke showed up about noon, shyly happy to see me. "You have been treated well?" he asked.

"Very well," I said.

"Good," he said. "That's very good."

That afternoon I met with the chief, a beautifully fat, serious-acting guy who spent a lot of time sitting cross-legged and sipping kava on a grass mat in the front room of his hut. Several other village men sat with him. The chief offered me a spot on the floor next to him. A traveler in Suva had warned me that if I was going to visit a village I should bring a gift of kava, the more the better. I'd come prepared. I leaned forward and put my gift on the floor. The chief nodded his approval. A woman brought a bowl with some brownish liquid sloshing in it. The next couple of hours we drank kava, the national pastime. Kava's a chalky-tasting substance, unimpressive at first. But then after a bit you notice that your lips and chin are numb and you *think* you remember they weren't numb earlier in the day. Next it's your cheeks that go slack, and before long, for no good reason, your whole attitude about life has shifted. You can't exactly tell where it has shifted to. But who cares? The sun's bound to shine tomorrow, the fish might be biting. And if they aren't, what the hell, you're living on the blue lagoon.

I stayed a week. Different kids joined me in my hut every night—just sharing me, it appeared. Through the whole time I had a sense of belonging without being told I belonged. My suspicions dissolved; I felt an intuitive trust of these people's actions. They were looking for nothing from me other than the opportunity to be generous. Apparently it never crossed their minds whether or not I could be trusted. Their reasoning, I guess, went that a person can be until he can't.

That's my impression of the native Fijian culture, for whatever it's worth, take it or leave it. I'm sure there are rivalries and differences in the villages, that the people are more complicated than I could ever know. But what I observed touched me deeply. A whole village—fifty or so adults—shared one bicycle. Apparently it was just understood how the bike would be used, what the priorities were for it. There were days it never moved from beneath the shed where it was stabled, because no one particularly cared to go anywhere.

On my last day there I went walking along the beach with Inoke. The sea gently pulsed against the shore. I squinted into the glare of the tropical sun. Out over the reef, a couple of small dugouts hung in equipoise on the water. Inoke stopped and sat beneath the shade of a spreading tree. I sat with him. Neither of us said anything for a while. We just watched the ocean.

He broke the silence. "You like it here?"

"Very much," I said.

"Perhaps you would like to stay?"

I didn't really have to go. But the restlessness that had begun in me in Alaska was still there and festering. Even though I was in paradise, I imagined something out there that was even better, that would take me from myself, that would feel like Alaska felt when I first entered it. "No," I said. "I have to go. But I've really enjoyed my visit here. Thanks for asking me."

"It has been very nice for us," he said. "You have been a likable guest."

SIMPLE THINGS

We sat quietly again. Then I had to ask him. "Inoke, you're an educated guy, you've studied other cultures, know about the world out there. Don't you ever want more than this?"

He looked at me curiously. "More?" He considered my question for several moments before he said anything else. Finally, in all seriousness, "How could I have more than this? If I want food I pick a coconut or I go fishing. I have many friends and family here." He extended an arm toward the shimmering blue sea. "How could I have more than this?"

It was humbling stuff for a Yankee boy raised in the belly of the great American Dream, a fellow on the run, looking for more. I'd grown up in a Mennonite culture, people dedicated to the idea of simplicity. My parents always talked of avoiding worldliness and the sin of covetousness. And I'd given some thought to what we're up to in the industrialized world, our obsession with consumption and possession, how it's most likely a dead end, a guaranteed abyss of dissatisfaction. But still, given my own dissatisfaction, I felt some conflict with what Inoke suggested. I couldn't let it go. "Maybe you'd like to travel some, have a car, a TV."

He thought about it very seriously, then shook his head. "No, that would not bring me pleasure. Some of my people, I know, would like those things. They go away to Suva or Australia to get them. But I don't see them happy."

I stayed on the move for seven years after that, all over the world. The path inward is often unintentionally initiated by an outward journey. Travel can open you, create a receptivity that's missing in everyday life. And travel can take you away. Movement can become just another way to keep the inner voice at bay, another way to forget, to avoid, to postpone. Though not always, not forever. There's a tricky paradox that you can inhabit on the run. In the act of detouring, you somehow circle

231

back to yourself. You can run but you can't hide. Wherever you go, there you are. Clichés become clichés because they're founded in the most basic truths.

Joseph Campbell says of the second stage of the mythological odyssey that once a person decides to take on the journey he "must survive a succession of trials." In the process of facing these trials the journeyer comes to recognize that he is aided and directed by "the advice, amulets, and secret agents of the supernatural helper whom [he] met before [his] entrance into this region. Or it may be that he here discovers for the first time that there is a benign power everywhere supporting him in his superhuman passage."

Campbell's words ring so true to me. For the seven years that I traveled, at every turn there were helpers. I was usually not capable of seeing them as such. No, often the truth of things comes in retrospect. But I was helped, and I still am.

As I write this, straining to remember the details of those years on the road, I know that some of the most essential things I began to see in Fiji, later all over the world, were the complexities that develop in people's lives when they begin to strive for what we in the West deem important. In contrast, people who have resisted the idea that they must have more to be happy, people who have chosen to stick with simple values, or by some quirk of fate have been isolated from the consumption message, are most often the happiest, most joyful and generous people you'll run into anywhere. The South Seas, Africa, Latin American, even North America.

I'll never forget an African man I met in London some years back. He was Oxford educated, had an important government position, a blonde English wife, a Mercedes. All he could talk about was how much he missed his home village back in Kenya. "I miss the company," he said. There he was in a city of millions, and he missed company. In his life he was experiencing spiritual poverty, and he was just coming to recognize it.

I think of those laughing children in Fiji, the ways that children the world over are born into innocence, and the ways that striving cultures deflate that innocence. In Fiji I came up against a counter-reflection of my own striving. I had entered Alaska twelve years earlier with a commitment to the simple life, a vision that honored what I intuitively knew as a child. Yet I put the dream aside for the lure of recognition and power, for money and accomplishment, all the measures of what we in the so-called advanced societies call success. I chose racing sled dogs—because the sport fit me well—but I could have put the same desire and energy into becoming the CEO of a corporation, or in striving toward academic recognition. Whatever I might have chosen, I remain convinced that I would have missed the most essential point of what my life was supposed to be about.

But one recognition does not make a journey. I was on the run.

17

the seduction of movement

There are writers like Evelyn Waugh, Graham Greene, and
V. S. Naipaul who seem to go looking for bad journeys, for
various reasons—political rage, an edgy personality, an appetite
for satire or disaster—to our profit, indeed. But there are others who can be counted upon to make no ado at all about a
bad trip—Marco Polo, John Muir, T. E. Lawrence—because
their agendas and virtues are different.

EDWARD HOAGLAND, "Balancing Act,"

It would take another book or two to capture those years
on the road. All I can hope to do here is write a quick
overview, something that tries to make feeble sense of how
those days of physical movement helped map my inward
journey. The events of those years hold a contradictory
power in me. I would take the adventure again; I crave it.
There are waking moments in this relatively sedentary life
that I live now when my heart aches for the feel of that
much physical freedom again, that kind of open, reckless

engagement with the world. But I know also, too well, the haunted look of the addicted traveler. I've seen them throughout the world, most often men, wanderers driven to the next horizon. Men looking for something, men running, men whose perceptions of domesticity and the "normal" life are so suffocating that there is no other option but to keep moving. I suspect my own face once bore that haunted look. I will always remember a woman I met in Hawaii who said to me, "I would like to get to know you, but you always give the impression that you're about to leave. Who can take a chance on that?"

I left Fiji, went to Australia, where I reentered the same overfed and striving culture that I had left back in America. Today I revisit my journals from those weeks in Australia and it's disturbing to me how much of that time I've forgotten; even with the journal's prompting I can't bring people, places, or events into my mind's eye. Perhaps it was because of the drinking, the nights of drunkenness that were only a reflection of the escape course I was on.

Only one particular event stands out in my time in Australia. Up in the tropical northeast, Caines, I had taken the next-to-the-last bed in the last room left in a cockroach-infested travelers' hostel. While I was spreading out my sleeping bag, a young blond fellow came into the room and threw his gear on the other mattress. "Howdy," I said. He replied and I could tell he was an American. "Where you from?" I asked.

"Alaska," he said. The two of us were probably the only Alaskans in northern Australia at the time, and we ended up in the same room, the last two mattresses available.

The synchronicity of that one event was interesting. But it was not the end. A year and a half later I was in a bar in Juneau, Alaska, a town I rarely visit. A woman sat down on the stool beside me. I struck up a conversation with her. She told me that she was shortly going to a play at the community theater down the street. I asked her if she thought there might be a ticket left, that I'd like to see a play. She said she'd call me from the theater if there was. The woman left. Ten minutes later the bartender handed me the phone. The woman told me there were two tickets left, that I'd better hurry. I hustled down to the theater and bought the next-to-the-last ticket, then took my seat in the back row. My eyes were adjusting to the dark when someone came in and sat in the single vacant seat beside me. I looked over at the new arrival. "Frank," I said. It was him, the same guy. We went out that night, talked about the chances of us meeting again in similar circumstances. We agreed that it was a strange coincidence, and we went our separate ways.

Two years after Juneau, I was just beginning a hitchhiking trek down through eastern Africa. A Nairobi hostel. I spread my sleeping sheet on one of the bunks in a dormitory room, then went out to eat. An hour or so later I came back, walked into my dormitory, and noticed a blond fellow spreading his gear on the last vacant bunk. He looked familiar. "Frank," I said. He turned and it was him. "We've got to quit meeting this way," I said. He agreed; it was just too weird. I was on my way south and Frank had been several months working his way north from Zambia. Our paths crossed again in the same room, one bunk left. It shook us both. Neither of us could call it coincidence any longer. There was some other force at play.

I don't know why Frank and I came together the way we did. I can guess. We were both on the run, seeking something, both trying to leave behind the memory of a woman. We spent some time together in Australia and recognized an affinity for each other. We were mirrors. Helpers. I haven't seen him now for sixteen years. But who knows where we might meet again? Or why?

There have been many other times since, particularly when I'm traveling, that I've experienced such statistical improbabilities. They most often seem to come when I've extended myself the greatest distance outside my comfort zone, when I'm the most open and vulnerable. I've come to believe that we are all held in an infinite web of interconnectedness, that there is no randomness to our actions and reactions. We move within a cosmic order that is so infinitely huge that from our nearsighted and limited perspectives, all appears random and chaotic. Yet we are constantly given evidence of our interconnectedness. But it's the same thing as the loss of a common language shared with other beings; we moderns have lost the ability to recognize the gifts.

In my travels I've been given the gift of having my perceptions wrenched from their moorings. This I believe is the single most valuable thing about leaving your physical comfort zone and entering another zone that's uncomfortable and foreign. Over time, I've come to recognize Joseph Campbell's words that the traveler discovers a benign power that supports him in his passage. There have been no smug religious connotations to this recognition. No, it has had more to do with the voice inside me, with a slowly growing awareness that my dissatisfaction with my life was propelled by a force that offers another path. This force is neutral, though. That is the hardest thing to understand. You want it to take over, to decide. But it won't. Even though it's an abundantly caring, loving presence, it insists on nothing. We all make our own choices. But with choice there's always a price to pay, either hard lessons or ones that eventually come with reward.

I went to New Zealand. There I touched the natural world again. It was hard to avoid, the mountains and green countryside, trout-filled rivers, friendly outdoorsy people. I "trekked," as the New Zealanders called it, over mountain trails, camped nights in my tiny blue tent—the Blue Hilton, I named it—or spent nights in mountain huts. In New Zealand, for a short time, I felt myself breathe easier, felt myself connect again with what mattered. But I couldn't stop moving. I needed to return to Alaska; it called me like a habit. I needed to see my daughter again.

In the spring of 1981 I left New Zealand and went back to my cabin on the river. But it felt alien and cold there. I lived with a consuming restlessness, my attention rocked between two allegiances. One, Cara and a desire to rekindle things with the woman I'd left, to settle into domestic life again. And the other that said go, run, take yourself back out into the world.

The woman announced that in my absence she'd met another man. She was torn, but decided in the end that she would go with him. I couldn't blame her; there was no way I could hide my conflicts. I spent three crazy weeks there in Alaska, trying to make sense of things.

But in the end there was no sense to be made. I was uneasy in my own skin; the place that I had loved and counted on for my identity felt hostile and dark. Movement and travel, escape, adventure, the spell of the exotic all pulled at me. I had money in the bank and a wad of cash from selling my dogs, enough that I could travel for years without needing to work. The go voice won. I sold most of what I owned, my boats and outdoor gear, anything that wouldn't fit easily in a twelve-by-twelve log shed. After experiencing the tropics, I had to admit to myself that I was damn tired of the cold. Although it didn't fit well the self-image I had projected for years, I didn't want to struggle with the harsh elements any longer. Early June I headed to Hawaii. I figured maybe I could make a life for myself there.

I lived a year in Hawaii, most of the time fighting a dark, hounding depression. My heart was broken in more ways than I could understand. The woman back in Alaska was the focus of my heartbreak and remained so for a long time. But I know now that she was more a distraction. My depression was actually instead about the loss of a lifestyle and a dream, about the diminishment of a place called Alaska. And most of all, it was about letting go of an old identity and attempting to discover something new about myself that I only had a vague intuition of. I was determined to inhabit a new me, but I had no models to aspire to. I was lost and afraid. My infatuation with a lot of things had come to an end. I saw nothing but movement and distance as replacements for them.

But I told myself I'd stay in Hawaii for at least a year. The whole time I fought the urge to run. To compensate, I forced myself to stay busy. I took a class on psychic awareness, another on meditation. I had always been a voracious reader, but in Hawaii I read even more prolifically. Buddhism, spiritual writings, philosophy. Books that spoke to me came in inexplicable ways. My mind began to open to ideas that I never knew existed before. I could not get enough of them. But the intellect alone is not the heart's salvation.

I let go of my first name, Richard, and my nickname, Dick. I wanted a symbol of change. I told a friend that I didn't want to be a Dick any longer. I began to use my middle name. I earned a dive master's certification and worked awhile as a dive guide on a tourist boat. But before long I grew tired of catering to tourists. Next I took a job building a house for a rich Chilean who had been forced into exile by Pinochet. I lived alone on his property in the country, a lush mountainside retreat with wild turkeys and pigs, and a stream tumbling down through black, volcanic rocks. I tried to meditate and get quiet. But after a few days the solitude would defeat me, and I would retreat into alcohol and the arms of women.

Once, climbing the Mauna Loa volcano alone, feeling despair for the rudderlessness of my life, in one of the most defenseless moments of my life, I let go and cried out for help. It was only a fleeting moment, a flash, an opening. But in that instant, with my defenses down, I felt the presence of God. I know of no other way to define what I experienced. For a wonderful moment I was aware of an immense, loving presence that could not be mistaken for anything else but the presence of the Divine. Beyond this, words are entirely inadequate. There is no rational way to describe that experience. It was a knowing, a recognition that has no rational equivalent. Of course, the skeptics will have their view of it— I *wanted* to feel something, I was delusional. They cannot know. Nor could I at the time fully understand the invitation, for an experience of God was not something that aligned with my own view of myself in the world. It was an opening in the process, though, a great moment of immense grace.

After serving my year in Hawaii I left. Like a migratory bird driven by the urges of spring I returned again to Alaska. But I knew I wouldn't stay. I just needed to check in. Maybe, I thought, I'd work at something for the summer, then be gone again.

Things had changed during my year away. With the new road at Thirty Mile, other people had begun to move into the land along the river; houses were sprouting up in the woods. I didn't like what I saw. And there was another thing that affected me.

Earlier that spring Denis had come down sick. True to his personality he didn't tell anybody much about it. "Got a kidney infection," he said when I first asked him. He toughed it out, made a man's game of it. But by late summer there was no getting around the fact that he had more than a kidney infection. He was growing shockingly thin. His voice was weak. His wife was doing most of the outside chores. I visited him one afternoon late in August. He stood on his front porch, bent, gaunt, his head bowed, one hand up on a canted hip. "What's really going on with you?" I asked.

"The doctor says I've got cancer," he said.

It was hard to believe. Here was the big man of our community, Grizzly Den, as we called him behind his back, just turned thirty years old and sick with cancer. "Is it bad?" I asked him.

"I guess it's bad enough," he said. "It's in my kidneys. Chances are it's in my lymph glands, too." He looked me solid in the eyes. "Doesn't matter where it is, I'm gonna beat it."

A month later I visited him in the hospital, a wracked, shrunken husk of a man with eyes hanging like dull moons in his skull. A crucifix hung above the head of his bed, the tortured body of Christ, head lolling in agony. Denis slowly turned his own head toward me. I could see the embarrassment in him, apology for appearing, in his mind, less than a man. In a voice cracked and dry as summer weeds, he said to me, "This damned cancer's not gonna beat me." He took a few faltering breaths and closed his eyes. "I'm gonna whip it. You'll see."

"You will," I said to him. And I badly wanted him to. I wanted a man who had promised so much to come out on top, to, as he said, whip it. Whip it the same way he had once taught me to pummel a dog. But it didn't work that way. Three days later he turned his head away from his wife sitting by his side, and he died. A lot of people came to his funeral. There was much talk about what a presence he'd been.

I went home the night after the funeral and sat alone in my cabin. I thought about what it meant to be alive. The cancer that had metastasized in Denis's body seemed like a reflection of the cancer that was ravaging Alaska. Denis, the big man, the quintessential frontiersman, the man who saw no limits, who lived by his own rules, had been struck down.

The messages were tangled and too complex for me to make sense of. But I understood one thing: too many things were changing too fast.

The voice kept nagging at me. I could not avoid the sense that something else needed doing in my life. There was something in it related to what I saw happening to Alaska, some sense of sorrow for the end of things as I'd first known them. I could not escape the fact that Fairbanks, the whole state for that matter, was continuing to change at a rapid rate. There was a mindlessness to it, a recklessness, an unconsciousness. In some way, I knew, I was part of that mindlessness; my own life was still unconscious. But I couldn't come up with what it was I needed to do.

I sat with Denis's death for a week. I imagined myself dying, tried to envision who would show up for the funeral. Would they have anything good to say about me? For a long time I couldn't shake the reflection of my own death.

I stayed in Fairbanks until Christmas, spent the day with Cara. The next day I headed out again. In Texas I teamed up with a fellow I'd met in Alaska. I barely knew Tom Rolls when we left Texas in his pickup. The second night, driving south through the swamps and bayous along the Gulf Coast of east Mexico, he started talking about his time as an Army ranger in Vietnam. The dash lights shone green on his face. "I was a cold-blooded killer then," he said in his slow drawl. "Every platoon had a guy like me. I *had* to kill, it was all I wanted. One night I got a gook down, a skinny little guy, and I figured I'd choke him to death, just to see what it would feel like. I started bearing down, could feel the bones breaking in his neck, and him struggling like hell to stay above it. I just about had him, and out of nowhere I started thinking the son of a bitch probably had a family. Had a kid and a wife, just like I once did. And I felt like I couldn't go on, couldn't do it."

He looked over at me, smiled in an embarrassed way. "Something snapped in me that night. I had to kill him. I did, but he was my last one. I went back to base camp and just quit. Stayed stoned the rest of my tour. Never been the same since."

Tom and I, the killer and the pacifist, lived on a beach in the Yucatan for a couple of months. When we tired of the inactivity we headed down into Belize. I wanted to go on into Guatemala, but Tom declined. Guatemala was experiencing the aftermath of the reign of terror by the psychotic general Rios Mont. Word from other travelers was that the country was in complete chaos. "I've had enough military bullshit to last several lifetimes," Tom said. "I'll meet you later up in Mexico."

I went on alone. Each mile hitchhiking or riding buses in Guatemala was a nerve-wracking push through the tragedy of a country where surly boy soldiers touted automatic rifles and systematically executed Indians. I kept on the move and ended up a month later despondent and sick with some tropical ailment. My intestines felt as if a callused hand was slowly pinching the life from them. In the morning I'd crawl weakly from my sleeping bag and piss blood. I moved on sheer determination, lived in a mental fog so thick at times that I could barely remember where I was. The roadblocks, the simpleminded, macho posturing of soldiers at checkpoints, dragging my body from one place to the next, it got to the point that I just wanted to go home, back to the States.

I hitchhiked to the northern border only to find it closed because of some fresh disagreement with Mexico. I told the soldiers there I was sick. Would they make an exception and let me cross? They laughed at me, stupid fucking gringo. They told me to get away from the border. I hitched south again, headed for Guatemala City. As foggy as my mind was then from the illness, I recall so very vividly a moment on that trip south. I was waiting for a bus at a backcountry crossroads. Indians were gathered there waiting for rides, dressed in their colorful garb. They all ignored me, rich white man. I left my pack sitting at the roadside and walked into the brush to pee. As I did I looked back at my pack and it hit me: the worth of that one pack and its contents was most likely more than any one of the Indians' total wealth, more money than one of them might make in many years. I returned to my pack. A country bus arrived, roof piled high with bags and goods. It took on some passengers. As it pulled forward again, one of the thin, mange-ridden dogs that were slinking around the place got caught under a back tire. The dog yelped and exploded, its intestines spilling like greased rope out on the roadway. What I remember most is how the Indians laughed. Perhaps it's true that people who have it bad take some delight in witnessing something else that has it even worse.

I made it back to Guatemala City, the capital, where I watched squads of armed soldiers hold drills in all quarters of the city, just to remind the populace that a real man was still in charge. At the virtually abandoned Guatemala City airport I bummed a ride from a couple of rough-looking Americans flying an old DC-3 with a strafe of machine-gun bullet holes running the length of its port side. They flew back into the Yucatan, the city of Merida. I thanked them for the ride, then hitched east into the state of Chiapas with some Mexicans driving a dilapidated Ford sedan.

In the quaint Mexican town of San Cristòbal de las Casas I rendezvoused again with Tom Rolls. We were glad to see each other. In a campground at the edge of town Tom had rented a one-room cabin with two cots and a tiny kerosene stove. It felt like luxury. "I'm pretty sick," I told Tom. "I need to rest up. Let's stay here awhile."

The man who owned the campground was a local *politico*, a fighting-cock of a man who on Sunday mornings decked himself in full *vaquero* regalia: black sombrero; tight black pants; black, tooled-leather boots; heavy-roweled silver spurs. He would mount a nice bay horse and spur it into a prancing froth, ride round and round the campground, taking long drafts from a bottle of bad tequila. With each pass he became drunker and more belligerent.

My second Sunday there I sat weak in the sunshine on the front porch of the cabin. Mid-morning, the *politico* came out of his house and mounted his horse. A short while later I noticed a Canadian fellow enter the campground. He walked up to the *politico* and demanded to talk with him. Within seconds the two of them began arguing, shouting at each other. The best I could make out from the Spanish was that the Canadian accused the *politico* of selling him a bad horse, and the *politico* felt his own honor was in question. The Canadian reached up and tried to pull the *politico* from the saddle. The *politico* kicked the Canadian away and pulled an automatic pistol from his belt in one swift motion, pointed it at the Canadian's head, and pulled the trigger. The gun clicked. The Canadian stumbled backward, wide-eyed. He turned and bolted, running quick zigzags down the entrance road. The Mexican wheeled his horse and spurred it into a run. He jacked the dud shell out of the chamber and fired once, twice, before the Canadian plunged off the road into heavy brush, apparently unhurt.

Tom saw the incident. "It wasn't the Canadian's time to go," he said calmly. "It's just the way it works. I saw it a bunch of times in Nam."

Not his time to go. I've thought of Tom Rolls's statement many times since. In the great scheme of things, for all the ways I was on my own self-destructive course, it was not my time to go. Today I'm thankful for that.

I wish I had kept in touch with Tom. A couple of months ago a friend called me and said that Tom had died up in Colorado. Cancer. It was his time to go, I guess. I wish I had known he was up there. I would have liked to have seen him before he traveled on.

That summer I made it back to Alaska, spent most of it trying to recuperate from my illness. The doctors in Fairbanks could come up with nothing wrong, just some tropical bug, they said, one of those foreign things that elude all tests. In the fall I was still too ill to travel, but good enough, I figured, to learn some things. So I enrolled in a state university in California to study writing. I stayed there the winter, pining the whole time to be on the move again. The following summer I went back to Alaska, where I went to work as a wildlife biologist, worked for the first time on a caribou study up in the North Slope oil fields. A couple of months, and I had enough money to go again.

That fall I headed for Europe. With an American friend I moved through Holland, Germany, and Switzerland, then spent a couple of months of the coldest winter in recorded European history trying to live the expatriate writer's life in southern France. People cross-country skied on the beaches of the Riviera that winter. It made the world news. By late December France made me claustrophobic; I wanted more than a freezing *pension* in a damned country where everybody talked like they had a head cold. I was tired of typing with gloves, and it was clear that Europe was not my beat. Too settled. Nothing wild.

My American friend and I drove up to Paris, where he bought a ticket to San Francisco and I bought a boat passage to London, where I knew I could get visas and a cheap ticket to Nairobi. That night someone broke into the rental car and stole everything in it: my friend's computer, the manuscript of a novel he'd written, several months' worth of my own writing, and my electronic typewriter. Free at last, I thought to myself. All I had left was my backpack.

In London it took me ten days or so to get my visas and a ticket to Nairobi. I felt lonely there, with only my restless thoughts to keep me company. I thought of Alaska, and Cara just starting high school in Hawaii, where B had moved to pursue graduate work at the university there.

I flew out of Heathrow on a gray and drizzling day, and landed twelve hours later in the tropical glare and heat of Kenya. From the moment I stepped off the plane I was entirely smitten by Africa.

18

meeting midlife on the serengeti

This is . . . the story of people who won their freedom on battlefields and at the negotiating tables, only to discover that
their white colonial masters had been replaced by black neo-
colonial leaders more concerned with personal power and
wealth than with national consensus or development. . . . The
colonists designed the scenario for disaster, and the Africans
seem to be trying their best to fulfill it. Calamity waits within
arm's reach, economies are collapsing, cities are deteriorat-
ing, populations are growing like weed-seeds turned loose in
a garden. Governments fall at the whim of illiterate sergeants
and disgruntled despots, prisons are as overcrowded as the
farmlands are empty.

DAVID LAMB, *The Africans*

It's interesting to me that I find it difficult now to write
about Africa. Of all my travels, the memories of my times
there are the most vivid and alluring, the ones I would most
choose to live again. Strangely, all of my journals and writings

for that time—other than a couple of typed and much whited-out essays written on onionskin—are missing. I have little record of even being there. Perhaps it's because Africa resists being captured by simple words. Writers much better and bolder than I have tried, and have eventually come up waving the white flag. Even some African writers seem to find it difficult to write about Africa. They find it challenging to place their continent in some relationship with the rest of the world. That huge, ornery, complex bulge of land below Europe plays, no, *dances,* by its own set of rules.

I sit here now, sixteen years later, trying to make sense of the months spread over two years that I traveled there. There's a jumble of scenes in my mind, colors and smells, a hundred black faces, and memories of both joy and despair. The scenes resist chronological order. All I know is Africa is a mystery, a siren, a big warring love affair of the heart. Hearing African music I'm immediately taken by a punch of rhythm that propels me into some mysterious place. It's something about accessing the edges of some deeply buried thing, a primal recognition that I crave to feel, yet have never felt the same way any other place. Seeing certain bright colors, smelling certain smells, I'm taken back to Africa. In an odd way, arriving there was like coming home, similar yet different from my first arrival in Alaska.

Amid the heat and dust and penetrating smells of sub-Saharan Africa—the charcoal smoke and sweet-scented blossoms, and acrid red dust, and sweat and urine and shit—every morning I woke up knowing that something wild or weird or wonderful was bound to happen that day. For all the time I traveled there that's how it went. Africa did something to me, it opened me. The lessons I learned there built on other lessons learned elsewhere along the way. But in Africa, because of what it is, the lessons come at you with an intensity and tenacity that I've felt no other place. It was hard to hide there. In some way that I still don't quite understand, Africa began to call me back to myself.

My first trip I spent a couple of days in Nairobi trying to figure out what I wanted to do next. It is the con men and thieves and *panga* (machete) gangs that I remember most about Nairobi, how they preyed on travelers. Throughout Africa destitute men from the country, from villages exploding with children and more children, flood to the cities. There they do their best to survive. But thieving from one another and from low-budget travelers is a thin way to make a living.

I could not wait to exit town, but I had only a vague idea of what I wanted to do, where I wanted to go. In the travelers' hostel I talked to others who had been there awhile, learned what I could about border crossings and black-market money exchange and places to avoid and others to visit. I met Mick O'Malley, a quintessential Irishman, fifteen years my junior but already an inveterate traveler. Mick was also newly arrived to Africa. Travel enough and you learn to size up people quickly. We instantly took a liking to each other. I told him that I was thinking of heading up into northern Kenya, then from there work my way south again. I asked him if he'd like to team up. "I would," he said, and that was it.

We hitchhiked out of Nairobi the next day, caught rides in heavily loaded lorries up into the thorny scrub desert along the east and north side of Lake Turkana, where the borders of Sudan, Ethiopia, and Kenya shape a tense political polyglot, where fierce, hawk-faced Sudanese and Ethiopian warriors smuggle goods and arms into Kenya. Our plan was to find the indigenous Turkana people there, supposedly one of the wildest tribes left in Kenya. We spent a couple of days stumbling around in the desert, and finally managed to run into some Turkana tribesmen, but they were anything but wild. They were more like walking symbols of what the twentieth century has done to indigenous peoples the world over. Dressed in a mix of traditional garb and torn T-shirts and tattered gym shoes, many had running sores on their arms and legs, festering eyes. The men tried to sell us some copper bracelets they'd twisted out of telephone wire, and little toy flamingos manufactured in Taiwan, with fluorescent pink chicken feathers glued on them.

Enough of the Turkana, we decided, and hitched for three days to southern Kenya, into the Masai Mara Game Reserve, where we saw lots of creatures. But the place was anything but wild. Scores of open-topped Land Rovers and Land Cruisers and minivans, all filled with safari-suited Americans and Germans, careened over a maze of vehicle tracks. The animals were virtually tame. It was like a zoo in reverse: the people in the cages and the animals the spectators. Kenya has done a land-office business of commodifying its parks.

Mick and I agreed that Kenya was not our idea of Africa. My fortieth birthday was only days off. "Mick," I said, "I'm thinking I'd like to be camped some place a little wilder than this on my birthday, maybe down on the Serengeti Plain in Tanzania. You interested?"

Mick smiled. "I wouldn't miss it. Besides, your fortieth, it's likely you're goin' to be needin' some geriatric assistance."

Reluctantly we went back to Nairobi, the center of all commerce in Kenya. The word among travelers hanging out in the hostel there was that there was nothing much to buy in Tanzania. Food was at a premium. Public buses and trains ran only when the government could get enough foreign exchange to buy fuel. Supposedly there wasn't a roll of toilet paper to be found in the country (cause for some concern, given the dietary quick-step one is sure to suffer sooner or later in Africa.) In short, one of Africa's political experiments with Marxist Socialism was grinding to a painful halt.

Kenya, though, was well stocked with basic goods. In a Nairobi general store we supplied ourselves with canned corned beef and rice and toilet paper. The next morning we got up early, hid greenbacks in secret places in our packs and on our bodies, then walked through a misty dawn to the downtown bus station. We bought passage in a *matatu,* one of hundreds of Peugeot station wagons used all over East Africa as public transport. After an hour or two delay, always the reality with any attempt at movement in Africa, we started out, seven adults and three children, packs and parcels and a couple of trussed-up chickens, all crammed together in what, in opulent Europe, was designed as a six-person vehicle.

It was once again good to be leaving Nairobi. I recall breathing deeply as we cleared the outskirts of the city and turned south. The countryside was beautiful, the dusty green grasslands of the tribal Masai. Here and there the horizon was broken by thin stick figures of herdsmen tending cattle and goats. In the hazy distance snowcapped Kilimanjaro reared alone into a superheated blue sky.

Across the border we arranged a ride in another *matatu* to Arusha, the town we'd been told was the place to outfit for the Serengeti. The word was we could change money on the black market there, with an East Indian named Sharif. And Sharif's cousin had an ancient Land Rover that we would rent for a run into the Serengeti Reserve.

The dry steppes of northern Tanzania stretched endlessly in all directions. I remember it as beautiful, exotic land, antithetical to the notion that we'd just entered one of the most hopelessly poor countries on the face of the earth.

The other passengers in our *matatu,* we learned shortly, were the district police chief (who had insisted on the unheard-of luxury of having the front passenger seat all to himself) and a couple of his cronies. It turned out that the chief and was smuggling *qat*, a mild amphetamine that's illegal in Tanzania. It took several hours to get to Arusha. Along the way we passed through a number of army checkpoints set up to intercept smuggled goods. The soldiers would look in the *matatu*, see the police chief, and wave us on. I was rapidly catching on to how things worked in Africa.

From a distance, the main structures of Arusha, built square and true during the German occupation of Tanzania in the early part of the century, belied the reality of what the country had come to since the departure of the colonials. Up close it was clear that the town was falling down at a high rate of speed.

Mick and I checked into a downtown hotel where we'd been told we could make contact with Sharif. A faded sign over the door read THE GREENLANDER and below promised LUXURY ACCOMMODATIONS. At the desk a surly African rented us a room. We told him we'd like to meet Sharif. "He will find you," he said.

Two plump, garishly painted ladies sat in the lobby on broken chairs. They smiled at us as we climbed a flight of rickety stairs. Our room smelled of urine, dirty socks, and curry. Green paint peeled off the walls in long strips. The mattresses on the two sagging beds were yellow-stained, with cotton batting leaking out of rat-sized holes. There were no blankets, no sheets. Cockroaches scurried across the floor between the beds.

An hour later there was a knock on our door. Mick opened it. A short, feral-looking Indian guy stood there, his long black hair slicked back gangster-style. He wore sunglasses, tailored polyester pants, and a white nylon windbreaker. Flanking him were two African henchmen. "I'm Sharif," he said in perfect Oxford English. "You wanted to see me?"

"We did," Mick said.

Sharif and his henchmen oozed into the room. We told him we wanted to exchange some money. He told us the risks he took working the black market and what it would cost us. We agreed to his fee. Sharif turned to one of the Africans. The guy reached into his pocket and pulled out a bank stamp and ink pad. Sharif held out his hand. "Your dollars." I handed him two one-hundred-dollar bills that I had ready in the pocket of my shorts, money we'd claimed at the border. Sharif pulled up one of his pant legs to reveal a red, mid-calf stretch sock so stuffed with wads of Tanzanian shillings that he looked like he had an advanced case of elephantiasis. He pulled out a couple of handfuls, counted out 12,000 shillings, and handed them to me and asked for our bank forms.

Mick and I produced the forms. Sharif stamped them, wrote twelve hundred dollars in the exchange column, which is what we would have had to exchange for the same amount of shillings at an official bank. "Twenty dollars each for the stamp," he said. I pulled out two twenties and handed them to him. He looked me in the eye. "You never saw me." With that he turned toward the door, nodded to his henchmen, and the three of them slipped out into the hallway.

That night we discovered that the ladies smiling at us in the lobby were doing a lively business of their own in a room down the hall. The Greenlander echoed through the night with the moans and groans of apparently satisfied customers.

So it went the months I traveled in Africa, one bizarre scene after the next, hundreds of outlandish encounters that made it a joy and a daily challenge to be there. I can't pretend to understand it well, but this is how it seemed to me: Africans viewed things differently. For example, time. In Africa time appears not to be a linear thing, something that one spends, a threatening specter that one races against.

Time is organic, a process, a slow spiral of endless proportion. Life does not necessarily begin with birth and end with death. Life just is. The spirits of one's ancestors are ever present and one's own life is intertwined in a timeless relationship with family and tribe and the ancestral spirits. Death is not finality but simply a transition into a different realm. To us life may appear cheap in Africa. We can perceive of Africans as cruel or careless with it. But this is only a Western perception. There, because life is not so sacred, not something to be coveted like a gold watch, ironically people seem capable of living it more fully. Death and suffering are simply acknowledged as an integral part of living. To learn to endure gracefully, to accept life's fates and to dance in the face of fate, this is the mark of a successful person.

Under this agreement Africa seems to work. It clearly seems to cease working when Africans attempt to embrace the Western way of doing things. When they strive to live by the colonizers' perceptions, with all the inherent spiritual disease and soul-numbing consumption, then things begin to fall apart. The covenant of timelessness and mutual acceptance gets broken, and the unrest and political turmoil begin. This is what's happening to Africa. But thankfully, some Africans are beginning to figure out that the Western way of viewing the world is an empty vessel. They are beginning to resist its pull, to call for a return to old ways.

It took Sharif's cousin a couple of days to buy enough fuel on the black market. Departure day, the back of the Land Rover was filled with five-gallon jerry cans of diesel. We paid Sharif's cousin some of our black-market shillings and a couple of hundred American under the table, then hit the road.

The Land Rover was a fifties-vintage relic from the glory days of the British Empire. The tires looked like they'd been hacked at with a machine. Anything over twenty-five kilometers per hour and the front end wobbled like a drunk go-go dancer. Second gear was missing. We were forced to travel in first gear most of the way, because in third, on anything but flat or downhill, the Rover didn't have enough power to pull itself.

We wobbled west and that evening passed into the Serengeti Game Reserve. I was not prepared for how strongly and instantly the Serengeti affected me, how it filled me with something that had been missing in Europe, that had been missing since my first days in Alaska. It was the vastness, the shift from human domination. It was the same primordial expansiveness I felt when I was in the Arctic, the same sense that I was coming home after a long time away.

Unlike the tourist zoos up in Kenya, we saw no other vehicles or tourists there. In a decade of political disputes with Kenya, the borders with Tanzania had been closed more often than not. Add to this Tanzania's worsening economic difficulties. Regular tourists, who demand predictability and comfort, had pretty much quit coming to the southern Serengeti. The Serengeti was a de facto wilderness then, only because of political realities. I wonder now what has become of it.

For the next several days we slowly traveled west. Along the way we spotted herds of gazelle, wildebeest, impala, and other species of antelope. We saw lions and a couple of cheetahs, giraffes, a single rhino (which had become increasingly rare due to poaching), herds of African buffalo, wild dogs, hyenas. And birds, so many. Hornbills and sunbirds. Egrets and herons. Storks and spoonbills. Small birds, large birds, birds of prey and birds preyed upon. The bird list grew by tens each day. One evening, in the angled light of the setting sun, the surface of a lake in the Nagorongoro crater was lit pink with flamingos.

We circled north and east, up toward the Kenyan border. On the eve of my fortieth we camped in a grove of spreading trees next to a beautiful little river.

At dusk I left Mick with the Land Rover and walked off alone with a tarp and my sleeping bag. On a little rise a half mile from camp I spread the tarp, threw my sleeping bag on top, and settled in for the night. The stars stood sharp in a liquid black sky. I lay awake for hours, staring at the heavens, listening to a cacophony of night screeches and moans and hollers. Far off I heard a hippo bellow. I thought about my life. What was I called to do? I fell asleep pondering the questions. Sometime in the night I was startled awake by lions roaring close. I listened. As I did I felt my fear fade, replaced by an unfamiliar contentment, a trust.

The morning of February 14 I awoke to a bold red sun rising out of low hills to the east. It was official, I'd lived forty years. I'd entered midlife. I sat up and took in the sights. Not far away two Masai giraffes stripped leaves from an acacia tree. Beyond, zebras and gazelles grazed, and farther off a herd of wildebeest. Birds sang riotously. I was as happy as I could remember being in a long time, in love with life, with the myriad possibilities of it all. I was where I most cared to be, a place with creatures big enough and wild enough to eat me, one of the last unspoiled places. How, I asked myself, had I come so far away from the things that I most cared about? How might I return?

19

turning

Compassion and love are precious things in life. They are not complicated. They are simple but difficult to practice.

HIS HOLINESS THE DALAI LAMA

The questions about my life lingered as Mick and I journeyed back to Arusha. We returned the Land Rover to Sharif's cousin, then hitched slowly southeast over rutted and broken roads into the rickety capital of Dar Es Salaam. For two days we waited in Dar Es Salaam, until the Tanzanian Federal Railway managed to secure enough foreign funds to buy fuel for the passenger train that ran down into the southern interior.

We boarded a battered rail car and rode it to the end of the line. From there we hitchhiked southeast again, toward Malawi. Tanzania and Malawi had been feuding for years, the ideological schism between Tanzanian Marxism and the iron-rule dictatorship in Malawi of Dr. Hastings Banda, who had been installed by the departing British. But, for some reason, the strain at that point had temporarily eased and the border was tentatively reopened. In Tanzania the border guards boiled beneath a hastily erected, ragged army tent. We paid our departure bribe, crossed a bridge, and entered Malawi. Instantly there was a noticeable contrast to the abject poverty and despair of Tanzania. Dr. Banda had ordered citizens there to be friendly to foreigners. He had ordered them to keep things clean and to smile. The guards asked if we had any travel guides. But we had been warned, if the guide said anything derogatory about Banda, the guards would confiscate it. We had our Lonely Planet guides well hidden and declared we had none. The guards welcomed us to Malawi and waved us on.

In Malawi things were clean, spare, orderly. We spent a week on the beaches of Lake Malawi, swimming and eating simple, abundant food. We were warned by some other travelers of thieves working along the lake, but paid little attention to the warning. One moonless night I awoke suddenly with a black face inches from mine. A hand was slowly working the zipper of the tent door. I hollered, my heart thumping like a piledriver. Two thieves ran off into the night.

I said good-bye to Mick in Malawi. I hated to see him go. He was a go-for-broke traveling partner. His pale Irish skin would burn pomegranate red under the searing tropical sun. But he rarely complained about anything, not the sand in our food, the nights sleeping on hard ground, his sore feet. But he needed to head back to Nairobi and on to Europe to make some money so he could travel more the following year. We agreed to meet up in Germany in the fall.

I left Malawi and hitched west across a corner of poverty-stricken Zambia, several days later south into Zimbabwe. Over the next months I took whatever conveyance I could to keep moving. Sometimes I'd wait hours, days once, just for a vehicle to pass. Once in southern Zambia it got to the point where I decided I'd take a ride going either direction, anything just to move. Often it was the backs of trucks, now and then a car driven by a missionary or a white development worker, a train occasionally, sometimes a country bus. But mostly it was the old thumb in the air, the wait at the side of the road. Who knew what character would pick you up next?

In Harare, the pleasant, flowering capital of Zimbabwe, I met a couple of former Rhodesians, the ex-ruling class. Privileged white people or not, they proved once again what I'd already found throughout Africa, that most people, black and white, poor and wealthy, were amazingly generous. These people didn't know me at all. I looked rough and tattered from my journeys. But they wanted to know me, to hear my story, so they asked me to stay with them, took me into their opulent home in the suburbs, told their servants to treat me well.

I took to the good life with them for a week or so. A servant brought me tea in bed in the morning and washed my clothes. I would take a dip in the pool in the heat of the afternoon, and evenings eat platters of rich food and drink too much beer. But the good life began to wear thin in short order. I felt uncomfortable having servants anticipate my every whim. Besides, the restlessness kept elbowing me, there was more to see.

I left Zimbabwe and entered the boiling pain and anger of South Africa for the first time, that heartbroken complexity of a country. I traveled from one end of it to the other. Nairobi to Capetown, it had taken me most of the winter into spring.

I circled South Africa twice. Back in Johannesburg I bought a little Underwood typewriter with a couple of strange Afrikaans letters on it, and for the first time in my life I formally began to write. The Underwood was just small enough to slip into my backpack. Every few days I'd stop and pitch my tent under a spreading mango tree or rent a hut in some lakeside retreat. There I would punch away at the keys, try to put down what I'd seen and experienced, attempted to express the experience of South Africa, of feeling anew what

I'd first felt in the American South during the civil rights marches of the sixties. Tried to capture in words what institutional hate and fear can mean to a whole country.

It was not an easy thing to get a call through to Africa from Hawaii. But Cara managed to track me down in Harare, where I was staying with a cousin. The phone line rattled with static. Her voice sounded small but determined to say what she had to say. "Dad, I wish you'd come home. I miss you. I worry about you."

"I can't come back right now," I said.

"Why?"

"I don't know."

"I need you closer."

"How close?" I said. "I don't think I can live in Hawaii."

"I don't know how close," she said. "All I know is I need a dad."

We stumbled then through some small conversation. After I hung up I felt trapped, hollow inside. I saw my desires, both my literal journey and what I imagined was my spiritual journey, competing with the needs of a tender girl bursting into adolescence. I lived in a boil of fear, afraid of being taken over by the shackles of a common life. The thought of settling, the alternative that I imagined—a boring job, a split-level in the suburbs, two cars, the cardiac track—felt grim beyond measure. For years my life had been about extremes. I couldn't see any way to have my old life back in Alaska, and the only other option I saw for settling "close" was the way that I'd grown up in the Midwest. In my mind it was either be a rogue traveler or go back and be my father.

Yet, despite my resistance, I was being led to consider a third path. It was in Harare that I read for the first time Scott Peck's *The Road Less Traveled.* Another moment of grace. What that bit of pop psychology was doing there in Africa I'll never know. But for the first time in my life I began to think about the nature of love. Love was a choice, not a romantic thing, not a wild ride, but a quiet decision. Love is ever present, available, yet humans most often refuse the offer of it and choose instead fear. Peck's thesis that love is the less-traveled road struck me hard. Yes, I was living differently from the norm. But was I really on a less-traveled road? My curiosity about the world and my resistance to a common life were not the issues. My running was. With it I was treading a well-worn groove. So what was an alternative? The practice of love, Peck said, is hard work. It requires a certain kind of discipline, something I was discovering that I had yet to develop.

I could not make up my mind. I left Zimbabwe and traveled through the Kalahari Desert into the Okavango Swamps of Botswana. I hired an African with a dugout and poled for days through those magic waters, the huge, wild oasis in the middle of the Kalahari. Next it was the desert pans and wilds of Namibia, then back into South Africa. In a perverse way South Africa held a fascination for me. There, in one place, it was possible to witness so many of the complicated pathologies of humanity. It's no secret that Africa is chaotic, that civilization as it's defined in the West is a thin veneer over a primitive, angry, pulsing core. It's no secret, either, that a couple of centuries of colonial rule imposed a stiff and illusionary order, and with its departure left the place bleeding at the jugular. If I may venture a postulate, though, I'd say that all the same chaos, all the same primitive notions lurk beneath Western veneers. It's just that our surface is thicker and slicker, patinated by our smug perceptions of technological safety and cultural superiority. With Africa, what you see is what you get, and what you get may well be a loud social and environmental warning signal of what's about to come for all of us, no matter where we are.

In March I traveled back into Zimbabwe. Constant movement, rootlessness, was beginning to lose its appeal. Although Africa still fascinated me, held me enthralled, my life was beginning to feel pointless. I needed something to do that made some contribution. Why not settle here some-where, get involved in wildlife research? But whenever I thought of settling in Africa, Cara's words, "I need you here," would tumble over and over in my mind.

Trains have always helped me think. It's the movement, I guess, the sway and lights passing through night black-ness. Some force enters the hidden crevices of my mind. As the miles click by, new possibilities come seeping through the misty edges. Thoughts coalesce into sensible patterns where none existed before. I needed to think. I boarded a train in Harare, unconcerned where it was going or where I would get off, but thinking I would find Mick, who had been work-ing on a farm down by the Botswana border.

The whistle blew and the train lurched out of the station. I stood at the open window in the passageway and watched the procession of city lights, and then the sharp, uniquely African interface where modern civilization gives way sud-denly to the night mysteries of countryside. Here and there a campfire glowed or a feeble kerosene lamp or the lights of a farm, but mostly all that was out there was a glorious, starlit African night.

The train rocked and lulled. I had bought a sleeping berth, but I remained standing in the passageway, out of long habit, relishing the feel of being on the move again. At the end of the corridor I saw a gray-haired man standing, his legs spread and braced as if riding a ship in high seas. He was urinating on the floor, drunk. Those around him, in the best African tradition, ignored him. Endure, brothers; don't acknowledge this unpleasant thing. In time, like all unpleasant things, it will go away.

What followed was one of those African scenes that I'd just come to expect. The huge African conductor and a diminutive train guard entered the car just as the drunk was finishing up. "Only an animal would piss on the floor of a train!" the conductor shouted. The two of them grabbed the drunk and pushed him against the wall. "Take your shirt off," the conductor ordered. With some shoving back and forth, the two of them finally got the drunk's shirt off. "Wipe up this mess now!" the conductor shouted. The drunk sank slowly to his knees. "Wipe!" the conductor ordered again. The drunk wadded his shirt and with it made some half-hearted swipes at the puddle. But a polyester shirt is not a sponge.

The conductor finally had had enough. "Stand," he said. The drunk staggered to his feet. "Put your shirt back on." The poor fellow pulled it on and stood there looking horribly soggy and downcast, his belly protruding like a bowling ball from the unbuttoned front. My berthmate, a young "colored" man (in the language of southern Africa, neither white nor black but in-between), had heard the commotion and was standing in the doorway of our compartment. He leaned and whispered in my ear with some empathy: "That is a very strong punishment for only pissing on the floor."

But it wasn't over. The conductor asked the drunk for his ticket. Of course he didn't have one. The conductor's anger dissolved into sighing regret. "Throw him off," he said to the guard. The poor drunk began to bleat and struggle like a trapped animal. The guard, who at one time must have been a force on the soccer field, delivered a couple of clean right-foot shots to the drunk's shins. With the conductor's bulk added to the melee it was no contest. They slid open the rear door and sailed the offender out into the night.

My berthmate looked at me knowingly and lit another cigarette. "It's not a good thing to board a train without a ticket." He turned and went back into the compartment. Yes, I thought, he's got that right. But then too it was just another day in Africa. I would miss this place where life, though not always pleasant, was so vibrant and full, so unpredictable. The thought of going back to the States, where everything was so orderly and safe, so sanitized and physically easy, held no appeal for me. The thought of living tamed and house-broken felt like slow spiritual death. Somehow I needed to think of it another way. But how?

In the early-morning cool the train stopped and I debarked at the small town where Mick had been working on a farm since our return to Africa. As always, we were glad to meet up again. The next few days Mick toured me around the area, meeting local farmers, hearing their stories, visiting the farms in the region that had not yet been taken over by the government for redistribution to black Africans. The soil on those farms had absorbed more than their share of blood. One man showed us some old Portuguese musket barrels found on his farm. Just behind his farmhouse were extensive ruins of the lost tribe of Zimbabwe, one of several sites on which a moderately advanced people of Stone Age Africa lived, people who disappeared suddenly, probably via a violent confrontation with the invading Portuguese. At the turn of the century the pioneering English, under the leadership of the pathologically insane empire builder Cecil Rhodes, slaughtered the people of Matabele tribe for possession of those farmlands. During the seventies blood was shed again in the war for independence, with the Africans regaining political control.

Violence and threat, guns and vigilance have been the daily realities for white settlers and their children and children's children from the beginning. As with most people who grow up with violence, they were casual about it. "It's the first bloody thing I put on in the morning," one farmer said about his pistol. "It's under my pillow at night. Never know when some bloody dissidents'll come pokin' around."

It was clear that the white farmers were living an isolated life, separated not only by physical distances, but also by the outdated and rigid rules of their old social order. There seemed to be a singular obsession to hang onto the good old days, to reject the idea that anything had really changed. But you got the feeling the attitude was a little forced, the social graces a little too contrived. When pressed, most of the farmers felt there was little more than a few years left before things got impossible economically, or the government simply took over their farms. This was where conversations usually lapsed into uneasy silence. Because most of them, like it or not, were African; they really had no other place to call home. Despite clinging tenaciously to a set of values that belonged in the cloistered fields of England, their roots were impossibly sunk into the baked and bloody soil of Africa.

These days I listen intently to reports of more violence in Zimbabwe. Blacks and whites still continue to die in a confused power struggle between the tribesmen of the Matabele and the Shona-dominated government. The government is taking over more white farms. I often wonder what has happened to those people I visited. I cannot imagine them anywhere else but on their farms. Yet I know some must be gone now, to Australia or who knows where.

One evening the farmer Mick worked for asked Mick and me if we'd like to go to the "social club," what had once been a community gathering place exclusively for the use of white Rhodesians. But since the war for African independence all clubs were forced to integrate or to close.

A sign at the door, PLEASE CHECK ARMS, summed up the past and the present. Our host put his pistol on a ledge over the bar. He explained how the club had been attacked during the war. Social night, and all the whites in the community were gathered there. A black nanny and her white charge were killed before the white farmers took up their arms and drove off the attackers. Shortly after, the club members built a tall block wall, complete with gun ports, around the entire premise. The wall remained, he said, only half jokingly, "because you never know when we may need the bloody thing again."

Three whites and three blacks, two separate groups, stood drinking at the bar. Our host introduced us to the white men, two other farmers and a little, rodent-eyed cattle buyer with the instant angry and belligerent demeanor of the incurable redneck. He was quite drunk.

The white men got into asking me the usual questions about Alaska and what it was like traveling down through Africa. To a man—and they were brave men who had survived a bush war—it was inconceivable that anyone would choose to travel through postcolonial Africa. And hitchhiking to do it—the very idea sent those hardy sons of pioneers into spasms of fear. The cattle buyer summed it up: "I'm not interested in going anyplace else the bloody black bastards have taken over. This country's bad enough, and she's gettin' worse by the day."

He was living proof of how hard it is to adjust to the reality of the present when you're still looking through the privileged eyes of the good old days when whites were in control. He bought me a beer. "Cheers," he said, and lifted his glass to mine. He squinted disdainfully and gestured with his glass at the three black men standing at the end of the bar. Loud, so everyone could hear, he said, "What'a you think of our *gentlemen* here? You know, we have to call them gentlemen now. And we've got to drink with them. It didn't used to be that way. This used to be a good goddamned country."

I glanced at the three Africans. They stared straight ahead at the black barman, wearing their best African endure-and-eventually-it-will-go-away expressions. But I noticed the muscles twitch in the jaw of the one closest to me. My host, a public gentleman, a rare former Rhodesian who grudgingly accepted the need to get along at least superficially, asked Mick and one of the blacks to play darts. They accepted, leaving me alone with the cattle buyer.

His red eyes narrowed even more. I had a general sense of what was coming. I'd been hearing the gist of it for months wherever the relics of the colonial past gathered. "Instead of these rich Americans coming over here and hunting elephants and lions and such, we ought to put 'em on a few of these buggers." He nodded toward the two Africans left at the bar. "Tell me if I'm not right. They'd be lining up in California and Texas to get over here and take a shot." He looked around, smiling, pleased with himself. "You may not say it, but I know you agree with me. Everybody hates a *kaffir*."

I couldn't let it go. "Seems to me you've already been doing this hunting stuff for some time," I said. "Only they aren't like elephants. They shoot back. And they kicked the shit out of you in the war."

His eyes widened. "You sound like a fucking *kaffir* lover."

"It's all how you look at it," I said. And with that I left him standing there, *Africanus rhodesia rodentia*.

You did good, I said to myself as I walked out into the starry night, beyond the gun ports, beyond the whine of the cattle buyer's voice, beyond the sad circle of light thrown by the social club. For once you got mad and you said something sensible. I walked until the night sounds of Africa took over: the harsh ratchet of insects, the long-drawn, twangy notes of some unfamiliar stringed instrument, and a woman's soft laugh from the village near. The air was permeated with the sticky sweet odor of night-blooming flowers.

I thought of Cara, her trusting face, a smile that could light up the world. I wished she could be there with me. Maybe then she would understand why I leave. Perhaps she would come to this same place: this desire to experience, to be touched by the unfamiliar, to move. But should I wish that for her? Would I want her possessed by this same restlessness?

No.

At the railroad tracks I stopped. Somewhere, way off, I thought I could hear a train, a moaning whistle, just a hint of movement on the soft breeze. My body reacted instinctually; time to move again. But in opposition something else surfaced. Suddenly I felt weary, worn down by the rigors of travel, defeated by the common vagrancies and hate and injustices perpetrated by men, by all the warring perceptions that humans project upon the planet. For some reason it came clear to me then. This was it, the exact point where I either gave up and headed back to the States and attempted to stay for a while, did my best to make a decent life there, or I kept moving and most likely slipped beyond the bounds of being able to return, gave myself to a life of ceaseless wandering. This meant, also, giving up on the idea of fatherhood, to become one of those men who abandon their children, who cannot suffer the responsibility, another one of the many who pass on the wounds, who fail to learn how to love.

I stood there for the longest time, staring off into the darkness. I was afraid that either way would lead to failure. But the voice came to me again. Return, it said. Return and let the fates decide. For once I listened. No more debate. I turned and walked toward the social club, preparing the words that I would use to tell Mick that I was going home, wherever that might be.

20

facing east

An ecologist without a conscience is doomed to failure, and
the same is true of an artist who does not bow to the laws of
nature. . . . In 1953 I realized that the straight line leads to
the downfall of mankind.

HUNDERTWASSER, "The Paradise
Destroyed by the Straight Line"

Infatuation, disappointment, retreat, awakening, return,
opening, love, commitment. The journey that carries us
away and away, then turns with a sigh and carries us back
again, hearts rent open by a succession of grace-filled moments, is the journey of waking after years asleep. Celebrate
awakening, rise to it and sing. For the sharp, breathing pain
of consciousness is exquisitely more rich than the dull, suffocating pain of existing asleep.

I visited Cara in Hawaii, told her I was going to do my best
to settle somewhere in the States, maybe back in Alaska,
maybe Hawaii, I just didn't know yet. Wherever I was, though,

she could be with me whenever she chose. I wondered, though, Could I pull it off? Like the gravity of the moon, Africa and travel still pulled at me. I had to keep reminding myself of the reasons why I had come back. The addict vacillates with the recognition of his disease. There is some kind of convoluted, pinched, and tragic nobility in succumbing to the poison. It ultimately, though, comes down once again to the discipline of love—for others, for oneself. But the fact remains, a recovering addict of any kind is just that, always recovering, never recovered.

After a couple of weeks in Hawaii, I headed back to Alaska and once again took a job in a caribou study up in the North Slope oil fields. Ironically, caribou, one of the most compulsive wanderers on the planet, paid for my journeys. Ironically, the petroleum industry, the beast that changed Alaska so and drove me away, brought me home.

Caribou. How I admire them. I know it may sound contradictory, but I have ever since, so many years earlier as a wide-eyed kid working with the Yupik up in the Crazy Mountains, I killed my first ones there.

Caribou are tough. They live and thrive by the thousands in one of the harshest environments imaginable. Winters are the worst, with twenty-four-hour-a-day darkness, punishing winds, and temperatures diving down to fifty, sixty, seventy below zero. Yet summer offers no relief. Mid-June to the end of July, temperatures can range up into the eighties, and parasitic insects proliferate. Mosquitoes, great black clouds of them, are just the beginning. Next come bots, stout, hairy flies that inject their larvae up the caribou's nose. The larvae migrate through the caribou's nasal passages and into the back of the throat, where they grow to be hacked out eventually by their host. If the bots aren't bad enough, there are warble flies, which lay eggs on the caribou's legs. The warble fly hatchlings burrow through the subcutaneous tissue and migrate up to the back, where they bore breathing holes through the skin and grow to the size of BBs. In the spring the larvae emerge painfully (for the caribou) and fall to the ground, where they pupate to keep the whole cycle going.

During fly season caribou stand spraddle-legged, heads down, listening for a fly's approach. When one comes, a single fly, whole herds will run off wildly across the tundra. Add to all this misery the large predators—gray wolves, grizzly bears, wolverines, humans—and there are not two weeks a year that caribou live in any kind of peace. Yet given a chance they can thrive in the Arctic.

I've watched caribou stream by in the thousands. To this day caribou migrating in the Arctic are for me one of the ultimate wild spectacles. It's the flow of abundance across the harsh cut of an Arctic landscape, a sea of antlers bobbing and catching the sun in a thousand ways. Witnessing it, you're privileged to feel something primal and ancient and important, a sacred gift. To witness it is to feel the divine.

It was not easy to feel the divine in the oil fields.

At the very southern edge of the development my wooden observation tower sat alone out on the tundra. I entered it via a wooden ladder propped beneath, popped up inside like a gopher through a trapdoor set in the middle of the floor. The view south through the Plexiglas windows was of tundra spreading endlessly, a dull green, polygonally patterned plain pocked with countless small black lakes. On the perimeters of the lakes waterfowl still nested—black brant, tundra swans, and pintail ducks; migratory species. On the drier ground, amid stunted willows, golden and black-bellied plovers and Lapland longspurs hid nests from the relentless predation of long-tailed and parasitic jaegers. Occasionally an Arctic fox wandered by, or a snowy owl floated past like a winged ghost. On still days I could hear the plaintive cry of a yellow-billed loon above the sounds on the road. Far out across the tundra it called, signaling like a prophet.

My view of the other three directions was significantly different. "The slope," as it's called by workers there, was even then in 1989 the largest contiguous industrial development on earth, several hundred square miles. (It's close to double that size today.) The oil companies boldly touted just how carefully they were developing the Arctic. But the reality was and is that petroleum production is a toxic, destructive, go-for-it business, dedicated to one thing only: profit, billions and billions of dollars taken at the expense of the earth.

The slope told the tale of it. Toxic waste bubbled in settling ponds and seeped into nearby lakes. Huge holes, where billions of yards of gravel had been mined, gaped like open sores on the landscape. Every turn of the horizon was broken by the works of man: a maze of pipelines and roads, drilling platforms, radio towers, transmission lines, camp buildings, oil wells, refineries, and production facilities. There was something surreal and sinister about it, a space-odyssey quality that confused the mind, a hard, angled, technological sterility. Being an observer of wildlife there, of observing living things juxtaposed against everything that was their antithesis, was a schizoid experience.

My part in the caribou studies was not glamorous, just interminable hours and days of waiting and of scanning an often empty tundra plain with my binoculars. There were only my idle thoughts to keep me company. Behind it all was the ceaseless blowing of the north wind, careening off the tundra, rattling and shaking my tower so hard at times that I thought it might tear the guy wires from the frozen earth and I would sail away over the white expanse of the ocean, like some reluctant space traveler. In time the north wind became part of my subconscious. But then one day it would suddenly die and the world would become loud with its absence. That was the moment when gray Arctic spring yielded to the heat of the round-the-clock sun and summer began. The time when the tundra world instantly became an angry, buzzing mop of mosquitoes and flies.

Like some daunting apparition the caribou would suddenly appear, a line of brown velvet antlers moving far off through the heat waves. Then they would take form, maybe ten or a thousand, moving quickly and determined, driven to the edge of panic by the bugs. They were headed for the cooler, mosquito-free shores of the Arctic Ocean that lay just a few miles to the north. This response to the torment of insects is a migration pattern that has gone on for as long as there have been caribou in the Arctic. But times had changed.

My job, if they came within my study area, was to count their numbers, map their movements, and note their reactions to the elevated pipeline and to the road adjacent to it, that ran along behind my tower. "Success rates crossing pipelines" was the scientific jargon we used, as if caribou were competing for something.

If I was on the ball, not lost in some far-off fantasy, when they appeared I would snap to attention and grab my binoculars and the four-finger hand counter, and begin clicking numbers. The caribou always came too fast. Stay calm, I'd tell myself. The sure way to blow a count is to panic. Also keep in mind vehicles on the road. Vehicles always made the difference.

I would watch them cross the outer fringes of my study area, note the time, and check for vehicles on the road. Too often then the same maddening scenario would develop. The caribou closed on the pipeline. A couple of hundred feet away the lead animal, usually a roman-nosed old cow, would throw up her head and stop. The others would immediately halt behind her, begin milling and shaking heads, twitching hides and tails, battling the mosquitoes. Then very cautiously the lead cow would advance toward the pipe, her nose held high in the air, like a bird dog on fresh scent. She would stop again, clearly mystified by this odd form looming over the tundra. Then a pickup truck or a belly dump or some other piece of heavy equipment would approach noisily on the road. The old cow would turn and begin paralleling the pipe, the others following her closely. The vehicle would blast by in a cloud of dust, more often than not with its horn blaring. Then it would happen: the herd would turn as one and run, eyes wide, nostrils flaring, stampeding back toward the horizon from which they had first appeared minutes earlier.

What I remember most is the anger, the frustration I felt when I watched the vehicles approach and the caribou fail at crossing. Each day the anger built and seemed to have no place to go. So many times I stood tense and hopeful, then watched the same scenario unfold, felt their defeat as the animals turned away. And with it I felt and began to actively articulate to myself a much larger defeat, the lunacy of this clumsy, arrogant game we moderns play with the natural world.

Over the course of the three summer seasons that I participated in the studies my colleagues and I noted some things. Gravel ramps built over lowered sections of the pipelines as crossing devices failed miserably. When confronted with any obstacle foreign to many thousand years of Arctic experience, caribou in numbers usually became confused and retreated. Given enough time, though, some would eventually figure it out and begin to cross under pipelines if they were elevated enough off the ground. The bulls would duck their heads in an exaggerated way, careful of their antlers, and then quickly shuttle under. But trucks and machinery on the roads—"vehicle interactions," we called them—would almost always foil any attempt. Bulls and dry cows clearly got through the oil fields more easily than cows with calves; cows with calves rarely succeeded, even with no vehicles on the roads. A few bulls did adapt to the oil fields, in fact seemed to prefer them—most likely, we speculated, because of the lack of predators.

My colleagues and I did not record the confusion, the white-eyed panic, the separation of cows from calves when pipelines and roads with traffic were encountered. We did not record the casual attitude of the workers in the oil fields, their lack of interest or even their outright disdain for living things. We did not record the caribous' beauty, their comic grace, the miracles of minute ecological adaptations that allow them to thrive in a punishing environment. Nor did we record the anger that some of us felt. All that we recorded was what was allowed within the narrow parameters of the study. We generated "data" to be run through the mathematical hieroglyphics of computer models, data that were then spit out as statistics, graphs, charts, and technological language devoid of any smells, colors, or feelings, all to be thickly bound in reports to gather dust on desks in Fairbanks, Anchorage, and Houston. Somewhere early on in the process, at the tip of my own pencil, caribou quit being living things, with all the miraculous interactions of any species, and they became an abstraction.

I felt frustrated by the parameters. I wanted other people to feel what I felt, to observe what I observed. I wanted them to know what it was like to see the Arctic change so rapidly, to have seen this same tundra world before development. To have seen it wild and unscarred, and then a few short years later to see the heart torn from it. When I expressed my concern to one of my colleagues, he reminded me that scientists pride themselves on being detached, on being objective. "You can't care about these animals and do the work," he said. He was the same one who called caribou "tundra maggots," referring, I guess, to their numbers and the way a large herd on the move seemed to squirm in the distance.

I could not help but witness that many research biologists in the oil fields go numb. The reductionist nature of the "science" they practice, the crush of bureaucratic and corporate demands, of seeing over and over again the destruction of wild places and of living things, all these things divorced some from their feelings. I know, though, beneath it, at one time most cared. Almost all the field biologists I have ever known are people who began their careers with a keen appreciation of the natural world. The consulting company I worked for was as reputable as they get, committed to good science, at least the kind of "science" that was required by governmental agencies catering to corporations tenaciously dedicated to getting what they wanted. I know, too, that most of us working there were uncomfortable at some level with what we were doing. But our reasoning went, if we don't do this study, some other, less ethical consulting company will. At least we'll do it the best that it can be done. And beneath that reasoning was one ever-insistent practicality: we all needed to make a living.

Yes, so many things we do in life are justified by the dual rationalizations of inevitability and economics. The voices of modern reason. By my third summer working in the oil fields, the voice of reason that I had employed was sounding more and more hollow. I couldn't help but feel that most of us working there were giving away something important when we sold ourselves to the oil corporations. It's hard to say this now, hard to make judgments about people I still know and care about, but there was a heavy price to it. Something died in all of us, some deep part, some vital idealism and passion that feeds the soul and gives us cause for full living.

When hearts are unengaged, any work becomes a paper cutout. Wildlife biology (or any science, for that matter) becomes an exercise dominated by technicians, computer-model addicts, people who have bought the notion that scientific practice is supposed to be completely value-free. Which of course it can never be. Because there are humans doing it, with all their human biases and value-based perceptions.

It bothered me that the old-time naturalist/biologists, those men or women who dedicated their whole lives to understanding intimately a place and the interrelationships of living things in that place, the biologist that I imagined myself being when I entered college, were no longer accepted. The patience and deep caring of that kind of observation was missing in everything that we did. Everything was speeded up, computerized, depersonalized, abstracted. It's become even more so today. Too much of biology has become the questionable science of risk assessment, an exercise dedicated to answer only this question: How far can we push a species with our industrial activities before it will fail entirely?

On the North Slope we took the science of abstraction and risk assessment to a new level. We studied caribou knowing full well that nothing would change in the oil fields if our study suggested harm to caribou populations. Our only intent with the study was to document what was already under way, to blanket with statistical jargon what anyone with a lick of common sense could see was a growing disaster for wildlife and for what was once a wild place. It was already well documented that cows had ceased calving in a major portion of their traditional calving areas because of human activities. This displacement was concentrating the cows into smaller areas, thus depleting nutrition sorely needed for calving. Speculation was that calves were being born weaker, making them more susceptible to mosquitoes and other stresses. It didn't take a science degree to figure out that cutting off access to mosquito-relief habitat added yet another complication to an already highly complicated existence. The effects could not easily be proved with a tidy, short-term study. All that was needed to see it, though, was a dollop of common sense. All it took was a willingness to look honestly, an openness to feeling.

One of the oil companies operating on the North Slope used to run an ad in national magazines with a glossy colored photo of some massively antlered bull caribou grazing contentedly by an oil rig. The text went something like this: "Working to protect our environment while providing for America's future." This catchy slogan used to turn me livid. I knew the truth. I wondered why scientists didn't speak up, go public, tell people what's really going on up in the Arctic.

As my third season drew to a close, I knew that I was in the wrong place, working in the wrong business. Each day I sat in my tower and fantasized about walking east. I saw myself walking quickly, leaving the oil fields behind. I walked effortlessly through the jumble of rivers and lakes, fifty miles, until I came to the broad, braided delta of the Canning River. Beyond the Canning was country devoid of oil structures, untouched and primal. Beyond the Canning lay the country I'd visited years earlier, the Arctic National Wildlife Refuge.

Autumn comes to the Arctic in a rush. One day the tundra is green and the next it's a palette of colors: reds and rusts and muted yellows. Newly feathered waterfowl begin to test their wings, restless, pushed by an inner whispering that warns of the hard hand of winter that will soon grip this place.

In my tower I could hear the same whispering.

It was well past midnight when I climbed down the ladder of my tower. The sun was still alive, a tepid orange orb set low on the northern horizon, casting a diffused yellow light over the tundra, a gentler touch than the pale, angled glare of daytime. I got in the company pickup. I could not go back to my room at the construction camp where I lived. I drove over gravel roads, through a maze of silver pipelines, the capillaries, veins, arteries of the giant. I passed dozens of well pads with rows of metal-sheathed pump houses standing like space-age knights in review; refineries with gas flares pulsing red into the night sky; and portable drilling rigs set on newly laid gravel pads far out on the tundra, towering ten stories high, aliens in a world where the tallest plant might rise a foot. I passed equipment yards with rows of dozers and graders and belly dumps; construction camps with lines of portable housing units connected in close rectangular patterns; and the ordered sprawl of a main operation camp, this one famed for an Olympic-sized swimming pool, full gym, and a tropical garden inside.

I drove northeast until I came to a long causeway that jutted like a finger into the Arctic Ocean, to a man-made gravel island that held another production facility. I pulled to the side of the road and parked. For most of the year the Arctic Ocean is icebound, covered beyond imagination with a solid white armor. Summer, though, the winds shift from the northwest to the southeast. By August the sun has weakened the ice enough that the winds can push it offshore. It lies far out to the north then, visually just a shimmering mirage, a refracted white band of light against the darker curve of the sky.

Escape. I shouldered a small pack and began walking quickly east. I waded shallow braids of the Sagavanirktok River, then gained the narrow beach along the deceptively placid Arctic Ocean. The beach, a slate-gray interface between the tundra and the ocean, was littered with chunks of Styrofoam and soda cans, survey stakes topped with tags of fluorescent red ribbon, frayed lengths of rope, and the ever-present symbol of modern man in the north: rusted, fifty-five-gallon drums.

I walked, zigzagging from the beach out onto the tundra, skirting ponds and small lakes, then back to the beach again.

Along the way I spotted an Arctic fox busily investigating a colony of Arctic ground squirrels, a snowy owl perched motionless on its hunting mound, and out over the ocean the white-on-black flash of king eiders in flight. I must have walked an hour or so before I came to the banks of a black tundra creek, too wide and deep at its mouth to cross.

At least I was out of the oil fields. I turned south and stared out over the tundra, the coastal plain that some call barren. In the distance, eighty miles at least, the peaks of the Brooks Range caught the early-morning light. Somewhere in those mountains the new Dalton Highway crossed a high pass, connecting the oil fields with the rest of the world. Its construction had speeded up time on the coastal plain, had brought it square and immediately into the insatiable hunger of the twentieth century.

I stood still and let the sounds of the tundra take over. Close by I could hear the whistled *chu-leet* of a golden plover, and somewhere in the distance the cry of an Arctic loon. I felt the wind gather itself, watched it touch the tundra, bend strands of cotton grass and riffle the surface of ponds.

I faced to the east again. I thought of my fantasy of walking to the Arctic Refuge. I knew that the oil companies, speculating there were paying quantities of petroleum in the refuge, were spending millions on a public relations effort to get permission from the federal government to develop there. It struck me then that I stood at a place on the planet that symbolically focused so many of our modern dilemmas. I stood at the north edge of the world, one of the last places that could be exploited in a big way. To the south, far beyond the Brooks Range, millions of North Americans were demanding more of everything, more goods, more oil, and, ironically, more wild places to escape to. West of where I stood, the oil fields were witness to what we've been up to for over three centuries, the ill-conceived notion of frontier, of resources unlimited, the unquestioned righteousness of industrial technology and an ever expanding economy.

And to the east, in stark contrast, there survived a remnant of unaltered nature, the priceless remains of a former world, the path back to something our overly denatured souls most certainly yearn for. It came to me then that I stood at the interface of choice. Do we modern humans continue to deface the world in order to keep the illusion of our progress alive? Or can we begin to face another direction, begin to make the hard choices of living here in a radically new way?

Awakening. The journey of the heart is an intricate weaving of small moments that build and build to finally turn us in a new direction. As I stood there it also came to me that I had to ask myself the same questions. I had to see my part in the scarring of Alaska, not always an active part particularly, more one of compliance by silence and avoidance. It angered me when I thought of oil development in the Arctic Refuge. But what was I doing about it? How was my participation in the oil fields, my assumptions and consumptions, any different or more righteous from those of the executive who signed my paycheck? If I wanted the guarantee of wild in my own life, and wild places for generations to come, what was I doing about it? If I cared about my own child, what was I doing to leave her a different legacy?

The sun was climbing the east flank of its orbit, casting a new, harsher quality of light across the tundra. I made some decisions then. It would be my last season in the oil fields. I would never again knowingly give my energies directly to any institution that was dedicated to profit at the expense of the earth. Of course, I understood the key word was "directly." I could not avoid the many compromises that each of us lives with each day, the ways that we are forced to participate in the destruction. But I could work for fundamental change. In that moment I decided that I had no choice. I could not run again.

It was time to follow the other voice. Whatever it asked, wherever it took me, that's what I had to do.

That moment up on the North Slope turned me in a new direction. Yet in another way it simply verified the course that I'd been on all my life. Like it or not, I was about to come out of the closet, to take a stand and announce publicly what I had avoided for many years. I cared about, no, I desperately *loved* this earth. It was time to begin to act on that love. I had journeyed, literally and figuratively, full circle, back to my beginnings, back to the instinctive desires of my early childhood, back to Alaska, back to the risks of caring for a place again, of beginning again with my own daughter, of facing my own self. In another way, also, I had come back to my pacifist roots. For I had decided to quit making war.

The practice of loving, of course, is not an easy thing. It's about letting go. It takes time. Yet, like any journey, it begins with the decision to turn and take a step.

I stood there a while longer, facing east. I felt the first outlines of a scary new freedom, an opening to something that I had long yearned for, a release from some long-held confinement. I turned back and began walking to the pickup. Ahead, far off over the coastal plain, a giant plume of black smoke, a flare-off in the oil fields, trailed northward across the sky.

return

21

the fear of nature, the nature of fear

And it is a strange thing that most of the feeling we call religious, most of the mystical outcrying which is one of the
most prized and used and desired reactions of our species,
is really the understanding and the attempt to say that man
is related to the whole thing, related inextricably to all reality, known as unknowable.

JOHN STEINBECK, *The Log From the Sea of Cortez*

There is a tundra plain up along the Arctic Ocean. There,
in the summer, countless tough, tiny flowers bloom. Dark
purples, faded yellows, delicate blues, they bend and nod in
the cold wind. The wind is like a restless breath, a warning
whisper of forces building. When I die I want my ashes to go
there. Promise me that. Take them there. That is, unless the
place has been lost to the spoilers, to the dealers that provi-
sion our addictions.

I would like to take you there. Perhaps we'll see an old
boar, grizzly, frenzied, and angry in the hunt. We'll watch him

tear up yards of tundra in a quest for parka squirrels. He will smell our human stink, swivel around hard, and rear up onto his hind legs. Through nearsighted eyes he will stare at us, nostrils flaring. His front legs bat the air, as if sorting and rejecting the scents that carry on it. The silver hair of his back riffles like waves in the wind. In his ferociousness for living, if we're open to feeling, we might begin to sense something infinitely large at work in the universe.

Later, we might see caribou stream by, thousands of them through a high mountain pass, like gold and silver coins poured from a purse. The summer-night sun will glow like slick polish on their antlers. And above, long-tailed jaegers will slice through the sky. In the far distance, the wavering yodel of a loon will fill the air with a sound so primitive and right that at that moment we will know there has to be a God.

Yes, the experience of this place could change us. It could change the world. And the world needs changing. Because the places where we might most easily feel God, we keep destroying.

My decision to quit the oil fields and follow another voice led me on new journeys, ones I could never have predicted. The following fall, with the help of several dedicated friends, I produced "The Last Great Wilderness," a multimedia slide show that explored the Arctic National Wildlife Refuge and exposed the reality of petroleum development in the Arctic.

I traveled with the "Last Great Wilderness" for three years, all over the country, did hundreds of presentations to thousands of people. To what avail? Early spring of 1989 it looked like the petroleum interests were going to get their way; Congress was on the verge of voting to give them the go-ahead to enter the Arctic Refuge. George Bush senior waited ex-

pectantly in the White House, pen ready to sign a development bill. I was touring in New England, Good Friday, March
24, 1989, when we got word that the Exxon *Valdez* had run
aground in Prince William Sound. If I had any doubts about
the scurrilous price of oil development in Alaska, that single
event made them vanish forever. Alaska had become a corporate fiefdom. The wilds of Alaska were at the mercy of men
who sat thousands of miles away at desks in Houston and
Washington, D.C., and Tokyo, men who cared for nothing but
bottom-line profit, who were careless and supercilious, lost in
old and destructive ways of thinking. The black petroleum
scum that sucked life from Prince William Sound was an apt
metaphor for their hearts.

I'll never forget a moment in Arcata, California, one of my
first presentations with the "Last Great Wilderness." A grizzled veteran of the timber wars in California stood during
the question-and-answer period. "For fifteen years I've been
trying to save forests here," he said. "I applaud what you're
trying to do for the Arctic. But I have to share with you one
thing I've learned. Maybe it will help you. You gotta know
that some people are soul dead; they will never hear. They
have no ability to do anything but promote evil. If I can say
one thing to you, focus your energy on those who can hear."

His words stayed with me. In believing in the power of
love, I didn't want to believe what he said was true. Yet I've
come to believe he shared something that's sadly accurate.
Some people are so lost in the blind canyons of dominance
and greed that they are beyond hearing.

There were unintended gifts that came from the Exxon
Valdez tragedy. Congress backed off; the Arctic Refuge
gained a temporary reprieve. Eyes were opened. People who
had never proclaimed any allegiance to the earth became
champions for it. Those of us working for the refuge renewed
our commitments.

There were gifts, also, of touring the country. Along the way I got to talk to a lot of people. I verified what I had already seen other places in the world and in Alaska. Communities the country over are facing their own Exxon *Valdez*es. They are being devastated by corporate machinations and by too many of their citizens who have retreated into cynicism and apathy, many who are lost in outright denial. Yet in every community there are those willing to see, people concerned about what's happening. Many want to change their lifestyles, but feel helpless, frustrated, up against huge odds.

My decision that day in the oil fields was the coming together of many growing recognitions. Environmental and social issues are all related; they spring from the same set of misguided, warring perceptions that have shaped cultures since the development of agriculture, and even more so since the industrial revolution. North American culture is the great culmination of these misperceptions.

My decision to no longer support war of any kind meant developing a more conscious understanding of the ways that fear underlies all violence and destruction and social ill. The journey is ultimately about courage. Ultimate courage does not take place on a battlefield or in a corporate boardroom. Ultimate courage takes place within the human heart, in taking a first step on a less-traveled path, in taking the risk of saying no to the forces of destruction and violence however or wherever they appear.

Environmentalist. Environmentalism. After leaving the oil fields that fall, the name *environmentalist* hit me. I was about to become one. No realization in my life had ever felt better or more right. I felt some discomfort with the popular misappropriations of the word, but in secret I liked the ring of it.

I suppose I might sound like a reformed smoker or a born-again Christian saying any of this. Of course, in taking on any cause there's always the danger of creating yet another brand of fundamentalism. The word *environmentalist,* as it's been used, is not accurate. It's not inclusive enough. And it's been maligned and misappropriated by those who would cling tenaciously to the status quo, those lost in denial. Tree-huggers, posy-sniffers, bleeding hearts, unreasonable people, radicals, people who are just too emotional, the list grows longer the more our biosphere spirals downward. People who care too much, who risk loving the earth, are too often singularly seen only as troublemakers, people who want only to throw a wrench into the great, munching jaws of the economic machine.

The meanings we assign to words, the powers of language, are huge. Labels are convenient but most often misleading. The *environmentalist* label has been used mindlessly by news media that have failed to grasp the quality and nature of the commitment inherent in the word. Like all labels, *environmentalist* and *environmentalism* have become abstractions, inaccuracies. They do not reflect people smart enough and feeling enough to actually step forward and proclaim an allegiance to the sacred circle that supports all life. Environmentalists, of course, have let it happen, let themselves be labeled. We have gone naively about the business of saving the world, all too often self-righteously. Too many of us have not seen that the issues run much deeper and more complex than just saving a spot of wildness, or of having clean air and water.

We need a new word now that reflects self-examination and is more inclusive, that celebrates those who have come to understand that all variations of war can no longer be tolerated. We need a simple metaphor that suggests a person who is willing to risk loving this intricately beautiful planet and all beings on it, a language that exposes the suicidal folly of behaving otherwise. Not a limiting word, but one that is inclusive. Not a word that suggests any nobility. Because there is nothing noble about doing what one knows intuitively and logically is right. There is, though, a great deal ignoble about *not* doing it.

I did what felt closest to my heart when I joined the effort to save the Arctic National Wildlife Refuge from petroleum development. But really, why get all misty-eyed over some "empty wasteland," as Don Young, Alaska's lone congressional representative, called the refuge? In response, I'd suggest that loving a place is a big part of what life's about. One of those frustrating paradoxes of our modern humanness is that we seem to deny, fear and resist, even destroy what we most yearn to experience. One of the ways we avoid feeling for a place is by staying on the move. I know this well. I know, also, that we Americans are perhaps the most restless people on earth. We migrate, not like nomads following seasons and food, but because we are unhappy, because we seek something outside ourselves, something that can never be found. My own running was no different. We resist learning to love a place, a landscape, resist risking that much intimacy with something so powerful, because doing so might mean we have to stay and take a stand. Government policies support such transience and detachment. The managers of National Parks, Refuges, and Forests are routinely transferred every few years to keep them from caring about a place too much. Loving a place, in the industrial/political mind-set, is a hindrance, a tragic flaw.

Once, a few years back, while visiting Washington, D.C., I had lunch with a veteran environmental lobbyist. He was a pleasant guy, balding and spreading soft in the middle. In the course of our conversation he admitted he didn't feel too comfortable being too far away from civilization. "I like my amenities," he said. "I'm more a theorist than I am a naturalist. I know it's just common sense to protect the planet, so I've made a career of it."

"How do you get up for it each day," I asked him, "without feeling some passion for the wild?"

He looked me straight in the eye. "When you lobby these politicians, passion's got nothing to do with it. You come here and these guys see you care too much, they'll discount whatever it is you have to say. My advice, keep feelings out of it."

I let it go at that, even though I wanted to pontificate a bit and suggest that buying into the other guys' game only adds to the problem. But I couldn't judge his motives; he was involved, doing what he thought he should. If I understood his reasoning, though, the idea is to approach everything as pragmatically as possible. Leave out the feelings, because feelings won't sway the policy-makers or pay the bills.

I get stumped here. How do I say what I want to say, tie the notion of caring for a place into the way some people think? How can I not sound like some emotionally over-wrought tree-hugger? It's the challenge of trying to describe something outside too many people's experience. It's kind of like trying to describe the experience of eating ice cream to primitive tribesmen from New Guinea, when their experience holds no references for the feelings of cold and melting, or the taste of cream and sugar.

But how long can we keep fooling ourselves? Our migrations are fueled, literally, with oil. The ultimate irony is that in the quest for and conquest of oil, we willingly destroy thousands of years of migratory evolution, all to keep ourselves moving at this desperate pace for just a few more years. A case in point is the mean estimate of the amount of oil that might be found in the Arctic Refuge. If it were our only source, it would last the United States six months. Of course, it could take a couple of decades to extract what might be there, twenty years of destructive activity imposed upon a profoundly delicate and precious ecosystem. What price are we willing to pay to keep the illusion of our progress alive, to avoid *feeling* the truth of our tenuous existence?

I look back to my days with sled dogs. In all the ways that I was becoming a better dog man, what was actually working for me, I know now, was a minutely budding understanding of the meaning of reciprocal relationships. I had an instinct for dogs, an intuitive sense that served me well. It helped me begin to understand that domestic animals, most wild ones even, given any kind of a truce, for the most part want to participate with us. At the risk of incurring the bemusement of my scientific friends, I'll admit that in recent years I've come to believe that animals are speaking to us, constantly trying to communicate important things. But in the way we moderns do most things, we push against them, we resist their offer. Taken by the conceited notion that we must dominate, that animals are only here for us to use, that they are inherently inferior, we have lost our ability to hear, or more accurately we have lost our ability to feel, to sense another language. In a dangerously arrogant and human-centered present, we industrialized ones have misplaced the code of common life.

Reciprocity. As always there seems to be a paradox, a duality involved in all experience. A number of years ago I quit hunting. Why? From a practical standpoint, I didn't need to any longer. More important, though, the sorrow of killing began to outweigh the pleasure of the hunt, and some things about the so-called sport began to bother me. I say all this, and as I do I also have to say that I don't believe hunting is inherently wrong.

I did not quit hunting naively or in a flood of emotion. Before I quit, I had read plenty about the nobility of the blood sports. My training at the university in wildlife biology also grounded me fully in all the "managed harvest" theories and justifications of modern hunting. None of this was enough, though. Simply, the act of killing had become empty for me.

Some sport hunters talk reverently of "closing the circle," of killing as the sacred culmination of the chase. In all the experiences that I've had with hunting in my life, I've seen very little of the reverent or sacred acted out by men in the pursuit of wild animals. I've come to believe it's the *way* most moderns go about hunting that's wrong. Most men who hunt have lost any sense of the sacred, of gratitude for the gift the animal makes to us. Hunting has become a huge industry, a complex commercial enterprise dedicated to the commodification of the natural world, to the manufacture and marketing of machines and firearms and all sorts of paraphernalia, all designed to destroy. At some point I had to begin to look honestly at a destructive element in my own psyche, in the industrial male psyche in general, that leads us to destroy what we most yearn to touch and understand.

But it's still not so simple. The issue carries beyond to hunt or not to hunt. Richard Nelson, a man who I believe hunts as consciously as anyone, sums up my dilemma: "My reactions toward predators and prey are terribly inconsistent, especially considering that I am a predator myself. How can I love the beauty of living things apart from the process that sustains them? Life feeds on life."

In recent years I've read volumes on the ethics of animal rights and the moral imperatives for taking up the vegetarian lifestyle. Certainly some of the arguments for meatless diets are excellent ones. Still, I resist drawing indelible lines. The fact remains that we live in a world made up of predator-prey relationships, be they animal or plant, fungus, bacterium or virus. We kill to live. I've tried vegetarianism and failed miserably at it. Despite all the agruments against it, I still eat meat.

I relish it. And every time I stalk the aisles of a supermarket, armed with my checkbook to buy the flesh of animals, I'm aware that I'm still killing. I'm simply hiring it done. But an animal living miserably in some factory-farm in a distant place, or dying in some distant slaughterhouse, is intangible enough that I'm not struck with the same discomfort as when I killed directly. In our modern distance from the source of most of the elements that sustain us—food, water, fuel, shelter—killing for most of us in these so-called advanced cultures has become a vague abstraction. I can't help but feel this a dangerous thing, the exact opposite direction that we need to travel.

I may hunt again. In many ways my life feels like it's coming full circle; I'm getting increasingly uncomfortable with the abstractions. If I want to eat meat, then I should be able to kill the animal that's bearing it. If I can't, then I need to get honest about it, face my fears, suck it up and become a vegetarian. So yes, I may hunt again. But not for sport, for antlers, or to support the killing industry. No, to take direct responsibility for the deaths that the perpetuation of my life relies on. If I do hunt, I'll hunt differently this time, with a lot more respect. It was in the denial of the feelings, in the pushing away from them and being callous about the act, that the emotions of killing became so deformed. This time, if I kill, I'll allow the regret and sorrow to come fully, acknowledge them, and feel them as part of the process. I'll create a ceremony of gratitude, a conscious solemnity that bows reverently to a life taken so that I might live.

In my mind I keep coming back to fear. In the striving cultures, we are so fearful of doing without that we end up not owning the most basic elements of our own selves. The farther up the accumulating and controlling strata a person or culture climbs, the more energy has to be put out in the form of fences and defenses and rhetorical devices and weapons to stay there, just to protect that position.

There are two types of fear: legitimate fear and projected fear. Legitimate fear is real. There is a clearly definable threat to some aspect of one's life, either carried from past experience or felt fully in the present moment. Projected fear, in contrast, is fear of the future, a fantasy of what *might* go wrong. Projected fear comes from the imagination; it takes people out of the moment and propels them into some fictionalized, negative situation in the future. Humans may be the only species on the planet with the capacity to project fear, to imagine what might go wrong, and then to create elaborate defense mechanisms—be they psychological or physical—to prepare for the possibility.

There's so much irony in it all. In wanting to have it our own way, in seeking what's missing in our overly civilized spirits, we so often tend to project fear on those attributes of nature that sustain us most, the very qualities that would lead us home to the missing parts, the wild, unscrubbed, unruly, arrogant, and at the same time soft nature that is ultimately us.

Audre Lorde says it another way: "We have been raised to fear the yes within ourselves . . . within our deepest cravings. And the fear of our deepest cravings keeps them suspect, keeps us docile and loyal and obedient, and leads us to settle for or accept many facets of our own oppression."

Our oppression is self-imposed. We live in terror of those wild, untamed, restless places within and without. They wake us at night and keep us running scared during the day. Most of us don't seem to understand how our fears control us. Instead, we push against them until our souls bleed. We run scared to the shopping centers and movie houses, plug into the TV, drown ourselves in a hundred addictions, all under the misperceived notion that such activities will somehow provide solace. There's more sad irony to it all: the more we run from our fears, the farther away from our essential, yearning selves we're taken.

L ove is an ever-present force in the universe. But to embrace that force remains a choice. The road of love is a commitment to the relinquishment of fear, to finding courage. The most common way we are offered a road to love is through organized religion. Since my early conflicts with Mennonite doctrine, I sensed that there was something deeply wrong with what many religions have come to. Christ was the great symbol of unconditional love. But Christianity and other religions have taken on fundamentalist forms. They have become neurosis, fear-based dogma, narrowing, a construct of men dedicated to control, the antithesis of love.

Since I was a child I've yearned for something. I looked the world over for it. Along the way I slowly began to understand that what I have hungered for was Spirit—the offer of love and beauty, the harmony and power of undiminished nature, connection with the sacred, the acknowledgment of an infinitely complex web of energy that permeates the universe. At some point I even allowed myself to begin to say the word, *God,* the summation of it all. I began to see that the Spirit I yearned for was not necessarily the same thing as religion, but a way of living and thinking that opened to all possibility instead of closing it out. A way of being that imagined a mystical universe where humans are only a most minute part of it, instead of the simpleminded conceit of one that is human-centered. But I've come to know that the more this mystery is sought after, the more it recedes. It comes when you are least expecting it, least striving to attain it.

Some of us thrive on the unknown. We take great pleasure in the adventure of an infinite universe that works so far outside human perception all we can ultimately do is celebrate it. But many more of us fear the unknown. Thus we create elaborately simplistic and arrogant schemes of how the world works. But life is too big a mystery for everyone to see things the same way. Fundamentalism of all kinds—from religions, to atheism, to blind allegiance to political and economic systems, to a myopic faith in technology and narrowly defined science—are all part of the same spectrum, people doing their best to hold the Great Mystery at bay. For cultures worldwide that have taken on these brands of fundamentalism, the cramp of doing so appears to be increasingly uncomfortable.

22

the rage of men

The tragedy of the old rites of manhood is that they made so
many of us morally tone-deaf. We have become so tough-
minded and tough-hearted, such experts in control and command, that we can hardly hear the crying needs of our time
or the first faint strand of melody the future is sounding. . . .
The historical challenge for modern men is clear—to discover
a peaceful form of virility and to create an ecological com-
monwealth, to become fierce gentlemen.

SAM KEEN, *Fire in the Belly: On Being a Man*

Write about what you know best. I have. In writing about
my own life I have written mostly about men, about
being a man. I've tried to say something about the way men
go into the world, about how we strive so to dominate, to ac-
cumulate power, to maintain control. Institutions worldwide—governments, militaries, corporations, universities,
families—reflect our single-mindedness. I have said little
about the women who enable us, who either out of fear of

alienation or for their lives have failed to examine the truth of their own bondage, who in serving us or in taking on our negatives give up the full potential of their own humanness. I bow to those courageous women who are doing otherwise, who are asking men to begin behaving another way.

I think back to that summer I worked on the pipeline. I see now that it was one of a number of events in my life that have collectively forced me to become more sensitized to the behavior of men. Through the lens of my own life I had to begin to see that so much of what we do is adversarial and destructive and violent, and unevolved. Wherever I've traveled on the edge, it usually came down to being worn down most of all by the fractiousness of men. There always came a point when I wanted to be away from it, to be back in my homeland, a familiar place. Ironically, my country is the one that leads the world with the highest rates of murder and abuse, a country with more prisons and prisoners than any other, a culture that has become institutional in its propitiation of violence by men.

Of course, America does not stand alone. America simply leads. America packages and commodifies men's rage, in wars, in the sale of arms and military equipment, in fear-laden fundamentalist religion, in TV programs and movies that glorify violence against men, against women, against virtually every decent thing on the planet; we sell violence all over the world. I don't know if we create the demand or if we simply fill it. I don't think it matters. All we need to know is that we are in a self-perpetuating, downward spiral of anger and abuse, a story of war against ourselves and all nature, waged on countless fronts.

Life is a process, an accumulation of choices that turn us either away from ourselves or toward ourselves. I believe that there are no accidents, nothing entirely random; in all events we are given the opportunity to heal our hearts, to come closer to our soul's needs. Here and there certain choices stand tall and beckoning, opportunities to turn toward all we can be.

Surgeon Bernie Siegel says in his book *Love, Medicine and Miracles,* "Each of us seems to be born with a 'blueprint' that not only turns us into a certain type of physical being, but also maps out the path of our psychological, intellectual and spiritual development as well. When we deviate from that inner blueprint, it often takes psychological or physical illness to get us back on course."

Three years after I began working for the Arctic Refuge, I almost died. The best that any of the medical people could figure is that it was a long-term tropical ailment and a couple of unidentified exotic parasites that were doing their best to eat my intestines. I know, too, that my intestinal disease was the residue of many years detoured away from the things I was brought here to do, from my deepest loves. Another part of it was a parasite called anger.

It's a complicated story, with lots of medical misdiagnoses and ineptitude in it. The short version of it, though, is that after months of intense pain and some long stays in hospitals in Fairbanks and Seattle, the surgeons cut several inches of gangrenous intestine from my gut to save my life. Before they got to it, though, on two separate occasions I faced death.

The first time was in the hospital in Fairbanks. I came out of a coma into a hazy consciousness. I was floating above the roof of the hospital, looking down at my body spread like a puddle on the hospital bed. For the first time in a long time I was pain-free, and it felt entirely possible to stay that way. I looked up, and above me in a dark sky was a tunnel of white light. It felt so inviting. Friends were sitting with me around the clock. I heard myself speak, a distant voice. "Am I still here in my body?" A friend by my bed replied, "You're right here, Glendon." Instantly, as he spoke, I slammed back into my body and felt the wracking pain begin again. I believe that if my friend had not been there to call me back, I would have gone on, entered the tunnel of light.

The doctors in Fairbanks could not figure out what was wrong. They flew me to a hospital in Seattle. There, several days later, lost in the fog of a body completely saturated with pain, I felt myself come to a barrier. A voice, or an awareness, asked me if I'd like to go. I had the undeniable sense that I could leave if I chose to. Very logically I considered the question. I felt no fear. It was very seductive to think of being pain-free, to be shed of a body that had betrayed me. I thought of people who cared for me, began to go through a list of friends and family who might miss me. When I came to my daughter, Cara, my decision was instant. I had to stay.

Three weeks after entering the hospital in Seattle, I left it in a wheelchair and was flown back to Alaska. It was several more weeks before I could even turn over in bed without help. For the first time in my life I was completely dependent upon someone else; I had no control of anything. I felt angry, cheated out of life; I struck out at whatever I could. Sometime into my healing, my friend Nancy, who had cared for me from the beginning, asked me why I was so angry.

"I didn't know I was," I replied.

"You are," she said. "There's just a tension in you. You carry it like a flag."

A year after my own brush with death I found myself at my father's bedside. He had had a long history of small strokes, attacks to his brain that over a span of ten years had taken him deeper and deeper into a distant and agitated senility. After his final stroke he lay comatose in a Mennonite nursing center. "I'm here, Dad," I said as I came to his bedside, knowing full well he could not reply, but hoping he could sense my presence. His eyes were strangely complicated, vacant, yet fearful at the same time. His barrel chest, now only ribs and soft folds of red, mottled skin, rose and fell with the slow effort of his breathing. His mouth hung agape, toothless. The skin of his face stretched like parchment over his cheekbones, so hot and dry that it looked as if it might split if touched.

I sat with him then, night and day, waiting for the inevitable. I held his hand, stroked his head, played a tape of his favorite hymns over and over. "It's okay to die," I said to him many times. "It's okay, you're loved." The sound of my voice, my presence, seemed to be a comfort to him. His breathing would slow and his face would settle into the most fragile countenance. In these moments I uncovered evidence of the progression of my own healing, because I discovered that I loved my father, without embarrassment; I deeply loved him.

I left his side for only short periods to help my invalid mother come to see him, or to get some food. When I returned each time he was agitated again, his eyes wide with fear. But as soon as I came into the room and spoke to him he visibly calmed.

He became weaker and weaker, yet he held on. I was astounded that he could continue to live without taking any water or food. Mid-morning of the third day I told him I needed to get something to eat, that I would be back soon. I left and was gone for no more than an hour. When I returned, something had changed in the room, not anything I can describe easily, more just a feeling that a decision had been made.

I sat beside him again, took his hand in mine, and said to him, "I'm back, Dad." He took one long shuddering breath. This is it, I thought to myself, he's actually going to die. But then he took another breath, and for an instant I thought he was going to hang on a while longer. Let go, I thought, just this once, let go.

His next breath ended differently, with a deep sigh at the end that seemed to say, "Enough, I've had enough."

I watched the blood drain from his face, the death mask, watched it fall like a curtain over his life. And then I tapped him gently on top of his head, signaling his soul that it was time to leave, a ritual carried from my Buddhist readings. Otherwise, the Buddhists say, the soul may stay with the body, confused about its departure time. I knew that my father had waited for me to return before he died. He waited, and as soon as he knew I was there by his side, he let go. This fact means a lot to me.

I sat quietly with him then, knowing I needed to mourn. I felt both sorrow and relief for his dying. A flood of memories rolled across my mind. I thought of all the ways he had pushed against life and against those who had tried to love him. I thought of the years he had come to Alaska, how he had seemed at peace there. I was glad he had those times. I began to cry. There was no apology to it. In my sorrow for his dying I uncovered evidence of my own healing. For I knew that I loved my father. For all his sins against me, a man who had never once in his life said to me "I love you," still, I loved him, and I had told him so before he died.

Not long ago I came across a journal entry I wrote while my father was dying. "Being here is such a gift," the entry begins. "I watch him hold onto life out of the fear of death. I see it: underneath all his religious trappings is a deep mistrust of his God. And rightfully so, for who could ever be good enough to meet a God so full of judgment? Who would *want* to meet such a God? How lonely this time must be for him."

It was after the funeral that I asked my mother if he had ever talked of dying, ever mentioned his fears or his questions. She thought about it for some time before she replied. "No," she said, "in all the fifty-five years we were married he never once mentioned death."

"But why?" I asked.

"I think he was afraid of it," she said. "Your father did not like to admit his fears." I recalled a time six months earlier when I had visited my father. He sat essentially mute, hunched over in a wheelchair, food stains dribbled down his shirt front. I thought of my own near-death, the tunnel of white light, the voice. "Dad," I said, "I think there's nothing to fear. It's okay to die."

He turned his head haltingly and looked at me. Like a storm building in a distant sky, his eyes filled with the old rage. "What are you saying to me!" he shouted. "What kind of craziness are you talking about?" And then as quickly as it had built, his rage ended. He turned away from me, back into his private and lonely world.

Awareness is the first step toward change. With Nancy's words I began to look seriously at my own anger, where it came from, where it had taken me, the things I desired that it kept me away from. I saw my father. My grandfather. I began to address the hard ball of anger in my gut. It has not been an instant change. But the dis-ease that I inherited from my father, my grandfather, a long line of men, began to soften and dissolve. Often now, I live free of it.

Rage acknowledged and turned outward toward some injustice is a great tool. Rage carried and turned inward, denied, becomes disease. In my pacifist father I saw elements of the same frustrations that turn men to war, to the obliteration of the earth. The rage of feeling inconsequential and impotent in the face of forces one cannot understand, the frustration of feeling something important and essential in one's life as being out of reach because of circumstances, the press of a judgmental God, all of these things gnawed at my father. I believe, too, that all these things gnaw at a lot of men, men in all walks of life, all levels of power.

My father was no different from most of us. We rage against the inevitability of our death, rage against the paltriness of our own existence. We fear the darkness. Against all of it we strive desperately for control, and in the pursuit of this illusion we subdue, conquer, manipulate, wage war, attempt to manage things from a myopic and limited perspective of how they need to be. Ravaged forests, rivers, farmlands, cultures, families, women and children, all bear witness to our disease.

We have to find another way. We need to make amends. It's no exaggeration to say that if we don't change, then there's little hope for this earth. I'm here, also, as a witness, to say that the rage we carry can be released. It's as simple and as difficult as that, *released,* like taking off a suit of armor or dropping a weapon. The world is crying out for us to do so.

A couple of years after my near-death experiences, one fine cloudless bluebird of a day, Cara and I carried backpacks along the continental divide of the northern Rockies. We had left the Forest Service trail the day before, and were now angling high along a ridgeline, through fields of dusty red boulders and carpets of yellow and deep purple alpine flowers. Once a band of bighorn sheep wheeled and ran away from us as we approached. Another time we stopped and watched a cow and calf moose break from the timber far below and move quickly across a meadow.

At the base of the tallest peak for miles around, we dropped our packs and began to climb. We climbed fast, both of us breathing hard. I reveled in the strength of my legs, my breath coming strong, the sheer joy of being alive in the wild.

We gained the peak and hunkered down out of the wind to take in the view—mountains stretching bold in all directions. It was some time before Cara broke the spell.

"Dad," she said.

"Uh-huh."

"Thanks for being here with me."

"Thanks back to you."

She turned and looked at me, her expression so kind. "Remember when you almost died?"

"How could I forget?"

"Well, if I haven't said so, I'm sure glad you didn't. Because I feel really lucky to have you as a dad."

"Thanks for saying so," I said.

"Sure," she said. "Anytime."

I dream of men the world over coming to live fully in their hearts. It seems so simple yet so very difficult for us to do so. It's about creating new visions of life, new stories. This is not to say we need to become entirely feminine, forsaking our best masculine selves. No, quite the opposite. Our best selves are those soft yet fierce qualities that we all carry, buried deeply perhaps, but nevertheless here in us. With the same vigor that we now destroy, we can turn toward healing and restoration. We can find a new voice and identity.

I have hope. My hope comes from looking back at that young man who stood on the Arctic plain years ago. Over time he was opened to a different view of the world. If it can happen to him, then it can happen to another. There is hope, and it comes with awareness, with choosing to open our fragmented minds, and then finding the courage to change them.

23

the stories we live by

Unless we can radically transform modern civilization, the wilderness and its people will be but a memory in the minds of a few people. When they die, it will die with them, and the wild will become completely abstract. . . . Our world looks backward, obsessed with a dim memory of a world that now seems more—the only word is—real. Something vast and old is vanishing, and our rage should mirror that loss.

JACK TURNER, *The Abstract Wild*

We are all defined by stories, ways we believe ourselves and our institutions and societies to be. Our memories and what we imagine—our fears and fantasies—form the collective evidence for our stories; from an infinite number of experiences and possibilities we select a few convenient impressions and say this is what we are, this is where we stand. Our perceptions rule us, even in error. All of our stories, I believe, circle around our soul's fundamental desires. Most of what life is supposed to be about is coming into alignment with the soul's calling. Too often, though, the soul's whispering voice, that inner yearning, comes up against one's family story or the confused, conflicted story of our culture; too often the soul's callings are put aside or entirely lost. Too many of us get detoured from our work by our fears of failure or of the unknown, fears of being misunderstood. Fear keeps us stuck in the old stories.

Perhaps it's simply human nature to want to hold on to the status quo, to what's safe and familiar, even if that something is greatly painful or ultimately self-destructive. Witness the ways so many in our culture are addicted to alcohol and drugs, to television, to video games, to the Internet, to food, to starvation, to shopping, to sex, to the acquisition of things, to movement, to power, to sports, to violence, all at great, suffocating expense to the human spirit. We live in a culture of deep addiction, one that suffers from such a penetrating discomfort with life, such a spiritual alienation, that we have come to think of our addictions as normal, as the way things are. We have bought into a story that is fundamentally in error.

But the stories of addiction bring us pain. It is the mounting pain of an old story that may eventually push us to figure out what we need for ourselves, to become determined to actualize our lives, to meet the soul's needs. Our stories are, as William Kittredge says in his essay "The Politics of Storytelling," "maps or paradigms in which we see our purposes defined; then the world drifts and our maps don't work anymore, our paradigms and stories fail, and we have to reinvent our understandings, and our reasons for doing things."

It is with breakdown, in the discovery of error, that our stories can begin to change.

I often wonder what it is that keeps us going, a nation of Prozac-eaters, lotus-eaters, addicts to a way of living that seems to produce only more speed and more desperation and depression. I hear of more and more North American children diagnosed with attention deficit disorder and anorexia, and I read that teenage suicide is growing. Who was it that said, if you want to understand a culture, observe that culture's children?

I think how our food and water and air are poisoned, how rates of cancer and heart disease grow each year. How new diseases appear regularly and old ones return. We spend millions researching cures and medicines for the diseases, and millions more developing more and more complicated poisons to make them. Yes, we live better chemically. We treat the symptoms, over and over again, refusing to acknowledge the source.

At some point we've quit being called citizens and we've become "consumers," machines in the service of our corporate masters, our only tasks to greedily munch up the products they tell us we need. There is a sad vulgarity to this, of a citizenry given to consumption, as if that were our highest good. We have willingly misplaced the best of our human potential, to become whores in the service of the ever-expanding growth economy.

The American dream. A surreal dream it is.

Of course, there will always be those who can make long lists of all the ways the world has benefited from technological "advances." They will ask, Would I be willing to retreat in time and die of smallpox or polio or the black plague? Would I be willing to give up my car? My computer? The airplanes that have taken me all over the world? I would counter that I am not at all eager to die of the cancers and viruses spawned by the activities of the twentieth century, or to live on a planet diseased and polluted by the manufacture of cars and airplanes and machines and the escalating burning of fossil fuel. Ask me whether I'd prefer to live with six billion people, nine billion people, twelve billion people, sit bumper to bumper on polluted freeways, strive to live on a physically and spiritually starving planet. Ask me about the escalating extinctions and population declines of other species and the loss of wild places. Would I choose animals and forests and wild places, or more people? Would I choose to live in a world where industrialized people spend much of their lives mesmerized by electronic gadgetry and the glow of screens—television, computers, video games, movies—all at great expense to meaningful human interaction, to developing and maintaining real community, to having soulful interaction with the natural world? Would I choose to live on a planet where humans are out of control, or one where humans have honestly grappled with the responsibilities of their own procreation and living habits and have chosen instead to limit their numbers and their activities so that other beings might live?

From a shaky platform of faulty perceptions we keep making trade-offs. And we keep making bad ones. We suffer from the disease of the rational mind. Rational minds justify war, invent nuclear bombs, build dams, create machines and economic ideas that destroy whole ecosystems, drill and mine and skin the living earth, all in the name of progress and profit. We are conditioned to believe and bow to the "authorities"—men talking in reasonable, flat, knowing tones, saying and justifying the most horrendous things.

But rational thought is only one cramped way to understand. Those who rely only on the rational can create all kinds of rational arguments for not letting go and exploring other realms. They live in a self-created illusion. But sometimes one has no choice. Things happen. Despite one's resistance, the universe delivers gifts that cannot be ignored. In my most hopeful moments I imagine a shift away from our mechanistic, linear, wholly rational view. I imagine a time when we will be ethically bound to examine thoroughly anything touted as a technological advance or as scientific truth. That whatever it is will have to pass a rigorous questioning by a large body of enlightened citizens. Of course these citizens will use the rational mind in their questioning, but one completely enjoined with the heart, one that honors the sacred. They will ask, Does whatever it is truly advance the quality of life on the planet or will it be just another addictive illusion that will in the long run do the planet more harm than good? I imagine a day when we will scorn those who would promote recklessness, a day when we will laugh at our collective ignorance as we laugh now at the notion of rational people who once believed the earth was flat.

I dream of another way. Sometimes, though, the absence of that way covers me with an obdurate sadness. I mourn the loss of a way of living, of a living world, that I can only sense was once here, and could, I believe, be here again if we modern humans were willing to create a new story. I wish I knew where to begin, how to say it so even the most hardened heart could understand, could begin to feel what's actually at stake.

We humans have not evolved consciously as fast as we have evolved technologically. This is a dangerous imbalance. We are spiraling downward. Most of us, I believe, know this at some level, consciously or subconsciously. While we may choose to ignore or deny it, or feel numb to it because of a deep sense of helplessness and despair, it nevertheless is where we are. We exist in a world gone crazy because of a failure by too many of us to live honestly, to insist upon the hard truth in all matters, to find the courage to examine both our personal stories and those of our culture. In the face of apparently insurmountable obstacles, denial and cynicism have become our *modus operandi.*

It may sound too simple to some, but I believe to come home, to begin to find our way back to something essential and sustainable, we must find a connection to the sacred

RETURN

again, to the all-living world, we must inhabit a new story that insists upon harmony instead of promoting discord. A story that honors in all ways the earth we inhabit.

There is an urgency in this. Just as a river tears at its banks, the currents of time are demanding that we quickly begin to imagine a new course. But as addicts to an old way, we are still resistant to the kinds of radical change that our new story will require.

Stories of place. Like many others who have struck out for the frontier, I pushed away from the story I was born to. I headed for Alaska, where I strove to create a new identity radically different from the one I had left. That story was of a world that revolved around the shame and restriction of conservative Christianity, a tale of provinciality. The story of landscape in the Midwest was one of fragmentation and hard use, a place of restriction and diminished nature. I was drawn to a place where the landscape opened like a dream. In Alaska, for the first time in my life, I could breathe and feel the wild earth.

Yet in so many ways I brought my old story with me. It is in the pushing away that we get caught in our own fictions. We hang on to ways of being that can be hard on the people we might hope to love, hard on places we deeply desire to honor. Both places, the Midwest and Alaska, were contrived of their individual fictions, ways I wanted them to be. My Alaskan fiction served me well for a lot of years, held me in its arms and nurtured me. It did until both my individual story and the story I had assigned to that place began to unravel.

Today, Alaska draws even more people to its wildness. We're drawn there because it's the only place left that's close to the way all of North America once was. The ultimate tragedy of this

314

is that in our desire to reinhabit something—the wilderness of the American mind—we are trampling one of the last remnants of a former world. With oil development, large-scale mining, clear-cut logging, overfishing, and with the latest boom—corporate-run tourism, which has spread like a cancer into virtually every corner of the state—we are creating a sad caricature of the world we yearn to inhabit. The issue is not solely about wilderness. It's about our diminishing world. The loss of wilderness is only one symbol. As we settle for more and more boundaries, more management, designer parks and "designated" wildernesses, we increasingly let go of the memory of a vital, inspired nature that ultimately holds our salvation.

The loss I've felt in Alaska, the diminishment of the dream, is still hard to bear. I will never be resigned to the destruction of wild places, of the earth I love. I want something of the old days back, the feel of a world so unspoiled and alive. I still dream of frontier. Only this time the frontier I dream of is a new way of living. It is true that we have no visible models to aspire to, that we cannot see what's over the hill. But at least we have a horizon to gaze at. It is beyond that horizon that the true frontier lies.

Change follows imagination. Never mind that those of us who are reimagining the world are belittled by the protectors of the status quo. As the philosopher Arthur Schopenhauer said, "Every truth passes through three stages before it is recognized. In the first it is ridiculed. In the second, it is opposed. In the third, it is regarded as self-evident."

A strong enough vision of change, shared by enough people, and it can happen; we can evolve. Our will will be reflected back in our political and religious institutions. The pillars of patriarchal control will topple. Say it can happen and we take one small step in the direction of change. On the other hand, if you say it can't happen, all you do is add to the inertia of our time; you perpetuate the status quo.

I'm willing to imagine another way. Because I want this earth to survive. If not for me, then for my daughter and for the children of my friends. If not for them, then for all species. I would suggest that real manly men and real womanly women take risks. The first risk anyone can take this day is one of reimagining our personal stories and the stories of our culture. The next is summoning up the courage to live and speak passionately from a new vision. As the bumper sticker says, "Speak your mind, even if your voice shakes."

I look back through time to that young boy standing on the sloping lawn, gazing across farm fields toward the green and mysterious woods. As I do I feel a great deal of love for him. He tempted life. Along the way he made mistakes, but they always led somehow, through convoluted passages, to growth. And he's not done yet. He is alive, whispering in me, telling me that in this lifetime we may yet witness a radical shift in human consciousness. We may be alive to inhabit another world.

In our new story we may not return to some Edenic primitivism or even to Jefferson's notion of a landed agrarian culture. No, we have entered another era. But in the reimagined world, our cities, our farms, our wildlands, our relationships with technology, all will look radically different. We will inhabit a world where there are no visible boundaries between wild and the places that humans inhabit. Instead of war and destruction, men will measure their manhood by what they can renew and restore, by their abilities to align with natural forces. Our new heroes will not be Hollywood celebrities and generals, but women and men who give their lives to healing. Our priests will be naturalists. Our leaders will be artists. Beauty, the simple evidence of the hand of God, will be the measure of our success.